The Rise and Fall of the Right of Silence

Within an international context in which the right to silence has long been regarded as sacrosanct, this book provides the first comprehensive, empirically-based analysis of the effects of curtailing the right to silence. The right to silence has served as the practical expression of the principles that an individual was to be considered innocent until proven guilty, and that it was for the prosecution to establish guilt. In 1791, the Fifth Amendment to the US Constitution proclaimed that none 'shall be compelled in any criminal case to be a witness against himself'. In more recent times, the privilege against self-incrimination has been a founding principle for the International Criminal Court, the new South African constitution and the ad hoc International Criminal Tribunals for Rwanda and the former Yugoslavia. Despite this pedigree, over the past 30 years when governments have felt under pressure to combat crime or terrorism, the right to silence has been reconsidered (as in Australia), curtailed (in most of the United Kingdom) or circumvented (by the creation of the military tribunals to try the Guantánamo detainees). The analysis here focuses upon the effects of the Criminal Justice and Public Order Act 1994 in England and Wales. There, curtailing the right to silence was advocated in terms of 'common sense' policy-making and was achieved by an eclectic borrowing of concepts and policies from other jurisdictions. The implications of curtailing this right are here explored in detail with reference to England, Wales and Northern Ireland, but within a comparative context that examines how different 'types' of legal systems regard the right to silence and the effects of constitutional protection.

Hannah Quirk is a Senior Lecturer in Criminal Law and Justice at the University of Manchester, UK.

The Rise and Fall of the Right of Silence

Hannah Quirk

Routledge
Taylor & Francis Group

LONDON AND NEW YORK

First published 2017
by Routledge
2 Park Square, Milton Park, Abingdon, Oxon, OX14 4RN

and by Routledge
711 Third Avenue, New York, NY 10017

First issued in paperback 2018

Routledge is an imprint of the Taylor & Francis Group, an informa business

British Library Cataloguing in Publication Data
A catalogue record for this book is available from the British Library

Library of Congress Cataloging in Publication Data
Names: Quirk, Hannah, 1973– author.
Title: The rise and fall of the right of silence/Hannah Quirk.
Description: Abingdon, Oxon; New York, NY: Routledge, 2017. |
"A GlassHouse book." | Includes bibliographical references and
index.
Identifiers: LCCN 2016021311| ISBN 9780415547710 (hbk) |
ISBN 9780203798867 (ebk)
Subjects: LCSH: Self-incrimination–Great Britain.
Classification: LCC KD8386.Q57 2017 | DDC 345.41/056–dc23
LC record available at https://lccn.loc.gov/2016021311

ISBN 13: 978-1-138-59098-4 (pbk)
ISBN 13: 978-0-415-54771-0 (hbk)

Typeset in Baskerville
by Wearset Ltd, Boldon, Tyne and Wear

MIX
Paper from
responsible sources
FSC
www.fsc.org   FSC™ C013985

Printed in the United Kingdom
by Henry Ling Limited

CROMWELL: Now, Sir Thomas, you stand on your silence.

SIR THOMAS MORE: I do.

CROMWELL: But, gentlemen of the jury, there are many kinds of silence. Consider first the silence of a man who is dead. Let us suppose we go into the room where he is laid out, and we listen: what do we hear? Silence. What does it betoken, this silence? Nothing; this is silence pure and simple. But let us take another case. Suppose I were to take a dagger from my sleeve and make to kill the prisoner with it; and my lordships there, instead of crying out for me to stop, maintained their silence. That would betoken! It would betoken a willingness that I should do it, and under the law, they will be guilty with me. So silence can, according to the circumstances, speak! Let us consider now the circumstances of the prisoner's silence. The oath was put to loyal subjects up and down the country, and they all declared His Grace's title to be just and good. But when it came to the prisoner, he refused! He calls this silence. Yet is there a man in this court – is there a man in this country! – who does not know Sir Thomas More's opinion of this title?

CROWD IN COURT GALLERY: No!

CROMWELL: Yet how can this be? Because this silence betokened, nay, this silence was, not silence at all, but most eloquent denial!

SIR THOMAS MORE: Not so. Not so, Master Secretary. The maxim is 'Qui tacet consentiret': the maxim of the law is 'Silence gives consent'. If therefore you wish to construe what my silence betokened, you must construe that I consented, not that I denied.

CROMWELL: Is that in fact what the world construes from it? Do you pretend that is what you wish the world to construe from it?

SIR THOMAS MORE: The world must construe according to its wits; this court must construe according to the law.

Robert Bolt (1960) *A Man For All Seasons* Act 2

For my grandmothers, Ellen Healy and Mary Frances Quirk

Contents

Foreword

Hannah Quirk is a rare thing; a legal scholar who can tell a story and do so from a legal, political, practical, historical, domestic and international perspective, capable of exciting a variety of disciplines across the academy and beyond.

In *The Rise and Fall of the Right of Silence*, she unpacks the roots, importance, demise and broader significance of a once cherished common law criminal justice principle; fiercely defended, but almost forgotten in a little over 20 years.

The Criminal Justice and Public Order Act 1994, such an important landmark in Quirk's story, is also perhaps the beginning of an authoritarian arms race in British politics from which our legislators have yet to recover. Michael Howard and Tony Blair faced each other across the House of Commons. Barristers both, neither was prepared to place fair trial tradition or even hard evidence above the raw politics which would, in time, elevate each to the leadership of his own party and guide one's onslaught on what he described as a 'nineteenth-century criminal justice system' in need of 're-balancing'.

Whilst never inflating the argument, the writer paints an ever-more vivid picture of a policy led by populism rather than reason and which failed to take account of the right of silence's philosophical foundations. It blundered through the delicate interconnected relationships between the right and other police station and court-room vulnerabilities and safeguards. It lacked the vision to anticipate the way in which such a fundamental change would be viewed and, to too great an extent, emulated elsewhere in the common law world.

So why a right of silence? Some would point to the inherent vulnerability of the suspect in custody (some even more than others), even with the provision of police station legal advice that some in politics and policing came to resent. Some now point to the potential inappropriate wedge between lawyer and client when the precise nature of complex advice as to possible inferences becomes a contested question of evidence at a subsequent trial.

Yes, the right relates to those against oppression and self-incrimination, privacy and discrimination. But ultimately, as Quirk conveys so clearly and compellingly, its demise has been a burden-shifter, dishonouring – at least in part – the notion of the prosecution having to make its case without compliance or cooperation from a suspect or accused. This surely goes to the heart of the presumption of innocence itself.

In telling her story and making her argument so well, Hannah Quirk also reminds us of the broader political crime climate of recent years. Due process was denigrated as a box of tricks for professional criminals. Legal professionals plunged from being servants of justice to being smeared as little more than the accomplices of their no doubt all-too-guilty clients.

Sadly, we must wait for a political class sufficiently constitutionally humble or literate to be interested in this important book. But at least when that moment comes, there will be many students, scholars and practitioners ready to explain its wisdom to them.

Shami Chakrabarti
March 2016

Acknowledgements

Writing this book has taken an inordinate amount of time and I would like to thank those both professionally and personally who have helped with the process. The good people of Routledge, Colin Perrin, Melanie Fortmann-Brown, Rebekah Jenkins, Laura Muir, Holly Smithson, Hannah Riley, Allie Hargreaves, Ashleigh Phillips and Katie Short have shown enormous patience and made the process much easier.

The book develops my PhD thesis, which was generously supported by the University of Wolverhampton. I am very grateful to those practitioners who gave their time to be interviewed or to complete the questionnaires.

Some of the research for this book was conducted whilst I was a visiting scholar at the University of Melbourne, Queen's University Belfast and Fordham Law School and I thank them for their hospitality.

Writing a book is, by definition, a solitary experience but some academic colleagues have eased the process with helpful advice, encouragement or answers to questions: Ed Cape, James Chalmers, Marleen Eijkholt, Paul Kearns, Rachel Murray, Paul Roberts, Clive Walker and Richard Young, and I thank them. I am very grateful to those who read chapters for me: Bethan Loftus with her expertise on policing read Chapter 3; Richard Glover cast an evidence specialist's eye over Chapter 5 and John Jackson, who has been a huge source of professional support to me since he examined my PhD, read Chapter 6. Rebecca Askew and Joshua Warburton provided very efficient research assistance and Ian Fishwick, our librarian at Manchester, has been very helpful in helping me track down obscure articles and books. I was very honoured when Shami Chakrabarti offered to write the foreword for this book

My friends and relations who have offered practical support and encouragement have been a huge help: Helen and Hughie Furlong, Angela Flower, Pauline and Frank McLynn, Matt and Firouz Thompson, Michelle Timoney, Gillian Ulph and, of course, my 'partner in crime', Lucy McLynn.

I owe especial thanks to my 'Irish team' who read so much of this book and encouraged me over the line. Elaine Dewhurst has been an enormous support; Colin King has been a good friend and 'bad cop' when necessary; and Kieran McEvoy has stuck with this project since it was a half-finished thesis. If in academia we stand on the shoulders of those who have gone before us, that is equally true in my family. I would not be doing what I am today without the sacrifices my grandparents and parents, Nuala and Joe, made. I thank them and my brother Justin for their love and support.

Somebody once asked me if my book had a happy ending – it does now!

Hannah Quirk
March 2016

Table of cases

Introduction

The right of silence (in broad terms, the right of the accused to refuse to answer questions before or during trial without sanction) has a long, if somewhat obscure, history. It is a controversial provision that has been both celebrated as a benchmark of justice and castigated as a refuge of criminals. Supporters of the right regard it as protecting against miscarriages of justice, as well as a practical and symbolic expression of the presumption of innocence (Greer 1994b; Leng 1993; RCCP 1981; RCCJ 1993). In contrast, Jeremy Bentham (1825:241) famously argued that if a team of criminals was assembled to design a legal system in its own interests, the right of silence would be the first feature to be included for '[i]nnocence never takes advantage of it; innocence claims the right of speaking, as guilt invokes the privilege of silence'.

Such a rogues' charter has yet to be drafted, yet the privilege against self-incrimination has been included in no fewer than 48 national constitutions, including the United States of America, India and South Africa (Bassiouni 1992–93:265). In countries where the right of silence is not protected by a constitution, it has been secured by other means, such as inclusion in the criminal procedure code or statutes, as in France, Germany and most of Australia. The right was a common law creation in England where there was held to be an 'ancient and deep-rooted privilege against self-incrimination' (*R* v *Director of SFO ex parte Smith* 1993 at 42). The right of silence features in international treaties, including the International Covenant on Civil and Political Rights (ICCPR) and the American Convention on Human Rights. It is included in the founding statutes of the international criminal court and the ad hoc international criminal tribunals for the former Yugoslavia and Rwanda. Whilst the right is not mentioned explicitly in the European Convention on Human Rights (ECHR), the European Court of Human Rights (ECtHR) declared that the right of silence and the related privilege against self-incrimination are viewed as 'generally recognised international standards which lie at the heart of the notion of a fair procedure under Article 6' (*Saunders* v *UK* 1997 at 314). Every subsequent relevant international instrument includes the privilege against self-incrimination as part of the right to a fair trial (Roberts and Zuckerman 2010:555).[1] In 1994, the Third Optional Protocol to the ICCPR was drafted, with the aim of guaranteeing under all circumstances the right to fair trial. It sets out that 'silence by the accused may not be used as evidence to prove guilt and no adverse consequences may be drawn from the exercise of the right to remain silent'. This definition was endorsed by the United States-based advocacy group, Lawyers Committee for Human Rights (2000).

It might be thought, therefore, that by the late twentieth century, the case for the right of silence had been won; that, as with the prohibition on torture and the entitlement to legal advice, there was a reasonably settled understanding of the requirements of a modern criminal justice system – but this was not so. There is an ebb and flow in support for due process rights, and fear of crime or terrorism can be a more powerful political weapon than support for an abstract notion, or concern about wrongful convictions. The symbolic value of the right has been acknowledged by its defenders (Dixon 1991a; Greer 1990) but what has not been considered previously is that it is also freighted with symbolism for its detractors. Despite its international prevalence and historical antecedents, a retrenchment regarding the right of silence has occurred, or is underway, in countries around the world, and much of that has to do with what has happened in England and Wales. The right of silence was exported from – or imposed by – Britain[2] across much of the globe. The English proposals to curtail the right of silence (Criminal Law Revision Committee 1972) and legislation to do so in the Criminal Justice and Public Order Act 1994 (CJPOA) caused shockwaves and restrictions to the right around the world. The CJPOA has had a continuing domestic effect as the courts have widened its parameters and it arguably facilitated the passage of subsequent evidential changes that were less favourable to the defence. The right of silence thus remains very much a live issue.

Whilst the right of silence has been analysed extensively in theoretical and legal terms, this book provides the first comprehensive, empirically informed analysis of the effects of its curtailment. The work is located in the broader international context concerning the right of silence debates, but the primary focus is upon the effects of ss34–38 of the CJPOA. These sections allow inferences to be drawn from the accused's: failure to mention part of the defence case under police questioning or charge; refusal to answer certain questions; and failure to testify. Whilst this legislation was

---

1 The African Charter on Human and Peoples' Rights does not include the right of silence in the main text but it is included in the associated (non-binding) Principles and Guidelines (secs M, N and O).

2 England and Wales have always had a separate legal system from Scotland. The system in Northern Ireland is similar but has significant differences (discussed in Chapters 2 and 6). Empire-building activities were undertaken as Great Britain.

contested fiercely at the time, there has been little evaluation of the changes in practice, other than a single Home Office 'before and after' study (Bucke *et al.* 2000) and of course, detailed scrutiny of the developing case law. Analysis of the judgments or quantitative studies of the prevalence of 'no comment'[3] interviews or defendants not testifying, whilst important, are insufficient. Such research cannot capture the symbolic importance of the CJPOA, its interaction with the working practices of those responsible for its implementation and its impact upon the broader culture of the criminal justice system. In this book, these wider effects of the CJPOA are assessed through a review of the debates surrounding its introduction, consideration of the associated research and analysis of developments in the case law. This is complemented by a programme of in-depth interviews and questionnaires conducted with a range of criminal justice practitioners in one region of England shortly after the provisions came into effect (see Methods for details).

Easton argues that '[t]he right to silence in English and American law has been shaped by policy issues, questions of utility and moral principles' (Easton 1991:1). This book charts how these considerations compete: the principled aims; the politically expedient incursions; and the practical effects of curtailing the right. The first part of the book explores the tension between the ideals of the right of silence and the criticisms of its opponents. Chapter 1 explores the obscure historical origins of the right, the principles underlying its exercise and its enduring appeal. It shows that the right of silence is still an important, aspirational first principle for 'new' legal regimes, including the ad hoc international criminal tribunals and nascent democracies such as South Africa. Those charged with considering the criminal justice process from first principles also tend to recommend it, largely because of its association with the presumption of innocence (see the two Royal Commissions in England and Wales, RCCP 1981; RCCJ 1993; Australian Law Reform Commission 1987; New South Wales Law Reform Commission 1988 and 2000a; Law Commission of India 2000).

Whilst it may be difficult to design a system that does not include the right of silence, a pure system can be difficult to defend in practice. Once exceptions are admitted, however, it can be challenging to defend the principle against the lure of expedient concessions. Chapter 2 considers the early incursions in England and Wales and how the right of silence became a 'crime control' target. The curtailment of the right was portrayed as a response to terrorism and organised crime, but applied to even the most trivial offences. The chapter examines the right of silence debate in the context of contemporaneous events: the conflict in Northern

---

3 Whilst the CJPOA inferences extend beyond 'no comment' interviews to include failure to mention any fact relied upon in a suspect's defence, the terms 'no comment interviews' and 'silence' are nevertheless used widely, and in this book, as a convenient shorthand.

Ireland, rising crime, industrial disputes and social unrest. The legislation was advanced as a 'common sense' reform, designed to re-balance the criminal justice system away from the 'criminals' who were supposedly benefiting from its exploitation. In reality, there was little objective evidence that the right of silence was causing undue difficulties in the administration of justice. Rather, the pressure to curtail the right of silence was part of a sustained campaign led by the police at a time of rapidly rising crime rates. It then became part of a backlash against the increased protections given to suspects by the Police and Criminal Evidence Act 1984 (PACE), in particular legal advice. This was driven by the police, certain politicians and senior members of the judiciary.

Extravagant and often unsubstantiated claims were made when the CJPOA was introduced. The second part of the book offers an empirically informed exploration of what curtailing the right of silence has meant in practice in England and Wales: its effects on the working practices and occupational cultures of the police and defence solicitors and how the provisions have come to be utilised more boldly in court. Jackson (1994:277) and others have criticised the failure of the courts to consider the 'procedural context' in which the right of silence immunities were withdrawn by Parliament. Chapter 3 therefore examines the detention and interviewing of suspects at the police station, the initial context in which suspects decide whether to exercise their right of silence.[4] Whilst acknowledging the improvements that have been made in the treatment of suspects, the chapter critiques the premise of the 'balancing' argument used to restrict suspects' rights, by demonstrating the inadequacies in the protections suspects received before the CJPOA and the deficiencies that continue to exist. Few suspects made no comment interviews before the CJPOA, of those who did, almost half were convicted (Leng 1993); even fewer remain silent now (Bucke et al. 2000). The chapter questions the ability of suspects to understand the revised caution and to make informed decisions as to whether or not to remain silent. It is argued that the Act reinforces traditional police expectations about compliant behaviour from 'good' suspects, and about the innocent having nothing to hide. This appears contrary to many of the improvements that had been made in police investigative interviewing techniques.

Chapter 4 develops the arguments made by Cape (1997) and Leng (2001c) that the most profound effects of the CJPOA have been on the relationship between suspects and their legal representatives. Those advocating

4 The CJPOA also 'applies in relation to questioning by persons (other than constables) charged with the duty of investigating offences or charging offenders' – for example, local authority officials and Royal Society for the Prevention of Cruelty to Animals inspectors (s34(4)). Differences exist between these agencies due to their statutory powers, organisational practices, the offences and the 'types' of suspects being investigated. This discussion focuses on the police.

the changes argued that the right of silence should be ceded in part because of the increase in custodial legal representation. This was based on a false premise; less than a third of suspects were legally represented in the police station when the changes were mooted; take-up rates are still below 50 per cent. The quality and adversarialism of this representation (often by para-legals rather than qualified solicitors) has been criticised repeatedly (Baldwin 1993; Bridges and Choongh 1998; McConville *et al.* 1994). Legal representatives have no formal power in interviews but previously some would use the threat of a no comment interview as a bargaining tool to enforce their clients' rights or to obtain disclosure of the police case. Repre-sentatives now have to assess whether the potential risk of inferences being drawn from a no comment interview, should the case be brought to trial, outweighs the risk of providing the police with information that may be used to charge or convict the client. By making custodial legal advice of potential evidential significance, perhaps requiring representatives to testify why they gave such advice, it is argued that the CJPOA has compromised the lawyer–client relationship, thus further eroding the protective benefits of legal advice.

Refusal to testify and the domestic and European human rights case law around ss34–38 CJPOA are the focus of Chapter 5. The CJPOA has gener-ated a great deal of domestic case law, arguably of disproportionate weight to any evidential benefit it has provided (Birch 1999). Whilst the legislation appears to have increased the number of defendants who testify (Bucke *et al.* 2000), it has had a direct effect in only a small percentage of cases. The dire predictions that the CJPOA would cause miscarriages of justice have not been borne out and it has not made a noticeable difference in terms of increasing charge, plea or conviction rates. It is argued, however, that the CJPOA has had a profound effect upon the prevailing climate in which suspects are investigated and tried. There now exists what Leng (2001a:246) describes as a 'normative expectation' that suspects will cooperate in the investigation and trial process. The judiciary has become increasingly emboldened in drawing inferences from silence at the police station; a process assisted by the, perhaps surprising, decision of the ECtHR that the provisions do not breach Article 6, the right to a fair trial provisions in Article 6, per se (*Condron* v *UK* 2001). Whilst the Strasbourg decisions have resulted in slight restrictions upon the interpretation of the Act, this ambivalence has allowed the domestic courts to widen the parameters of the legislation in favour of the prosecution (*Howell* 2003). Inferences are no longer restricted to subsequent fabrication but can be used, in effect if not explicitly, for punitive as well as evidential purposes against suspects for not cooperating with the police at the earliest opportunity. This has essentially made the police interview a part of the trial but without the benefit of the safeguards or the rules of natural justice that attend a fair trial (Jackson 2001a:147). This has reduced the protections offered by legal representation, as the provision of legal advice to remain silent will not, of itself, protect the suspect from adverse inferences at trial. The Court went even further in *Seaton* (2010) and allowed incursions into legal professional privilege, previously also regarded as a fundamental protection for defendants (Quirk 2013). Whilst the presumption of innocence remains, the judgment in *Howell* (2003) suggests a significant judicial shift towards an assumption that the innocent have nothing to hide.

This book concludes that the right of silence, for a complex mix of political, legal and symbolic reasons, is a keystone of criminal justice. Just as Chapter 1 shows how the right had become part of a virtuous circle of international standards, the final chapter examines the destabilising effect of the English debate across much of the common law world. Rather than using traditional notions of 'policy transfer' (Dolowitz 2000), I argue that the initial plans to curtail the right of silence (CLRC 1972) caused a policy *tremor* that led to the right being curtailed in Singapore, Malaysia and Ireland. The CJPOA drew upon legislation from Northern Ireland and the Republic of Ireland. Other countries in turn drew on the English experience to change (Ireland again, parts of Australia) – or at least reconsider – their approach to the right of silence (India and states in Australia). English law still has persuasive effect in many common law jurisdictions and a backlash against suspects' rights starting from the 'Mother of Parliaments' proved influential – even in countries that retained the right of silence. The endorsement of the English and Strasbourg courts allowed curtailing the right to become almost a hallmark of an advanced legal system. Their validation also facilitated changes in countries with fewer protections for suspects.

David Garland has explored how the UK and USA governments reacted to their inability to reduce crime by 'acting out' through aggressive law enforcement measures and harsher sentencing policies. The object of such policies and the accompanying punitive rhetoric were primarily expressive, 'to denounce the crime and reassure the public' (Garland 2001:133). Criminal evidence rules have played a significant and under-examined role in the spread of this 'culture of control'. The CJPOA marked a new departure in the prosecution of crime in England; a declaration that defendants have too many rights and should cede some of them in order to restore equilibrium. This re-balancing narrative, which differed significantly from how the right of silence argument was framed in other jurisdictions, fed into the 'populist punitiveness' (Bottoms 1995) of criminal justice policy that subsequently took hold, coupled with subsequent legislation and an increasingly managerialist approach by the courts. Whilst the CJPOA has had limited direct effects upon the outcome trials, it has had profound consequences at the police station and upon the benefits to suspects of legal representation and far fewer defendants now decline to testify. Suspects' rights to a fair trial, now guaranteed formally under Article 6 of the ECHR, appear stronger than ever. In reality, however, the working practices of, and relationships between, suspects, the police and legal representatives have been distorted by this legislation, which has made it easier for the prosecution to discharge the burden of proof. In effect, for the first time, suspects are expected to cooperate actively with the investigation and trial process, an assumption of 'coerced participation', which runs contrary to the principle that it is for the prosecution to prove its case (Leng 2001c:128). This change has fundamentally altered the legal landscape in ways that were not envisaged by those on either side of the debate at the time. The danger of such a cavalier approach is that, in the face of a continuing need to be seen to be tackling crime, the boundaries of what is acceptable have to be pushed further.

Chapter 1

The right of silence – a benchmark of justice?

The background to the debate

The right of silence and the privilege against self-incrimination are 'two closely related but discrete rights' (Jennings 2001:207). Some (notably the ECtHR) use the terms interchangeably, but they vary in scope, have differing rationales and are protected to differing extents. The right of silence refers only to spoken communication, whereas the privilege can apply more widely to compulsory questioning by inspectors (*Saunders* v *UK* 1997), the requirement to produce documents (*Funke* v *France* 1993; *JB* v *Switzerland* 2001) or even to regurgitate a bag of cocaine (*Jalloh* v *Germany* 2007). The right of silence applies to any verbal statement, not just an incriminating one, thus protecting all suspects, whether guilty or innocent, from having to answer questions (the innocent cannot incriminate themselves by answering truthfully). A 'privilege' implies favourable treatment, whereas a 'right' is an entitlement that makes no judgment as to the guilt or motivations of the accused but 'denotes an interest protected as an expression of basic values' (Greer 1990:710). Suspects may decline to answer police questions or to testify for a number of reasons unrelated to their guilt, discussed below.

> The privilege against self-incrimination is firmly established judge-made law … It entitles any person to refuse to answer questions or to yield up documents or objects if to do so would carry a real or appreciable risk of its use in the prosecution of that person or his spouse.
> (*Bishopsgate Investment Management Ltd* v *Maxwell* 1993 at 63)

Witnesses are compelled to disclose information in criminal proceedings under threat of contempt of court but they can refuse to answer any question that might expose them to criminal liability.[1] When defendants first became allowed to give sworn testimony in their trials, they were exempted from the

---

1 In relation to civil proceedings, a person can refuse to answer any question or produce any document, if to do so would 'tend to expose' that person to proceedings for a criminal offence or criminal penalty (s14(1) of the Civil Evidence Act 1968).

compulsory process ('The failure of any person charged with an offence ... to give evidence shall not be made the subject of any comment by the prosecution', [s1(b) Criminal Evidence Act 1898]), but, once they began to testify, the privilege against self-incrimination was waived (s1(e)). International treaties and constitutions tend to refer to the wider privilege against self-incrimination. Whilst the privilege is generally considered a fundamental right, beyond information given in answer to compulsory questioning 'there is little agreement on its content or effect' (Choo 2013:113) between – and sometimes within – jurisdictions. Qualification of the privilege against self-incrimination is permissible if directed towards clear and proper public objectives and if the qualification is no greater than the situation calls for (*Brown* v *Stott* 2003). Compulsory questioning is permissible in certain circumstances (for example, company directors can be required to provide information), but the resulting answers could not be used in criminal proceedings (*Saunders* v *UK* 1997; *Heaney and McGuinness* v *Ireland* 2001). The ECHR now undertakes a 'balancing' exercise in deciding whether the use of such compelled testimony breaches Article 6(1) (*O'Halloran and Francis* v *UK* 2007; Choo 2013: ch 4). Much of the relevant jurisprudence of the ECtHR relates to the wider privilege. There are many excellent discussions of the privilege (for example, Choo 2013; Helmholz *et al.* 1997; Moisidis 2008) and, where the issues overlap, some of the literature will be used, but the focus of this book is on the right of silence in relation to the accused in criminal proceedings.

Lord Mustill (*SFO ex parte Smith* 1993 at 30–31), in what has become the key judicial reference point for the right of silence, identified six meanings of the 'disparate group of immunities, which differ in nature, origin, incidence and importance, and also to the extent to which they have already been encroached upon by statute'. These are:

1   A general immunity, possessed by all persons and bodies, from being compelled on pain of punishment to answer questions posed by other persons or bodies.
2   A general immunity, possessed by all persons and bodies, from being compelled on pain of punishment to answer questions the answers to which may incriminate them.
3   A specific immunity, possessed by all persons under suspicion of criminal responsibility whilst being interviewed by police officers or others in similar positions of authority, from being compelled on pain of punishment to answer questions of any kind.
4   A specific immunity, possessed by accused persons undergoing trial, from being compelled to give evidence, and from being compelled to answer questions put to them in the dock.
5   A specific immunity, possessed by persons who have been charged with a criminal offence, from having questions material to the offence addressed to them by police officers or persons in a similar position of authority.

6   A specific immunity (at least in certain circumstances, which it is unnecessary to explore), possessed by accused persons undergoing trial, from having adverse comment made on any failure (a) to answer questions before the trial, or (b) to give evidence at the trial.

It illustrates the lack of clarity in this area that some of what Lord Mustill referred to as subdivisions of the right of silence appear to refer to the wider privilege. His first point reiterates that in liberal democracies, just as individuals are entitled to freedom of expression, they are entitled to refuse to answer questions, or – in the more colourful phrasing of an Australian inquiry – everyone 'has a right to privacy and independence and can tell any officious enquirer to jump in the lake' (Northern Territory Law Reform Committee 2002:19). The importance of the right as protective of personal autonomy and privacy should not be underestimated. Even questions not related to criminal liability can have serious personal and professional consequences for an individual, such as the infamous 'are you now or have you ever been a member of the Communist Party' questions of the House Un-American Activities Committee in the 1950s (Bentley and US Congress 1971). Lord Mustill's points 3–5 relate to compulsory questioning relating to suspected criminal liability. Article 3 of the ECHR prohibits torture and it was a common law rule before the Police and Criminal Evidence Act 1984 came into force that confessions were only admissible if made voluntarily (Practice Note (Judges' Rules) 1964). The CJPOA, and thus the focus of this book, relates only to point 6 where the accused face the 'indirect compulsion' (*Murry* v *UK* 1996) of adverse inferences from failure to answer questions or to testify.

Many of those opposing the changes made by the CJPOA referred to the 'abolition' of the right of silence. Whilst it may be argued that a right which incurs penalties in its exercise has effectively been abolished (Greer 1990:710), this overstates the case. It is not possible to force an individual to speak, certainly not truthfully, and people cannot speak honestly of that which they do not know. It would be difficult, although as the revelations of 'extraordinary rendition' show, not impossible, for established democracies physically to coerce testimony from suspects (Open Society Justice Initiative 2013). Failure to answer questions is not, of itself, an offence (an important distinction for the ECtHR, see Chapter 5) in most situations. Rather than abolishing the right of silence, the question now is whether or not inferences can be drawn, to what extent and in what circumstances. Whether the inferences weaken the defence case, bolster or corroborate the prosecution case is largely a question of semantics. The CJPOA changes have been described variously as 'amending' (RCCJ 1993:50), 'modifying' (Easton 1991:viii), 'attenuating' (Mirfield 1997:246); 'curtailing' (Fenwick 1995a:132), 'emasculating' (Sanders and Young 2008:305), 'abolishing' (Greer 1990:710) or 'eviscerating' (Walker and Starmer

1999:12) the right of silence. As the right may still be exercised, often resulting in no charge being brought or an acquittal, the terms preferred here are 'curtailing' or 'changing'.

The origins of the right of silence

It has been claimed that the maxim *nemo tenetur seipsum accusare* ('no man is bound to accuse himself') 'goes back to the very origins of western legal tradition' (*Jalloh* v *Germany* 2007 at 702). There is also a Talmudic precept *Ein adam meissim atsmo rasha* ('no man shall show himself as wicked'). There are conflicting scholarly accounts of the origins of the right of silence. The classic or orthodox accounts of Leonard Levy (1968) and John Wigmore (1906) date the origin of the privilege to the seventeenth century opposition to the Courts of Star Chamber and High Commission. John Langbein's more recent account (John H. Langbein, 'The Historical Origins of the Privilege Against Self-Incrimination at Common Law, 92 Mich. L. Rev. 1047 (1994)) dates it to the eighteenth and nineteenth centuries and the transition from the 'accused speaks' system of trial to one of 'testing the prosecution' made possible by the rise of defence counsel. This view has latterly gained significant support from historians (McInerney 2014:108–109), although Alschuler (1996) claims that the confusion arises because Wigmore refers to the right of sworn witnesses to refuse to answer questions on the grounds of self-incrimination and Langbein the right of unsworn defendants to remain silent.

Since the twelfth century, the church had deployed compulsory sworn interrogations on matters ranging from heresy to Sabbath breach and sexual incontinence (Wolchover 2001:2). As religious dissent came to be associated with political insurrection, the Privy Council adopted the canon law oath procedure into its inquiries. In the late fifteenth century, the Star Chamber was established under the Royal Prerogative to ensure the fair enforcement of laws against the powerful whom the ordinary courts would not convict. This discretion meant that the Star Chamber could also punish actions that it deemed to be morally reprehensible but that were not against the law. The Court exercised its arbitrary powers against the Parliamentary and Puritan opponents of Charles I (1625–49). The Star Chamber's sessions investigating treason and heresy were held in secret and extracted evidence by torturing witnesses. Those summoned (often on the basis of mere rumour) were not told whether they were accused of a crime, or of the nature of any charges against them. Individuals were required to take the oath *ex officio* (so called because the judge could administer them by virtue of his office) to answer truthfully all questions that might be asked. Those who refused to take the oath, failed to give an answer or a sufficiently detailed response were convicted *pro confesso* – as though they had confessed. There was no jury, the common law did not apply and there was no right of appeal. Punishments included the pillory, corporal punishment, branding and mutilation.

The prosecution of John Lilburne, the leader of The Levellers, for importing seditious books into England in 1639 proved to be 'a victory for the right to silence and a devastating defeat for inquisitorial procedures in England' (O'Reilly 1994:417). Lilburne refused to take the oath or to answer any of the inquisitor's 'impertinent questions, for fear that with my answer I may do myself hurt'. He was found guilty of contempt for his refusal to take the oath, jailed until he agreed to do so and sentenced to corporal punishment. At his flogging, Lilburne denounced the unjust process before a large crowd (O'Reilly 1994:417). Langbein disputes Lilburne's significance, but 'Freeborn John' became part of the mythology of the right of silence. In 1641, the Long Parliament abolished the Star Chamber and made reparations to some of its victims. The right of silence appears as item 16 in The Levellers' *Agreement of the Free People of England* (1649), although not the Bill of Rights (1689). For many supporters of the right of silence, it 'is thus bound up historically with a rejection of authoritarian, "foreign", methods of criminal investigation, and consequently stands for the victory of freedom and justice over tyranny and despotism' (Roberts and Zuckerman 2010:538).

Many of the Puritan dissenters left for New England and the right appeared in a limited form in the Massachusetts Body of Liberties 1641.[2] Following the American Revolution, six states included the privilege against self-incrimination in their constitutions (Massachusetts, New Hampshire, North Carolina, Pennsylvania, Vermont and Virginia; Killian *et al.* 2004:1392). Lilburne's trial has been cited as a factor in the Fifth Amendment to the US Constitution, including in the landmark US Supreme Court decision of *Miranda* v *Arizona* (1966). The Supreme Court made clear that the right was more than an evidential rule – it expressed something profound about American ideals:

> It reflects many of our fundamental values and most noble aspirations; our unwillingness to subject those suspected of crime to the cruel trilemma of self-accusation, perjury or contempt; our preference for an accusatorial rather than an inquisitorial system of criminal justice; our fear that self-incriminating statements will be elicited by inhumane treatment and abuses; our sense of fair play which dictates 'a fair state-individual balance by requiring the government to leave the individual

2   45. No man shall be forced by torture to confess any crime against himself nor any other, unless it be in some capital case where he is first fully convicted by clear and sufficient evidence to be guilty, after which if the cause be of that nature, that it is very apparent there be other conspirators, or confederates with him, then he may be tortured, yet not with such tortures as be barbarous and inhumane.

alone until good cause is shown for disturbing him and by requiring the government in its contest with the individual to shoulder the entire load ... our respect for the inviolability of the human personality and of the right of each individual 'to a private enclave where he may lead a private life' ... our distrust of self-deprecatory statement; and our realization that the privilege, while sometimes 'a shelter to the guilty' is often 'a protection to the innocent'.

(Murphy v *Waterfront Commission* 1964 at 55)

Langbein in contrast argues that the true origins of the common law privilege 'are to be found not in the high politics of the English revolutions, but in the rise of adversary criminal procedure at the end of the Eighteenth Century' (1994:1047). In the sixteenth and seventeenth centuries, the accused were not allowed representation by counsel. Judges examined witnesses and the defendant, which meant that remaining silent was merely 'a right to commit suicide' (Alschuler 1996:2654). By the late eighteenth century, lawyers had taken over trial preparation and the examination of witnesses. Questioning defendants did not cease until the early nineteenth century and justices of peace questioned the accused before trial until 1848, when they became obliged to caution suspects that they were not bound to answer and the practice ended (Jackson and Summers 2012:243). Until the Criminal Evidence Act 1898 defendants were forbidden from testifying, through 'incompetence of interest'; before that, they would give unsworn evidence from the dock. Langbein argues that rather than the Star Chamber:

[I]t was the capture of the criminal trial by lawyers for the prosecution and defense, together with the important developments of the rules of evidence ... that made it possible for the criminal defendant to decline to be a witness against himself.

(Langbein 1997:83)

Mulcahy (2013:1144) observes that the development of the use of the dock to physically isolate defendants increased with the greater use of lawyers. She notes that '[r]ather than facilitating their participation in the trial, the use of the dock appears to signal the expectation that the defendant remains silent and passive'. Another factor in the development of the right of silence was the over-prescription of capital punishment. Evidential safeguards were created to avoid convictions for those accused of offences such as stealing fish or being in the company of gypsies at a time when 'too much truth meant too much death' (Moisidis 2008:15).

Wigmore describes the privilege against self-incrimination as 'creeping ... by indirection' into English life rather than being a major constitutional landmark as in the United States of America. Critics of the right have observed how its reach has extended far beyond that originally intended. 'The scope and function of the privilege have shifted over time ... While this flexibility may explain the privilege's longevity, the history does little to show why we should respect the privilege today' (Redmayne 2007:210). In reviewing the historical and contemporary debates, it becomes clear that an individual's view of the origin may influence whether the right is seen as 'a matter of high constitutional importance, or an accidental by-product of struggles over other issues which has limited value in comparison to the problems it causes' (MacNair 1990:66). Defenders of the right tend to claim its long heritage as a protection against state oppression and coercive questioning; its opponents point to its obscure origins and obsolete concerns as a reason for regarding the right as rather like the appendix – a redundant evolutionary remnant that is occasionally troublesome, and can be removed without ill effects.

While there may be different reasons in societies for adopting the right of silence, the fact that so many did suggests there is something in the right that resonates. As Allen and Mace (2003:246) argue 'while there is no general theoretical justification for the Fifth Amendment, there is a powerfully explanatory positive theory' that governs government–citizen encounters. Some judges have expressed contentment with the mutability of the right. Lord Gardiner (in terms that owed much to L.J. Frank's dissenting opinion in *United States* v *Grunewald* 1956) observed:

> The privilege against self-incrimination has always been as broad as the mischief against which it seeks to guard ... As a noble principle often transcends its origins, the privilege has come rightfully to be recognised in part as an individual's substantive right, 'a right to a private enclave where he may lead a private life' ... The constitutional foundation underlying the privilege is the respect a Government must accord to the dignity and integrity of its citizens.
>
> (House of Lords Official Report, 14 February 1973, cols 1567–1568)

Lord Diplock, in considering the exclusionary rules around confessions, noted today that:

> It has a long history dating back to the days before the existence of a disciplined police force, when a prisoner on a charge of felony could not be represented by counsel and was not entitled to give evidence in his own defence either to deny that he had made the confession, which was generally oral, or to deny that its contents were true. The underlying rationale of this branch of the criminal law, though it may originally have been based upon ensuring the reliability of confessions is, in my view, now to be found in the maxim *nemo debet prodere se ipsum*, no one can be required to be his own betrayer or in its popular English mistranslation 'the right to silence'.
>
> (*Sang* 1980 at 197)

Although crime, policing and court proceedings bear little relation to their seventeenth, eighteenth, nineteenth or even twentieth century equivalents, expectations and standards of rights have also evolved. For example, the bar for what the ECtHR considers torture has lowered over the last 50 years. The 're-balancing' argument is explored further in Chapter 2, but to argue that improvements in the treatment of suspects means that fundamental principles can and should be eroded sets a dangerous precedent. To follow this logic, it might equally be argued that the burden of proof no longer needs to be discharged beyond reasonable doubt or that legal representation is not essential. What matters instead is the goal which the right is designed to protect.

Police conduct of interviews has transformed (see Chapter 3) but this progress should not be taken for granted. Roberts and Zuckerman assert that 'judicial torture – and worse besides – is part of the dim and dark distant history of criminal investigation' (2010:543). The conflict in Northern Ireland and the practices of the West Midland Serious Crime Squad (Kaye 1991) offer examples within the last 40 years in which the police have abused suspects (*Ireland* v *UK* 1979–80; Bennett Report 1978–79; Committee for the Prevention of Torture or Degrading Treatment or Punishment 1994; Amnesty International 1995). In addition, the 'extraordinary rendition' techniques used by the US authorities and the proposals for the UK to withdraw from the ECHR should further caution against complacency. Whatever the recent pressures, in the words of Lord Devlin (1986:176) in the infamous murder trial of Dr John Bodkin Adams:

> The law on this matter reflects the natural thought of England. So great is and always has been our horror that a man might be questioned, forced to speak and perhaps to condemn himself out of his own mouth, that we grant to everyone suspected or accused of crime at the beginning, at every stage and until the very end, the right to say, 'Ask me no question. I shall answer none. Prove your case.'

Curtailing the right of silence: the debate

The lack of a definitive historical explanation of the origins of the right of silence means that a 'dozen justifications have been suggested' (Wigmore 1961). As with the version of history preferred, views about the right of silence are entwined with beliefs about the overriding priorities of the criminal justice system. The English criminal justice system is a complex organic entity. It is uncodified and, prior to the Human Rights Act 1998, the unwritten constitution meant that there were no formal, overarching concepts to guide or limit the extent of any changes. Instead, judges have articulated what they consider to be fundamental principles underlying English criminal law and procedure, designed to ensure that defendants receive a fair trial. As Leigh (1997:658) explains:

> The notion of fair trial in its application to criminal law incorporates three closely related, albeit distinct, principles. These are: that the accused be presumed innocent until proven guilty, that the State bear the burden of proof on the issue of guilt and innocence, and that the accused be not obliged to incriminate himself.

The right of silence was a practical expression of the principle that the prosecution should be able to prove its case, notwithstanding any answer by the defendant. In one of the most quoted aphorisms in English law, Lord Sankey stated that '[t]hroughout the web of the English Criminal Law one golden thread is always to be seen, that it is the duty of the prosecution to prove the prisoner's guilt' (*Woolmington* v *DPP* 1935 at 7). Whilst technically the burden of proof remains unchanged by allowing inferences to be drawn from silence, such legislation is based on an assumption that reluctance to speak or testify is indicative of guilt; innocence cannot be inferred from silence (*Murray* v *DPP* 1993). Ashworth (2006:256) cautions that 'a law that permits adverse inferences from a defendant's failure to answer questions may well have a strong impact on the presumption of innocence, by effectively reducing the prosecution's burden in matters of proof' (see also *Murray* v *UK* 1996 at 52, partly dissenting opinion of Mr E. Busuttil).

The bulk of the recent debate has tended to focus upon the right to silence in the police station rather than in the courtroom. Ashworth (2006:256) argues that this is 'an important normative distinction'. He contends that allowing inferences from failure to give evidence at a trial is not inconsistent with the presumption of innocence because the prosecution must first establish a case to answer. It does, however, make it easier for the prosecution to discharge that burden. Others separate the types of silence on the basis that the defendant enjoys greater protections and knows the prosecution case at trial. If the argument is framed solely in terms of protecting suspects against the risk of false confessions, that is a reasonable position, but it misses a number of other important aspects of the debate.

The approach taken to the right of silence shapes and is shaped by the priorities of the criminal justice system. In Packer's (1968) archetypes, 'crime control' systems prioritise the expeditious repression of criminal conduct through police interrogation, minimal safeguards and the encouragement of guilty pleas, and assume the police have apprehended the right suspect. 'Due process' systems emphasise the protection of individual rights and the integrity of the system by testing evidence, requiring a presumption of innocence and providing remedies for mistakes.

Bentham's well-known caricatures of reasons for endorsing the right of silence assume the guilt of the accused. His 'old woman's reason' for defending the right ('tis hard upon a man to be obliged to criminate himself') was echoed in the reasoning of the CLRC (1972) and the politicians endorsing the CJPOA who referred to 'criminals' exploiting the right of silence. Whilst the English system is broadly adversarial in nature, it cannot be truly so as the disparity in resources between the prosecution and defence could not result in a fair trial for defendants (McEwan 1998:2–3). Bentham's mocking 'fox hunter's reason' for the right of silence (that it is only sporting to give the quarry a chance to escape) ignores the need for compensatory measures in an adversarial system in which the prosecution holds superior resources to the defendant. Compensatory measures, such as the right to legal advice and exclusionary evidence rules, have been adopted to ensure that suspects are not at a disadvantage to the prosecution in preparing and presenting their defence. The conventional understanding was that it was better that ten guilty men should escape justice than one innocent man should suffer (*Hobson* 1823 per Holroyd J). This asymmetry has been exploited by proponents of crime control measures and the protections provided to achieve this – in particular, legal representation – were used to attack the right of silence.

The High Court made clear that 'though every citizen has a moral, or if you like social, duty to assist the police there is no legal duty to that effect' (*Rice* v *Connolly* 1966 at 419). Others have argued, notwithstanding this, the accused should 'respond to the promptings of conscience by co-operating with such enquiries … It is a moral failing, and in this context also a derogation of civic responsibility, always to stand on the strict letter of one's legal rights' (Roberts and Zuckerman 2010:543). The handbook for the 'Life in the UK Test' that those wanting to become a British citizen must pass states that:

> All good citizens are expected to help the police prevent and detect crimes whenever they can … If you are stopped by the police you should give the officer your name and address. You do not need to answer any more questions, although usually people do.
> (*Life in the United Kingdom: A Journey to Citizenship Handbook*, p. 88, in Gray and Griffin 2014:304)

The remaining arguments around the right of silence can be utilitarian, instrumental or symbolic (Greer 1990) and are sketched below; the 're-balancing' argument is explored in Chapter 2. Those commentators, sometimes referred to as *utilitarian abolitionists* (Greer 1990), regard the right of silence as inhibiting accurate truth finding – impeding 'rectitude of decision' in Benthamite terms. This chimed with the increasing managerialism in the criminal justice process as cases progress more quickly and cheaply if suspects cooperate. Modern utilitarians prefer 'common sense' assertions about the innocent having nothing to hide (CLRC 1972; Michael Howard in his speech to the Conservative Party Conference in Travis 1993). It is, superficially, a persuasive view but common sense is 'unreliable, impressionistic and unsystematic', and therefore 'a curious model for the law to follow' (Easton 1998a:114).

The equating of silence with guilt makes a number of untested assumptions about the 'natural' behaviour of suspects. It ignores the social, physical and emotional context within which suspects decide whether to exercise their right of silence.

There are many reasons, unrelated to guilt or innocence that may operate on an individual's decision to answer questions or testify. Cotterill (2005:12) distinguishes 'unintentional' silence ('I cannot respond' due to lack of knowledge, incomprehension, inhibition); 'intentional' silence, internal ('I will not respond' [lack of willingness]) and 'intentional' silence, external ('I must/may not respond' [coercion, lack of permission]). Suspects may have 'innocent' reasons for not wishing to answer police questions: such as protecting family or friends, a fear of reprisals, a sense of bewilderment, embarrassment or outrage at being investigated, or a reasoned decision to wait until the allegations against them have been set out in detail and they have sought legal advice. It may be a response to inappropriate police behaviour or the suspect may just believe, whether factually guilty or innocent, that the prosecution should have to prove its case unaided. Silence can be a resistance strategy against institutional power (Kurzon 1995). Pattenden (1995:602) suggests that Jesus did not respond to the questioning of Pontius Pilate (*Matthew* 27:11–14) as he rejected his authority. (A comparison also drawn by the folk singer Pete Seeger when asked to identify himself in a photograph by the House Un-American Activities Committee, 18 August 1955.) Members of minority groups may be more reluctant to answer police questions (Phillips and Brown 1998). Refusal to answer police questions has been described as a governing norm within the criminal fraternity (Hobbs 1989); the most famous example of this being the Mafia's code of *Omerta*. In Northern Ireland, some Republican suspects routinely refused to answer police questions. The Republican newspaper *An Phoblacht* regularly advised its readers not to answer police questions, once under the much-quoted headline 'Interrogation: Whatever you say, say nothing' (6 February 1986). Michael Murray, one of three men tried alongside the Birmingham Six, refused to testify. The judge advised the jury that they might consider him 'to be in the same position as a soldier taken prisoner and refusing to give more than his name, rank, and number' to his captors (Chartres 1975).

Testifying can be a daunting prospect whether guilty or innocent – even experienced legal practitioners told me that they found the prospect frightening. Defendants may be inarticulate, irritable, anxious or unintelligent. Some defendants may have unattractive characteristics, an objectionable manner or be unable to present their defence well – what Surtees (2000:122) described as 'chatting himself to the gallows' (see Chapter 5). There may be cultural, language or emotional barriers to presenting their own case. Kiranjit Ahluwalia would not give evidence at her trial for murdering her abusive husband because she was ashamed of his sexual abuse of her and did not want her family hearing about it at the trial (www.justiceforwomen.org.uk/kiranjit-ahluwalia/). A refusal to recognise British courts was also 'an integral part of [Irish Republican] political and military strategy' for 150 years (McEvoy 2001:140–150). Although this tactic dissipated from the mid-1970s, Jackson *et al.* (2000:147) found that refusal to testify remained a strategy, almost certainly against legal advice, amongst a substantial minority of defendants in 'scheduled' trials in Northern Ireland. Defendants with a sense of injustice about the proceedings may not wish to testify but other factors may be at work. Paul Hill, one of the Guildford Four, had been beaten by the police to force a confession from him. He wrote to his mother when he was waiting for his trial in 1975 that:

> I wasn't going to go into the box because I know, mum, that anything I say will be looked upon as a lie but I think you would like me to go in, so I told my brief that I would and so he's all happy now.
>
> (*Archive on 4*, 4 October 2014)

The campaign against the right of silence gained momentum after PACE was enacted. This *exchange abolitionist* (Greer 1990) view was divided. One camp believed that suspects would be better protected by a more cooperative enquiry at the police station and the most effective way to persuade the police to accept this would be to concede to their demand for the right to be abolished (Zuckerman 1989b, 1994; Blake 1990). The other group resented the inhibitions that PACE places on the police and, realising that the repeal of PACE was politically unlikely, sought to reassert police superiority by abolishing the right of silence. It was contended that defendants had been given so many rights, particularly the right to have a legal adviser present at police interviews, that the right should be ceded to even up the 'contest'.

Instrumental retentionists maintain that the right to silence is a vital part of an accusatorial criminal justice process. It protects the courts from the false testimony of those who may feel obliged to lie if they cannot remain silent and – more stirringly – acts as a counterbalance to oppressive custody conditions, prevents torture and safeguards against miscarriages of justice. In their support of the right of silence, the Law Society, the Bar Council and the Criminal Bar Association pointed to the 'disorientating and intimidating' nature of police custody which may lead suspects to falsely incriminate themselves – particularly when they do not know the nature of the charges against them and may not understand the legal significance of their answers with regard to concepts such as intent or honesty (RCCJ 1993:52). Suspects may be confused, distressed, intimidated, intoxicated or unwell. Answering questions in such a state may be detrimental if suspects' mistakes or omissions cast doubt on their account at trial. Others have argued that not allowing inferences from silence encourages the police to seek evidence from other sources, improving the robustness of any conviction.

Of itself, clearly the right of silence is inadequate to protect vulnerable suspects, as shown by the numerous miscarriages of justice based on false confessions. Despite its limited protective value and the fact that it never attracted the level of public support of the American Fifth Amendment, the right of silence was of great symbolic value in England and Wales (Dixon 1991a; Leng 1997; Easton 1998b). *Symbolic retentionists* acknowledge its practical limitations, but argue that the right of silence should be retained for its emblematic significance and as 'a touchstone against which broader criminal justice commitments have been tested', such as the presumption of innocence. Such symbolism can be positive, reinforcing the principle that the burden of proof lies with the prosecution; or negative, expressing lack of trust in the police (Dixon 1997:266). This symbolic value had been recognised as a reason for retaining the right of silence; my research suggests that this was as much a motivation for its curtailment – what I term *symbolic abolitionism*.[3] Police hostility to the right has been seen as an attempt to regain authority lost by PACE, which many regarded as a criticism of their previous activities. It also suited an unpopular government to be seen to be 'doing something' about crime (discussed further in Chapters 2 and 6). As Moglen (1994:1089–1090) explains:

> It is not the story of a timeless natural right, growing in recognition as society became more 'free'. Instead, the history of the privilege reveals how procedure makes substance, and how legal evolution, like natural selection itself, adapts old structures to new functions. If the revised account is less heroic, it nonetheless brings us closer to the real mechanisms of legal development.

New legal regimes: founding principles and fair trials

The post-World War Two Nuremberg and Tokyo War Crimes Tribunals were the first international attempt to hold wartime leaders accountable for the crimes against humanity committed by their armed forces. The privilege against self-incrimination was not included in the founding charters of either court. At the Yokohama War Crimes Trials (for lower ranking

---

3 Greer mentions in a footnote that '[e]xchange abolitionism could also be considered a form of symbolic abolitionism' but does not elaborate on this.

Japanese officers), the prosecutor could comment on the failure of the accused to testify and 'the commission was permitted to draw such inferences from his failure to testify as might seem fair and competent to a reasonable mind' (Spurlock 1950:388). The trials were undoubtedly flawed; 'most international standards relating to the protection of fundamental rights in the administration of criminal justice had not yet been the object of international law-making' (Zappala). Whilst British Prime Minister Winston Churchill took some persuading of the benefits of the judicial process over the merits of summary execution, others advocated using the rule of law to enhance the legitimacy of their decisions. As Chief Prosecutor Robert Jackson stated in opening the Nuremberg trials: 'We must never forget that the record on which we judge these defendants is the record on which history will judge us tomorrow.'

The ECHR was the first comprehensive human rights treaty to emerge from the post-World War Two law-making process (Schabas 2015:1). As noted above, the ECHR does not mention the privilege against self-incrimination explicitly ('presumably because the Convention was something of an international human right law prototype and the privilege was overlooked' (Roberts and Zuckerman 2010:555)). The Committee of Experts that considered the differences between the international and European treaties reported that the privilege was the 'very essence' of a fair trial (Council of Europe 1970, para 141 (vi)). The European Commission of Human Rights recognised a general right of silence as the negative counterpart of the freedom of expression protected under Article 10 (*K* v *Austria* Series A no 255-B, 2 June 1993), but this approach was not pursued. Article 6(1), was preferred. This ECHR provides defendants in criminal proceedings with certain basic rights. These include the right to: a fair and public hearing within a reasonable time by an independent and impartial tribunal; to be informed promptly and in detail of the accusation faced; to adequate time and facilities to prepare a defence; to legal assistance and to examine witnesses.

The European jurisprudence concerning the privilege against self-incrimination is 'somewhat inconsistent and problematic' (Dennis 2002:27; Leigh 1997:660; Chapter 5). The ECHR first recognised the privilege against self-incrimination in *Orkem* v *European Commission* (1989) but *Funke* v *France* (1993) was the first major decision and was expanded in *Saunders* v *UK* (1997). 'This was an important symbolic statement of the importance of the right across European jurisdictions straddling both common law and civil law traditions' (Jackson 2009:835). It was held in *Saunders* v *UK* (1997 at 68) that:

> The Court recalls that, although not specifically mentioned in Article 6 of the Convention (art. 6), the right to silence and the right not to incriminate oneself are generally recognised international standards

which lie at the heart of the notion of a fair procedure under Article 6 (art. 6). Their rationale lies, *inter alia*, in the protection of the accused against improper compulsion by the authorities thereby contributing to the avoidance of miscarriages of justice and to the fulfilment of the aims of Article 6 ... The right not to incriminate oneself, in particular, presupposes that the prosecution in a criminal case seek to prove their case against the accused without resort to evidence obtained through methods of coercion or oppression in defiance of the will of the accused. In this sense the right is closely linked to the presumption of innocence contained in Article 6 para 2 of the Convention.

While the ECtHR did not have as significant an effect on the CJPOA as had been anticipated, it has had an important influence in international law. For example, Article 6(1) of the Convention is thought to be the primary reason for the right to silence existing within both the International Criminal Tribunal for the former Yugoslavia (ICTY) and the International Criminal Tribunal for Rwanda (ICTR) that they attempt to mirror principles within the ECHR (Croquet 2011).

Mindful of the critiques of Nuremberg and Tokyo, the various international tribunals created at the end of the twentieth century (such as the ICTY, ICTR and the International Criminal Court [ICC]) as well as the hybrid tribunals in Sierra Leone and Cambodia and the Special Tribunal for Lebanon appear to have been determined to demonstrate that the rights of the accused were being protected, precisely because of the gravity of the charges faced by the accused. As Baum (2001:197) has argued:

it is precisely at those times when moral outrage is at its highest that the burden on adjudicating bodies is heaviest both to satisfy society's collective need for condemnation and punishment of war criminals and simultaneously to assiduously protect the rights of those accused of war crimes. In order for a war crimes tribunal to possess legitimacy, it must ensure that rights of the accused are protected by the principles of due process and fundamental fairness.

What is interesting for current purposes are the deliberations on the right of silence in these contexts. There were difficulties in forging a coherent system given the very different legal traditions of those establishing the tribunals. Antonio Cassese, the first President of the ICTY, argues that the Continental system is 'more geared toward the protection of the interests of society' whereas the Anglo-American approach is 'bent on enhancing the rights of the accused and more generally on ensuring respect for the fundamentals of "due process"'. An accommodation was reached and the Tribunals are evolving a distinctive style. Silence was a contentious issue during drafting (Creta 1997–98); however, it was deemed that a 'clear international consensus has emerged that the right to silence is an essential component of any system that is designed to enforce criminal law standards' (Berger 2012:14).

By way of illustration, Article 21(4)(g) of the Statute of the International Criminal Tribunals of Yugoslavia (1993) states that an accused has the right 'not to be compelled to testify against himself or to confess guilt'. The right of silence applies only after the suspect becomes an 'accused' (has been charged). It is unclear why this distinction was made but the Rules of Procedure and Evidence of the ICTY developed to give the suspect the right before this point. There is no mention in the Rules as to whether an adverse inference may be drawn from silence. The Tribunal could have followed the post-CJPOA English approach (which the ECHR had approved). Instead it held that there 'is no duty in law or morals for the accused to fill a vacuum created by the investigative procedural gap of the Prosecution' (*Prosecutor* v *Delalić* 2001 at 49). The ICTY found that 'an absolute prohibition against consideration of silence in the determination of guilt or innocence is guaranteed within the Statute and the Rules, reflecting what is now expressly stated in the Rome Statute' (*Prosecutor* v *Delalić* 2001). It held that if the drafters of the ICTY had wished for adverse inference to be allowed in court then they would have expressly stated it. It has upheld the right in another decision referring to the presumption of innocence and the requirement that the prosecution prove its case beyond reasonable doubt (*Prosecutor* v *Naletilic and Martinovic* 2003). The ICTY has also taken a 'notably expansive conception' of the privilege against self-incrimination (Choo 2013:61) extending to physical evidence created under compulsion, such as a handwriting sample from the defendant, whether or not it could be incriminating. The ICTY has also declined to consider the accused's silence in sentencing (*Prosecutor* v *Plavšić* 2003 at 58).

The drafting of the Statute of the International Criminal Tribunal for Rwanda followed a similar pattern to that of the ICTY. Article 20(4)(g) of the Statute of the International Criminal Tribunal for Rwanda states an accused has the right 'not to be compelled to testify against himself or herself or to confess guilt'. The right of silence was explicitly included in the Rules of Procedure and Evidence for the ICTR at Rule 42A(iii). This states that any suspect has '[t]he right to remain silent, and to be cautioned that any statement he makes shall be recorded and may be used in evidence'.

The International Criminal Court, a permanent international tribunal to prosecute individuals for genocide, crimes against humanity and war crimes when national courts are unwilling or unable to investigate or prosecute such crimes, was established under the Rome Statute 1998. The UN Secretary-General stated that it 'is axiomatic that the International Tribunal must fully respect internationally recognized standards regarding the rights of the accused at all stages of its proceeding' (Secretary-General's Report

1993). 'The ICC represents the most advanced level of protection to date of the rights of defendants in international criminal proceedings' (ibid.). At the pre-trial phase 'persons in respect of an investigation' have 'the right not to incriminate oneself or confess guilt' Article 55(1) (2)). Persons for whom there are grounds to believe committed a crime within the jurisdiction of the Court' have 'the right to remain silent, without such silence being a consideration in the determination of guilt or innocence' (Article 55 (2) (b)). Once on trial, the individual has the right '[n]ot to be compelled to testify or to confess guilt and to remain silent, without such silence being a consideration in the determination of guilt or innocence' (Article 67(1) (g)). In contexts where the political stakes could not have been higher or the crimes more serious, the drafters and judges on these various international courts have been committed to protecting the right of silence. DeFrancia (2001:1437) argues that:

> it is better for the credibility of a budding international criminal common law to err on the side of stronger protections rather than weaker. In this respect, support for these institutions will not dry up on the basis of a lack of procedural integrity.

Conclusion

The right of silence is an emotive subject that 'arouses strong but unfocused feelings' (*Director of SFO ex parte Smith* 1993 at 31). Its origins lay in a time when the judicial process was abused for political and religious ends. It is a principle upheld in many jurisdictions and there are practical and symbolic arguments for and against its retention. Even though that is no longer the position, that association still resonates as the anecdote cited in the 1895 US Supreme Court case of *Coffin* v *United States* (156 US at 455) captures:

> Upon being accused of a crime, Numerius, the governor of Narbonensis, came to trial before the Emperor Julian. There, Numerius simply denied his guilt, offering no proof of his own. In response, his adversary, Delphidius, realizing that he was not going to win a conviction due to his own insufficient proof, exclaimed, 'Oh, illustrious Caesar! if it is sufficient to deny, what hereafter will become of the guilty?' To this, the emperor replied: 'If it suffices to accuse, what will become of the innocent?'

The right of silence is the nexus of other fundamental rights, such as the presumption of innocence and the burden of proof lying with the prosecution. Gradually jurisdictions had evolved towards developing the right of silence so that it had become an expected right in new constitutions. This was seen as part of an evolving standard – it appears now that this may have been the peak of due process protections.

Chapter 2

The right of silence – a crime control target?

Although generally considered a cornerstone of British justice, the right of silence has never rested on entirely secure foundations. Having explored how the right of silence came to be regarded as a prerequisite for any credible judicial system in Chapter 1, this chapter examines in some detail how the tide began to turn in England and Wales. A significant imperative was the political desire to 'do something' about rising crime. The right of silence is intertwined with the presumption of innocence. Andrew Ashworth (2006:241) identifies four threats to the presumption of innocence in the 'risk society' (in which governments prioritise minimising the security threat over individual liberties): *confinement, erosion, side-stepping* and *evasion*. These do not map across exactly, but the right of silence faced similar dangers. The police exercised a strong influence in shaping that response.

Following the Criminal Evidence Act 1898, which permitted suspects to give sworn evidence at trial for the first time, the English courts at first largely followed the American approach of not permitting inferences from silence (Williams 1955) and the Royal Commission on Police Powers and Procedure (RCPPP 1929) endorsed the right of silence. The last three decades of the twentieth century, however, saw significant developments. Events are traced in chronological order through legislative incursions; judicial interpretation and a series of official reports: the Criminal Law Revision Committee (CLRC 1972) recommended abolishing the right; the Royal Commission on Criminal Procedure (RCCP 1981) favoured retention; and the Home Office Working Group (HOWG 1989) was directed to investigate how to implement restrictions. After the Criminal Evidence (Northern Ireland) Order 1988 curtailed the right of silence in Northern Ireland, the Royal Commission on Criminal Justice (RCCJ 1993) recommended its retention in England and Wales. These reports are examined in the broader social context in which they operated, including crime rates, social unrest, terrorism and the backlash against the Police and Criminal Evidence Act 1984 (PACE). The academic research relating to the use of the right is examined, and finally the provisions of the Criminal

Justice and Public Order Act 1994 (CJPOA), which curtailed the right of silence in England and Wales, are set out.

Zuckerman has described the undermining of the privilege against self-incrimination in English and American law as 'a process of attrition' (Zuckerman 1989a:549). Exceptions swiftly become the norm regarding particular types of evidence or crimes ('it is clear that statutory interference with the right is almost as old as the right itself' (*R* v *SFO ex parte Smith* 1993 at 40)). Significant legislative inroads had been made into the right of silence by the requirement that the defence must disclose before trial any alibi (s11 of the Criminal Justice Act 1967) or expert evidence (s81 of PACE) it proposes to call. These obligations were introduced on the basis that it was too difficult for the prosecution to rebut such evidence (or 'ambush defences' as they were pejoratively known) without notice and could lead to unmeritorious acquittals. In practice, these statutory incursions made little difference, as the only sanction – of excluding the evidence – was so potentially catastrophic for the defence that judges usually exercised their discretion to allow the evidence to be called (Zander 1996). Other statutes created specific penalties for non-compliance – for example, section 172(2)(a) of the Road Traffic Act 1988 requires the keeper of a vehicle to disclose the identity of the driver in certain circumstances (such as if it has been recorded speeding). Significant extra powers are given to those investigating fraud and serious financial misconduct (see *inter alia*, s447 of the Companies Act 1985, s219 of the Insolvency Act 1986, s105 of the Financial Services Act 1986, s41 of the Banking Act 1987 and s2 of the Criminal Justice Act 1987). These exceptions were rationalised because of the particular difficulties caused to the prosecution of investigating such offences without the suspect's cooperation. One of the examples that was cited as a reason for curtailing the right of silence was where a child dies and it is not possible to establish which parent was responsible if both remain silent. Legislation was subsequently introduced of 'causing or allowing the death of a child or vulnerable adult' (s5 of the Domestic Violence, Crime and Victims Act 2004).

Forty per cent of offences triable in the Crown Court put the onus of proving at least one element of the offence or a statutory defence on the defendant (Blake and Ashworth 1996), which makes it harder for the defendant not to give evidence. For example, s1(1) of the Prevention of Crime Act 1953 provides that '[a]ny person who without lawful authority or reasonable excuse, *the proof whereof shall lie on him*, has with him in any public place any offensive weapon shall be guilty of an offence' (emphasis added). In summary proceedings, 'the burden of proving the exception, exemption, proviso, excuse or qualification shall be on [the defendant]' (s101 of the Magistrates' Courts Act 1980). This is not a recent mechanism; s4 of the Explosive Substances Act 1883 placed the burden of proving lawful excuse for the possession of explosives on the accused – this was before the accused was allowed to give sworn testimony.

Counter-terrorism and wartime have been a fertile source of exemptions from the right of silence. Section 7 of the Official Secrets Act 1911 made it an offence for a person to refuse to disclose 'any information which it is in his power to give', relating to others who might reasonably be suspected of spying. The Defence of the Realm Regulation No 53, issued during World War One, made it an offence for any person not 'to stop and answer to the best of his ability and knowledge any questions which may be reasonably addressed to him' by a member of the armed forces or a police officer. It was suggested that more suspects gave statements to the police after World War One because '[t]hese powers and the circumstances of the time, bred in the Police a war mentality which has not yet wholly disappeared' (RCPPP 1929: para 267). A version of these powers could be found in the Emergency Provisions Act 1973 and appears in subsequent iterations of counter-terrorism legislation (see Walker 2014). This fear of terrorism and crime was a powerful motivating and justificatory force in curtailing the right of silence.

The right of silence has also been subject to circumvention, primarily through developments in forensic evidence and increased surveillance opportunities. If the police can access mobile telephone records, watch CCTV, bug legal consultations or use 'covert human intelligence sources' then the need for the suspect's participation in the investigation is rendered almost redundant.

Judicial comment

Parliament was not the only source of exceptions to the right of silence. It was not the case, as was sometimes suggested by those advocating the changes, that the courts were unable to consider a defendant's refusal to answer police questions or to testify before the CJPOA. When the Criminal Evidence Act 1898 permitted defendants to testify for the first time, it prohibited the prosecution, but not judges, or counsel for a co-accused, from commenting on a defendant's failure to give evidence. Historically the judiciary took what Jackson (1994:270) has described as 'a rather Janus-faced attitude towards the right of silence'. The court made clear from the start that:

> There is nothing in the Act that takes away or even purports to take away the right of the court to comment on the evidence in the case, and the manner in which the case has been conducted. The nature and degree of such comment must rest entirely in the discretion of the judge who tries the case; and it is impossible to lay down any rule as to the cases in which [the judge] ought or ought not to comment on the failure of the prisoner to give evidence, or as to what those comments should be ... That is a question entirely for the discretion of the judge.
>
> (*Rhodes* 1899 at 83)

The Judicial Studies Board issued a specimen direction to guide judges in their summings-up to juries about defendants who did not give evidence; this was known as a *Bathurst* direction, after the 1968 judgment on which it was based. Although the court later declined to rule that the judge must *always* direct the jury that it is wrong for them to assume that a defendant who does not testify is guilty, as 'that would be changing the law as it has stood ever since the court first started to consider the consequences of the Criminal Evidence Act 1898. We are not prepared to make new law' (*Harris* 1987 at 81). Judges were supposed to say:

> The defendant does not have to give evidence, he is entitled to sit in the dock and require the prosecution to prove its case. You must not assume that he is guilty because he has not given evidence. The fact that he has not given evidence proves nothing one way or the other. It does nothing to establish his guilt. On the other hand, it means there is no evidence from the defendant to undermine, contradict or explain the evidence put before you by the prosecution. However, you still have to decide whether on the prosecution's evidence you are sure of the defendant's guilt.
>
> (cited in *Martinez-Tobon* 1994 at 394)

The courts appeared more willing to permit judicial comment on an accused's refusal to testify than from a no comment interview (*Bathurst* 1968; *Mutch* 1973; *Martinez-Tobon* 1994). The Judges' Rules, first set out in 1912, gave the first official guidance to the police on interviewing and taking statements from suspects. This required that suspects should be cautioned before being questioned: 'Do you wish to say anything in answer to the charge? You are not obliged to say anything unless you wish to do so, but whatever you say will be taken down in writing and may be given in evidence' (cited in RCPPP 1929:71). The Rules also required that suspects should be entitled to consult with a solicitor in private at any time during questioning. In 80 per cent of cases where the defendant had been silent at the police station, the jury learnt about it (Zander and Henderson 1993). The Court of Appeal found, however, that it was not possible to reconcile the conflicting authorities as to what constituted proper judicial comment on a defence revealed for the first time at trial (*Gilbert* 1977 at 244). Lord Parker C.J. said in *Hoare* (1966 at 765) that the jury ought to be told that they should not assume that a defence was untrue simply because it had not been mentioned until trial. Inferences drawn from silence could not be corroborative of guilt, but they could be drawn in order to weaken defence evidence, to strengthen prosecution evidence or to affect the inferences drawn from other evidence (*Sparrow* 1973; *Mutch* 1973). Stronger comment could be made where the defence case consisted of facts which differed from the prosecution case, or were additional to it and exculpatory and which, if true, would have been within the defendant's knowledge. The nature and strength of such comment were for the judge's discretion and depended on the circumstances of the individual case. They could not contradict or nullify the essentials of the conventional direction (*Martinez-Tobon* 1994). It was held that a direction to the jury that the accused's silence was evidence of guilt went too far (*Leckey* 1944) and the judge must not have detracted from the proper direction on silence by saying an innocent man was likely to answer questions (*Sullivan* 1966). The judge could, however, 'remind' the jury if a defence was first advanced at trial (*Gilbert* 1977); in *Fisher* (1964) the judge issued such a reminder ten times during his summing-up. As Greer (1990:712) summed up:

> The reality is that 'the law' is vague and judges have interpreted it more or less restrictively according to their personal assessment of the proper balance between two conflicting considerations: (a) the view that in certain circumstances even the silence of suspects under caution may have some probative value; and (b) the basic assumption of accusatorial systems that the accuser should be obliged to prove his case without any assistance from the accused.

Whereas the Bar Council and Law Society (the representative organisations for barristers and solicitors, respectively) were consistently opposed to curtailing the right of silence (RCCJ 1993:52), judges have been less committed to the right of silence. In 1972, the CLRC reported that judicial comment on a defendant's refusal to testify was made 'much more sparingly' than it once was, that the emphasis had shifted towards stressing the right of the accused not to give evidence and, where comments were considered appropriate, these were sometimes given 'almost apologetically' (para 109). This appeared to provoke an immediate judicial response in *Sparrow* (1973) and *Mutch* (1973). Thoresby (1973:1047) expressed concern that the CLRC Report revealed 'that judges themselves wish English criminal procedure, traditionally a model of due process for the world ... [to] change in the direction of a crime control model'. In the later case of *Gilbert*, the Court of Appeal endorsed the suggestion of the CLRC that juries and magistrates should be allowed to draw inferences, citing its view that to forbid it appeared contrary to common sense and gave an unnecessary advantage to the guilty without helping the innocent:

> We regard the present position as unsatisfactory ... It is not within our competence sitting in this Court to change the law. We cannot overrule the decisions to which we have referred. A right of silence is one thing. No accused can be compelled to speak before, or for that matter, at his trial. But it is another thing to say that if he chooses to

exercise his right of silence, that must not be the subject of any comment adverse to the accused. A judge is entitled to comment on his failure to give evidence. As the law now stands, he must not comment adversely on the accused's failure to make a statement.

(*Gilbert* 1977 at 245 per Viscount Dilhorne)

After PACE provided the right to legal advice at the police station, certain judges took an overtly abolitionist perspective (Greer 1990:712), suggesting there should be a right to comment on a suspect's failure to reveal a defence before trial as a *quid pro quo* (Zuckerman 1989b:327). In *Alladice* (1988 at 385), Lord Chief Justice Lane commented *per curiam* (on behalf of the whole court):

[I]t seems to us that the effect of section 58 [PACE] is such that the balance of fairness between prosecution and defence cannot be maintained unless proper comment is permitted on the defendant's silence in such circumstances. It is high time that such comment should be permitted together with the necessary alteration to the words of the caution.

Some senior judges (Denning 1987; Taylor 1994) and the Director of Public Prosecutions expressed similar views in a personal capacity (Sir Thomas Hetherington QC in Gibb 1987). Michael Zander, a member of the Royal Commission on Criminal Justice, later said:

I have a sense that over the last twenty or thirty years, judges broadly have favored the approach of the Criminal Law Revision Committee in its 1972 report on the question of the right to silence, and would regard this change [the CJPOA] as generally beneficial.

(Zander 1996:672)

Official inquiries and political debate

The Royal Commission on Police Powers and Procedure (RCPP 1929:1) was asked to consider the general powers of the police in investigating crime and to report whether such powers were being exercised 'with due regard to the rights and liberties of the subject, the interests of justice, and the observance of the Judges' Rules both in the letter and the spirit'. Although noting that there was minority support for the idea of dispensing with the caution, the RCPPP cited Wigmore's (1906) argument that 'a right to question gives rise to the impression of a right to an answer, and a right to an answer seems to create "a right to the expected answer – that is to a confession of guilt"'. Given the risk that this would breed a readiness to bully and to use force, the RCPPP recommended 'a rigid instruction to the Police that no questioning of a person in custody, about any crime or offence with which he is or may be charged, should be permitted'. It concluded that those in custody should not be questioned, other than to remove ambiguities in any statement they had given (1929:paras 164–169).

Attitudes towards the right of silence appeared to change during the 1960s. It was a decade of enormous social change – reflected in the courts by the obscenity trial of Penguin Books for publishing *Lady Chatterley's Lover* (1960), the abolition of capital punishment (1965) and the partial decriminalisation of homosexuality and abortion (1967). A number of evidential changes were made during the 1960s – some to the benefit of suspects (revisions to the Judges' Rules, the appeal system and the expansion of legal aid provision); others more helpful to the prosecution, such as the introduction of majority verdicts for juries. It was a time of great social unrest across much of the western world, marked by protests against the Vietnam War, civil rights campaigns and, closer to home, the 'riot' in Clacton (1964) that inspired Stan Cohen's *Folk Devils and Moral Panics*. There were widespread industrial disputes; the 'Troubles' began in Northern Ireland (1968); Enoch Powell made his infamous 'Rivers of Blood' speech about immigration (1968) and crime rates doubled during the decade.

In 1960, JUSTICE (the UK section of the International Commission of Jurists) had reported that to deprive the accused of the right to remain silent was 'alien to the general conception of justice in this country'. In a 1967 Report, it performed an abrupt *volte-face*. It concluded that, as a result of rising crime, 'the climate of opinion ha[d] become less favourable to criminals' and more accepting of the criticism of the fact that 'a sentimental sporting rule for which there was no justification should enable a guilty man to escape'. It recommended a new procedure of 'controlled compulsory interrogation before a magistrate' (1967:2) and that the police should be able to apply to a magistrate for a summons to interrogate a suspect. JUSTICE remained agnostic as to whether suspects should be compelled to testify as 'the questions which it raises are so complex, involving as they do matters going to the root of the English criminal trial process' (1967:7).

In 1964, the Home Secretary asked the Criminal Law Revision Committee:

> to review the law of evidence in criminal cases and to consider whether any changes are desirable in the interests of the fair and efficient administration of justice; and in particular what provision should be made for modifying rules which have ceased to be appropriate in modern conditions.
>
> (CLRC 1972:para 1)

Its Eleventh Report (CLRC 1972) adopted 'a Utilitarian Approach' (RCCP 1981:9). It started from the premise that 'the object of a criminal trial should be to find out if the accused is guilty' (CLRC 1972 para 14). Wrongful convictions and acquittals were reduced to equivalence, with 'fairness' being due to both sides (para 27). The Report referred to a 'large and increasing class of sophisticated professional criminals'; a group who were accused of exploiting all means to evade justice. There was 'a good deal of feeling in the committee and elsewhere that the law of evidence should now be less tender to criminals generally' (para 21). The CLRC solicited a range of views but did not consider or commission any empirical research. It took the view that the historic disadvantages faced by the defence no longer existed and that the restrictions on the admissibility of evidence should be abolished so far as possible.

> Our main object, then, has been to go as far in getting rid of restrictions on admissibility of evidence as is possible in the 'modern conditions' referred to … We have also aimed at reducing the gap between the amount of relevant evidence which could be given and the amount which is in fact given. This is done chiefly by provisions designed to discourage the accused from refraining from giving evidence if a *prima facie* case has been made out against him … and by abolishing certain privileges of refusing to answer questions. We justify the reforms which we recommend for this purpose not only because of the changed conditions to which we have referred but mainly on the ground that there is no clear reason why the restrictions should ever have existed.
>
> (CLRC 1972:para 24)

The CLRC proposed dispensing with the caution, reasoning that it was illogical for the police to have to warn suspects that they did not have to answer questions and that such a practice risked dissuading innocent people from advancing their accounts (para 43). The majority recommended that courts should be allowed to draw 'such inferences … as appear proper' from the failure of an accused to mention to the police, before or at the point of charge, any fact upon which he subsequently relied in his defence. 'To forbid it seems to us contrary to common sense and, without helping the innocent, to give an unnecessary advantage to the guilty' (para 30). It also proposed the drawing of appropriate inferences from a defendant's refusal to be sworn, and to answer questions at the trial 'without good cause'. The majority also took the view that silence on the part of both the suspect in the police station and the defendant in the courtroom should be capable of amounting to corroboration of other evidence. The minority agreed with the general thrust of these proposals but wanted to delay their implementation until tape recording of police interviews was implemented fully. The CLRC made no reference to a suspect's right to legal advice. Birch (1999:770) observes that:

> [t]he notion that the proposed law might put unfair pressure on a suspect was rejected in terms that suggest the risk was assessed only in relation to a guilty suspect 'pressured' into lying or incriminating himself: the prospect of an innocent man being disadvantaged was not seriously entertained.

The controversy engendered by the CLRC Report caused the effective suspension of debate about curtailing the right of silence for the rest of the decade: 'Both within and outside Parliament a formidable body of professional and lay opinion stood aghast, and loudly, often emotionally, protested...' (RCCP 1981:9; Evans 1972; Tapper 1972; Zander 1974). There was a brief, heated debate – initially only three months were given for responses. The abolition of the right of silence was supported by the Conservative Political Centre (*The Times*, 15 June 1972) and the Justices' Clerks Society (*The Times*, 19 January 1973), but the National Council for Civil Liberties published a pamphlet arguing for an improvement in suspects' rights and the protection of the right of silence. JUSTICE then weighed in with a 12-page memorandum which was particularly critical of the impact these proposals would have on police abuse and it reiterated its 1967 proposal for reforming the system along Continental lines. Following the 1974 General Election and the change of government, the proposals were shelved.

Thoresby noted presciently, however, that whilst the opposition to the CLRC would see off the changes to the right of silence at that stage 'that does not mean that the mode of thought exemplified by the proposals has been eradicated' (1973:1047) – and so it proved. The CLRC Report 'was to provide the "law and order" lobby with one of its most powerful intellectual supports' (Christian 1983:10). The Report received weighty endorsement from Lords Diplock, Hailsham and Widgery when the House of Lords debated the matter (14 February 1973). The authors of the leading criminal evidence textbook both argued for the curtailment of the right (Colin Tapper served on the JUSTICE Committee and Sir Rupert Cross the CLRC, as did Glanville Williams). The methods as well as the arguments of the CLRC returned in the 1980s and 1990s: the casual deployment of terms such as 'guilty' and 'criminal' to refer to those who were entitled to the presumption of innocence; and the 're-balancing' calculations that focused only on changes beneficial to the defence, ignoring the rapidly developing imbalance in resources between the prosecution and defence (Tapper 1972:623). The legislation proposed by the CLRC provided the template for the Criminal Evidence (Northern Ireland) Order 1988 and for ss34 and 35 CJPOA.

Dworkin argued in a speech to Haldane Society that the criminal procedure rules were being used as a scapegoat for the increase in crime, diverting attention from its social causes (*The Times*, 4 December 1972). The 1970s were the decade of 'nothing works' in criminal justice policy (Martinsen 1974). Recorded crime in England and Wales passed the two million mark for the first time in 1977. The conflict in Northern Ireland worsened and industrial relations deteriorated to the widespread strike action of the 'Winter of Discontent' in 1978. The Conservative Party's winning election manifesto in 1979 promised a growth in police numbers, deterrent sentences, a 'short sharp shock' for juveniles, and a free vote on the re-introduction of capital punishment. Following the reorganisation of the criminal courts in 1973, a court duty solicitor scheme was created, legally aided representation of defendants in the Crown Court became the norm and expanded rapidly in the magistrates' courts (McConville *et al.* 1994:4–5). Baldwin and McConville's Home Office-funded study found 'little evidence to justify amending rules of evidence or procedure on the basis of the supposed ability of professional criminals to exploit the system' (1979:126).

The police acted as 'moral entrepreneurs', lobbying for legislation that advanced their 'crime control' interests (Thoresby 1973:1047). Sir Robert Mark (Commissioner of the Metropolitan Police 1972–77) was '[t]he first to realise the potential political role which could be played by Chief Constables' (Christian 1983:9) – what Reiner dubbed the 'Marksist revolution at Scotland Yard' (2010:89). Mark took the view that, post-war, the role of the police changed from law enforcement to 'contributors in the moulding of public opinion and legislation'. Despite the failure of the CLRC Report, Mark kept the issue of curtailing the right of silence alive – including in his Dimbleby Lecture in 1974. The Police Federation launched a campaign in 1975 to influence politicians to 'support the rule of law' and two weeks before polling day in 1979, it took out advertisements in most national newspapers blaming the Labour government for rising crime and setting out policies that were then agreed by the Conservatives (Reiner 2010:89). They followed this up in 1982 with an unsuccessful campaign calling for the re-introduction of the death penalty. Sim (1982:65) argues that certain newspapers and television programmes gave an uncritical platform for the views of senior police officers. Between 1979 and 1984, police expenditure doubled, whilst notifiable offences increased by 37 per cent (Newburn 2003:69). The spring and summer of 1981 saw widespread civil disorder and rioting in predominantly black areas of the major English cities and the hunger strikes in the Maze Prison in Northern Ireland. Senior police and army officers in Northern Ireland were 'increasingly angry and frustrated' at suspects remaining silent and engaged in 'intensive behind-the-scenes lobbying'. The Official Ulster Unionist Party produced an internal policy paper as part of an intensifying plan. It called for a specific offence of refusing to answer questions (Thomas 1980). Sir

David 'The Hammer' McNee, Commissioner of the Metropolitan Police between 1977 and 1982, followed his predecessor's approach. The 'law and order' lobbying became less overt when Sir Kenneth Newman took over (Bridges and Bunyan, 1983:86; Reiner 2000:73), but the police role in responding to civil disorder during the Miners' Strike of 1984–85 meant that they were closely identified with the Conservative government of Margaret Thatcher (Reiner 2010:35).

The 'Phillips' Royal Commission on Criminal Procedure (RCCP 1981) was established in 1977 in response to public anxieties about rising crime rates and police malpractice. Concerns had also been expressed following the quashing of the convictions of three teenagers who had falsely confessed to murder (House of Commons 1977). Its deliberations were 'accompanied by a concerted police campaign for further powers', including for the curtailment of the right of silence (Friend and Metcalf 1981:165.) The RCCP (1981:15) noted that:

> [c]rime has both increased and diversified ... sophistication of crime, particularly of major frauds. Criminal groups now operate not merely locally or regionally, but on a national and international scale. Hijacking, hostage-taking and terrorism add new dimensions of violence, fear and consequential security provisions.

The research it commissioned (Softley 1980) suggested that the right of silence was rarely exercised in practice (see Table 3.2 in the next chapter). The RCCP rejected any limitations upon the right of silence, with one dissension for silence at the police station; unanimously for silence at trial. It raised both principled and practical objections to curtailing the right: '[t]he accused should not be obliged, indeed, in the ultimate event he cannot be obliged, either to enter the witness box or to mount any defence' (RCCP 1981:90). The majority concluded that the right was a fundamental feature of the adversarial system, ensuring that the burden of proof remained on the prosecution. It appeared to find the 'burden of proof' arguments more persuasive. It had little discussion of inferences at trial (para 4.39) and did not discuss judicial comment (McNicol 1984:275). The argument that prevailed within the RCCP appears to have been that for any limitations to be fair, a more inquisitorial system would be necessary to make suspects fully aware of the police case before deciding whether to answer questions. It concluded:

> It might put strong (and additional) psychological pressure upon some suspects to answer questions without knowing precisely what was the substance of and evidence for the accusations against them; and in consequence what they needed to tell the police in order to allay the suspicion against them. This, in our view, might well increase the risk

of innocent people, particularly those under suspicion for the first time, making damaging statements ... any attempt ... to use a suspect's silence as evidence against him seems to run counter to a central element in the accusatorial system of trial. There is an inconsistency of principle in requiring the onus of proof at trial to be upon the prosecution and to be discharged without any assistance from the accused's silence in the face of police questioning under caution as any part of their case against him at trial.

(RCCP 1981:para 4.50)

The RCCP recommended 'a carefully constructed package of proposals' (Zander 1985:4) in which stricter control of police detention and interrogation of suspects, most notably access to custodial legal advice, counterbalanced the increased powers to detain and question suspects to be given to the police. Its report led to the momentous Police and Criminal Evidence Act 1984 (PACE), that first codified both parties' rights in relation to stop and search, arrest, detention, questioning and charge. The Prosecution of Offences Act 1985 followed, which removed prosecutorial powers from the police, establishing the independent Crown Prosecution Service.

The Parliamentary progress of PACE was painfully slow and was interrupted by the 1983 general election and the version that eventually made it into law was less driven by the 'law and order lobby' (Reiner 2000:168). Meanwhile, s72 of the Criminal Justice Act 1982 abolished the right of the accused to make an unsworn statement from the dock; a recommendation of both the CLRC and RCCP (1981:91). Many of the additional powers that the police were given by PACE came from 'the highly assertive evidence presented to the Royal Commission by various police spokesmen and pressure groups' (Bridges and Bunyan 1983:86). PACE balanced increased powers for the police with protections for suspects; most significantly, the right to legal representation at the police station (see Chapters 3 and 4). Although now generally regarded as a landmark act that has improved the treatment of suspects in police custody, at the time even the *Daily Mail* (15 March 1983) took the view that the Bill gave too much power to the police. Many viewed the powers of the police to detain suspects for questioning as an attempt 'to revive the attack on the right to silence in a devious and underhand way' (Geoffrey Bindman, Letter to *The Times*, 31 October 1983; Law Society memorandum on the Police and Criminal Evidence Bill, cited in *The Times*, 13 September 1983; Christian 1983:5).

The backlash against PACE was immediate and focused on the right of silence (Keel 1987; Denning 1987). The broad thrust of the criticisms was that improvements in the investigation and trial process had rendered the right of silence redundant as a protection and an unfair handicap to the police and prosecution. The police directly attributed a fall in the number of crimes 'cleared up' in 1986 to the effects of PACE, in particular the presence of legal representatives (HOWG 1989:17). The revival of the case against the right of silence was characterised by '[t]he evasion and distrust of detailed investigation and rational public debate' (Dixon 1991a:29). As is discussed in Chapters 3 and 4, many of these safeguards offer little protection in practice. There was scant objective evidence to show that the right of silence or legal advice was hampering police investigations or prosecutions. PACE has undoubtedly improved police conduct (see Chapter 3) – but curtailing such a fundamental right of suspects is a curious *quid pro quo* for achieving appropriate police conduct. Opponents of the right of silence seized upon the correlation between legal advice and no comment interviews to argue that, because solicitors might be more likely to tell their client to exercise their right to say nothing, then that right should be removed. This balancing exercise was based upon a flawed premise as the RCCP (1981) had included the right of silence in its calculations on striking the balance between the right of silence and the needs of the police and had concluded that the right should be maintained.

PACE came into effect on 1 January 1986. On 30 July 1987 the then Home Secretary, Douglas Hurd, unexpectedly announced his intention to re-examine the right of silence during the annual Police Foundation Lecture. As Zander (1996:659) argued, '[t]his was distinctly odd ... The signs were that the police had persuaded the Home Secretary to reopen the topic'. In September, the new Metropolitan Police Commissioner, Sir Peter Imbert, argued that the right of silence 'might have been designed by criminals for their special benefit and that of their advisers. It has done more to obscure the truth and facilitate crime than anything else this century' (*Guardian*, 30 November 1989). The Police Superintendents Association supported this view and Lord Chief Justice Lane then added his support in a speech to the Bar Council. A seminar held by the Law Society and the Police Foundation (November 1987) concluded that it would be dangerous to make changes to the right of silence at least until the effects of tape recording interviews had been evaluated, but called for pre-trial disclosure of the defence case (cited in HOWG 1989:5). Mr Hurd established a Home Office Working Group on the Right of Silence (HOWG 1989) to investigate how 'best' to curtail the right of silence in England and Wales. Despite its restrictive terms of reference, the HOWG recommended some modifications to the CLRC proposals. It rejected proposals that silence should be corroborative of other evidence or should be considered positive evidence of guilt, by itself, or with other evidence, as this would shift the burden of proof from prosecution to defence (para 86). The HOWG considered that failure to mention when questioned a fact that is relied upon at trial may weaken a defendant's credibility, but the only inference that can be drawn safely is that the fact given is untrue. It recommended statutory guidance for the drawing of inferences. It also recommended pre-trial disclosure of the defence case for Crown Court trials. In response to the HOWG, there was, once again, furious protest against any changes to the right of silence, including from the Criminal Bar Association, the Law Society, academic lawyers and civil liberties groups. By the end of 1987, it was reported that the government had been persuaded by the strength of this reaction not to proceed (Williams 1987:1107).

Before the deadline for submissions to the HOWG had passed, matters accelerated in relation to Northern Ireland. The Northern Ireland (Emergency Provisions) Act 1987 had not addressed the right of silence, but the proposal re-emerged in the independent review of the counter-terrorism legislation (Colville Report 1990). Recommendation 67 of the report was that '[t]he Government may wish to consider whether special provision is needed for Northern Ireland in relation to a failure to explain incriminating circumstances'. Viscount Colville argued that, as those detained on suspicion of terrorist acts increasingly remain silent and, in the absence of convictions, witnesses decline to give evidence 'there is in my view a real possibility that the rule of law may break down, or be seen to be in that condition' (1987:para 15.1.4).[1] Again this showed the power of the police as lobbyists – the Royal Ulster Constabulary had indicated to him that, unless they caught terrorists in the act, they found great obstacles to achieving prosecutions and suggested that courts should be allowed to draw inferences where a person found in an incriminating situation remained wholly silent. There was a widespread belief among the security forces that maintaining silence was evidence of training in 'anti-interrogation techniques';[2] '[t]errorist training manuals now contain detailed techniques whereby a person under interrogation may devote his mind to something which enables him to resist the temptation to answer even the most innocent sounding question' (Colville Report 1990:13). Viscount Colville argued that appropriate safeguards had been incorporated in the equivalent legislation in the Republic of Ireland. He noted, however, 'I would not suppose that a convincing argument for such a change could be made out in Great Britain' (para 15.1.6).

The following year the Criminal Evidence (Northern Ireland) Order 1988 was introduced. It was announced in rather curious circumstances, in statements to the Commons Press Gallery that purported to be written answers to

---

1 In a fascinating parallel, the IRA had similar difficulties in its courts martial procedures. Harkin and Ingram (2004:98) note that 'standard IRA procedure seemed to be that unless an individual made what the interrogators deemed to be a full confession they would not be killed'. The informer known as Kevin Fulton (2006:235) described how he survived an IRA court-martial:

> I had escaped execution ... because Michael and the boys hadn't managed to secure a confession. Nor did they have any proof, and they needed one or the other. Some may find it surprising, but the IRA is rigidly strict about such matters.

2 Home Office Circular, para 41, cited in Walker (1992:74, fn. 30).

questions that had not in fact been tabled (HC Debs, 20 October 1988: col. 1040). Despite Viscount Colville's reservations, the Home Secretary stated that he would seek the earliest opportunity after receiving the HOWG Report to bring forward similar legislation for England and Wales as the government saw 'a clear need for substantial changes to be made in both [jurisdictions] if the law is to be effectively enforced' (Written answers (Commons), 20 October 1988). The enactment was made by means of an Order in Council, rather than under prevention of terrorism legislation, which resulted in the changes being applied to all suspects, 'ordinary' as well as paramilitary. The Order was 'a clear extension of the emergency regime into the ordinary criminal law' (Ní Aoláin 1995–96:1384). This Parliamentary procedure, which meant that the wording was unamendable in the debate, was condemned as a 'constitutional outrage, and a monstrous way to proceed' (Robert Maclennan, 140 HC Debs, col. 202). Parliament had to vote in the absence of crucial details, such as the wording of the revised caution and the circumstances in which it would be issued. The Labour Party opposed the measure, which was also criticised by the Irish government.

The Northern Ireland Order is worth examining in some detail as it paved the way for the CJPOA.[3] The Order was justified in terms of removing the right from those involved in terrorism and other serious violence, particularly racketeering (Tom King, to deflect over 140 HC Debs, cols 183–187, 8 November 1988). It had been a particularly difficult year in the conflict. Republican violence surged in 1987 following a decline since 1981. The second most senior judge, Lord Justice Maurice Gibson, and his wife were murdered in April; six soldiers on a fun run were killed by a bomb in County Antrim on 15 June; and a bomb at the Enniskillen Remembrance Day ceremony killed 11 and injured 63 others. The government was struggling to contain the violence from the paramilitaries, to deal with the furious ongoing Unionist protests against the 1985 Anglo-Irish Agreement, calls from the Northern Ireland Police Federation for the re-introduction of internment in both Northern Ireland and the Republic of Ireland, and to manage national and international concern about the security forces abusing their powers. Disciplinary proceedings had been started against 20 RUC officers regarding 'shoot to kill' incidents in 1982 (Taylor 1987). The government was also facing criticism of its own conduct – in particular, regarding the fatal shooting of three unarmed IRA operatives by the SAS in Gibraltar on 6 March 1988. The funerals of these IRA members were attacked by a Loyalist gunman who killed three mourners. At the funeral of the mourners, two British soldiers drove into the cortege and were beaten to death. Both incidents were captured on film and events appeared to be spiralling out of control.

---

3 See John Jackson's work (1989, 1991, 1993, 1994, 2001a) for the background to the provisions, their implementation and effects.

Although the level of violence in Northern Ireland was extreme (there were 104 murders in 1988), the police had far greater powers under the existing 'emergency' legislation for combating terrorism than their counterparts in England. PACE did not apply to Northern Ireland until 1990, there was no statutory duty solicitor scheme and suspects were routinely denied access to solicitors in the holding centres (Dickson 1984; Greer 1980; Committee for the Prevention of Torture or Degrading Treatment or Punishment 1994; Quirk 2013). Interviews did not have to be tape recorded and confessions did not need not be excluded unless obtained by torture, inhuman or degrading treatment or violence (s6(2) Northern Ireland (Emergency Provisions) Act 1973), a higher threshold than ss76 and 78 of PACE. Trials took place before the jury-less 'Diplock' Courts. Greer (1995:207) suggested that this was a motivation for change as Diplock judges had to give reasoned judgments, which impeded the covert drawing of inferences from silence. An additional factor was the ending of the use of 'supergrass' testimony in 1986.

Tom King, the Secretary of State for Northern Ireland, sought to distinguish the situation in Northern Ireland from the RCCP's findings. He observed that its conclusions were based on a study showing that only about 4 per cent of suspects refused to answer any questions but that 'anybody with any knowledge of Northern Ireland will know that in Northern Ireland the figure is very different'. The minister stated that the government preferred the arguments of the CLRC and that it believed 'the arguments against change are overstated and that the CLRC's arguments are stronger, full of common sense and significantly reinforced by the deliberate and extreme exploitation of the present position'. Mr King noted the great difficulties faced by the police and the prosecuting authorities:

> in bringing to justice hardened, professional criminals – often assisted by able legal advisers – who are thoroughly trained in resisting police questioning, and in the case of terrorists, who even publish in their news-sheets detailed instructions on techniques for resisting questioning under the heading, 'Whatever you say, say nothing'. That is a measure of the importance attached to silence by those who are engaged in a sustained and systematic assault on the rule of law and the institutions of our democracy.
>
> (HC Debs, 8 November 1988, col. 185)[4]

---

4 The implicit criticism of defence solicitors was taken further on 17 January 1989 by the Home Office Minister Douglas Hogg, who criticised a 'number of solicitors in Northern Ireland who are unduly sympathetic to the cause of the IRA'. On 12 February 1989, Patrick Finucane, a Belfast solicitor who had represented a number of Republicans, was shot dead by Loyalists. The Stevens Inquiry found that: 'To the extent that [these comments] were based on information passed by the RUC, they were not justifiable and the inquiry concludes that the minister was compromised' (Stevens 2003: para 2.17).

Although Mr King claimed that the government 'had before them a formidable body of persuasive evidence for change', the changes were based on unpublished statistics provided by the police. As Seamus Mallon MP noted, with characteristic understatement, the government's own figures showed a conviction rate of between 90 and 95.4 per cent of those charged between 1980 and 1988 (HC Debs, 8 November 1988, col. 215). In contrast to England, the senior judiciary in Northern Ireland were opposed to the changes (McKittrick 1988).

With no apparent sense of irony, the curtailment of the right of silence was announced one day after the Home Secretary had announced the 'broadcasting ban' on organisations believed to support terrorism as part of the ongoing strategy to deny them the 'oxygen of publicity' (Edgerton 1996). Indeed the timing of Mr King's statement was particularly curious as it came during the trial of the 'Winchester Three' for conspiring to murder him (two of the three had refused to answer police questions and none had testified; Coles 1990a). In April 1990 their convictions were quashed after the Court of Appeal held that comments made by Mr King and Lord Denning during their trial to the effect that that silence was the refuge of the guilty could have prejudiced the proceedings.[5] Lord Chief Justice Lane disqualified himself from hearing the appeal on the grounds of previous comments that he had made advocating the curtailment of the right of silence (Dyer 1990a). According to the *Law Society's Gazette*, the Winchester Three verdict made the Home Office even more cautious about legislating on the right of silence in England and Wales.

The government's plans to introduce corresponding legislation for England and Wales as soon as the HOWG reported (25 July 1989) were thrown into disarray by the disbanding, in disgrace, of the West Midlands Serious Crime Squad (14 August 1989; Kaye 1991) and the Court of Appeal quashing the convictions of the Guildford Four (*Hill and Others* 1989) on 19 October. This was followed by a succession of high-profile Court of Appeal judgments quashing convictions, mostly based on false confessions, that included the Tottenham Three (*Silcott, Braithwaite and Raghip* 1991), the Birmingham Six (*McIlkenny and Others* 1992), the Maguire Seven (*Maguire and Others* 1992), Stefan Kiszko (*Kiszko* 1992), the Cardiff Three (*Paris, Abdullahi and Miller* 1993) and Judith Ward (*Ward* 1993). These cases exposed a catalogue of wrongdoing in the process of criminal investigation, leaving the criminal justice system in turmoil. There were calls in Parliament and in the newspapers for the Lord Chief

---

5 In an extraordinary post script, Lord Denning said 'section five of the Contempt of Court Act 1981 gives us the right to comment on matters of general public interest if the risk of prejudicing particular legal proceedings is merely incidental to the discussion ... "Tom King and I were condemned unheard ... British justice has been betrayed by the Court of Appeal, in my opinion. Justice was done at Winchester Crown Court."'

Justice to resign. For a brief period, there appeared to be wider recognition of the vulnerability of suspects and a desire to ensure that such travesties could not recur.

The government established the 'Runciman' Royal Commission on Criminal Justice (RCCJ) on 14 March 1991, the day the convictions of the Birmingham Six were quashed. Given the context in which it was established, it was, perhaps, surprising that the RCCJ should have as the fifth of its terms of reference, to consider whether changes were necessary to:

> the opportunities available for an accused person to state his position on the matters charged and the extent to which the courts might draw proper inferences from primary facts, the conduct of the accused, and any failure on his part to take advantage of an opportunity to state his position.

Getting this into the terms of reference represented a triumph for the police and the Crown Prosecution Service, who 'viewed the Commission as a vehicle for the promotion of crime control policies' (Leng 2001c:108). The RCCJ was given only two years to report. It commissioned a number of research studies but these were constrained by the timeframe. Leng's report (1993) found no evidence that the right of silence was impeding prosecutions, or that no comment interviews led to 'ambush defences'. Zander and Henderson (1993) found that between 70 and 74 per cent of defendants testified in the Crown Court. The police, the CPS and the majority of judges who gave evidence to the RCCJ were of the view that inferences should be permitted to expedite investigations. The police highlighted the problem of ambush defences by experienced 'criminals ... taking advantage of a feature of the criminal justice system left over from a past era when there were far fewer safeguards to protect the defendant than there are today' (ibid.:51).

The RCCJ recommended that, once the prosecution case has been disclosed fully, defendants should be required to answer any charges made against them or to risk adverse comment from this. (Two members dissented, advocating that, subject to added safeguards for the vulnerable, adverse comment should be made at trial about a suspect's failure to answer police questions.) The RCCJ came to a different conclusion about failure to testify. The Report concluded that this raised different issues as, once in court, defendants are protected both by knowing the prosecution case and because they are legally represented. Where the defendant does not give evidence, it recommended that the prosecution and the judge could comment upon any explanation advanced through counsel or the calling of other evidence, but the jury should not be invited to infer that the explanation is less deserving of belief.

The RCCJ's analysis was criticised for its failure to explore the social and organisational context within which the miscarriages of justice that led to its establishment occurred (McConville and Bridges 1994; Maguire and Norris 1994). It did not refer to the ECHR or examine the effects of the Northern Ireland Order in relation to the right of silence. The RCCJ interpreted its terms of reference in a way that afforded equal weight to the conviction of the guilty, the acquittal of the innocent and the efficient use of resources. Unlike the RCCP, it endorsed the right of silence at the police station only in pragmatic terms about protecting the vulnerable (Zander 1996:667). This absence of a principled argument by the RCCJ report in favour of the right of silence, that it distinguished the arguments in favour of the right at the police station and at trial, and its recommendation of a pre-trial defence disclosure regime, represented hostages to fortune for those who sought to preserve the right of silence. The government was able to counter opposition to curtailing the right of silence by offering 'safeguards' to address the RCCJ's concerns with regard to protecting the vulnerable (Sanders and Young 1994:197; Easton 1998b:45; Leng 2001c:112).

By the time the RCCJ reported, the prevailing political climate had changed. The Home Secretaries in office during the life of the RCCJ (Kenneth Baker, Kenneth Clarke and Michael Howard) 'espoused successively more extreme law and order policies' (Sharpe 1998b:86). In what Professor Zander, an RCCJ member, described as a 'debasement of decision-making', the government decided to override the view of the RCCJ and legislate to curtail the right of silence. Despite having won a fourth consecutive general election in 1992, the Conservatives were unpopular and had, in Michael Howard, a Home Secretary who played the 'law and order' card enthusiastically. Crime had become a highly contentious political issue. Officially recorded crime had risen sharply since 1989; a tenfold increase over the previous 40 years, despite a doubling of expenditure on the criminal justice system as a whole since the Conservatives took office in 1979. The number of police had almost doubled since the 1950s, whilst the clear-up rate of crimes had fallen from 46 per cent to 41 per cent in 1979 and 29 per cent in 1991. There were a number of high-profile crimes that led to what has been termed a moral panic: 16-year-old Suzanne Capper was murdered in December 1992. Her killers were said to have taunted her with lines from a horror film as they tortured her for several days. In February 1993, in a case that attracted worldwide attention, toddler James Bulger was abducted and murdered by two ten-year-old boys, the abduction captured on camera. The racist murder of Stephen Lawrence occurred in April of the same year. In the same month, the IRA set off a bomb in Bishopsgate in the City of London, a year after it had destroyed the Baltic Exchange there. It also bombed a shopping area in Warrington, killing two children and injuring 54 people. Prime Minister John Major said that: 'I would like the public to have a crusade against crime and change from being forgiving of crime to being considerate to the victim. Society needs to condemn a little more and understand a little less' (*Mail on Sunday*, 21 February 1993).

As the Labour Party sought to improve its electoral credibility, 'there was a cross-party search for punitive policies, and particularly punitive rhetoric, that could be used to convince an electorate to cast their vote for those who could be trusted to be toughest on crime' (Newburn and Jones 2004:188). At the 1993 Conservative Party conference, Mr Howard announced his 27-point 'crackdown on crime' that he claimed would correct the 30-year in-built bias in favour of the criminal against the public. He declared:

> The so-called right to silence is ruthlessly exploited by terrorists. What fools they must think we are. It's time to call a halt to this charade. The so-called right to silence will be abolished. The innocent have nothing to hide and that is exactly the point the prosecution will be able to make in future.
>
> (Travis 1993)

The Criminal Justice and Public Order Act 1994

The CJPOA, the first piece of legislation resulting from the RCCJ, marked a significant turning point in the criminal justice system; the start of what Shami Chakrabarti (2008:369) has described as 'the modern law and order arms race'. Labour, returning towards electoral popularity, was anxious to appear equally 'tough on crime' (Newburn 1995) so criticised the proposals but abstained rather than voted against them. The CJPOA was one of the most controversial Acts passed in recent years. It provoked fierce public protest, in particular against new public order offences, which targeted groups such as travellers, protesters against foxhunting and those attending unlicensed outdoor raves (Mullin 1994). Unlike in the 1970s, most academic opinion condemned the changes to the right of silence as unfair in principle and likely to cause wrongful convictions.

The CJPOA provisions permit comment upon, and the drawing of inferences at trial from, the failure of suspects to:

- mention when questioned or charged any feature of their defence that could reasonably have been mentioned then (s34);
- answer questions relating to the presence of any substance, object or mark about their person (s36);
- answer questions relating to their presence at the scene of an offence (s37);
- testify or, having been sworn, their refusal to answer questions without good cause (s35).

The Act provides no guidance in defining what inferences are 'proper'. (The consequences of this are discussed in Chapter 5; the full legislation is set out in the Legislation section.) Section 34 extends beyond 'no comment' interviews to include failure to mention any fact relied upon in a suspect's defence. It is a partly subjective test, referring to anything the accused could reasonably have been expected to mention when questioned or charged. Silence under questioning cannot, of itself, establish a *prima facie* case, although it can contribute to one (s38(3)) as inferences may be drawn in determining both whether there is a case to answer and whether the accused is guilty (s34(2)). The common law assumption is preserved that if a suspect, not under caution, remains silent in response to an accusation from someone with whom they are on 'even terms' (such as a witness or victim), then this can be considered an adoption of the allegation (s34(5); *Christie* 1914). Section 34 was intended to thwart 'ambush defences' (Hurd 1987; Howard 1995) but it does nothing to overcome the vague or inscrutable 'I bought it from a man in a pub, I don't know his name' type of response.

Sections 36 and 37 are the most problematic in terms of the presumption of innocence but have received less scrutiny than the other provisions. They are concerned with facts that point to a suspect's involvement with a specified offence, rather than with any defence. Inferences can be drawn from the failure of suspects when arrested, to account for the presence of any object, substance or mark about their person, or to explain their presence in a particular place, whether or not this forms part of the defence case: 'It is not so much the accused's failure to mention facts which could help him in his defence which is in issue but his failure to explain facts already known to the police and which point to his guilt' (Wasik and Taylor 1995:60). Such failure could already be used as circumstantial evidence of guilt at common law (ss36(6) and 37(5) preserve this); under the CJPOA, it can now be used effectively as corroboration. For example, the suspect was not only found at the scene (common law inference) but also failed to account for his or her presence there (additional CJPOA inference). These sections were not recommended by the CLRC but came from the equivalent Irish and Northern Irish provisions. These had been mentioned by the HOWG but not expanded upon and there was little mention of them in the debate preceding the CJPOA (Marks 2013:821). The sections 'impose a participatory burden on the accused, affecting not only the freedom to choose whether or not to respond to police questioning, but also shaping the response that should be given' (Owusu-Bempah 2014:135). 'Failure to account' assumes an ability to do so; but a suspect may be unable to provide an account of how drugs came to be in his or her possession if, for example, they have been planted there. They may not have sufficient knowledge – in some cases, even expert witnesses have been unable to offer a definitive explanation for drug traces on money (Marks 2013). Unlike s34, there is no proviso as to the reasonableness of expecting such an account. The questioner must have a reasonable belief that the presence or condition of the object, substance or mark may be attributable to the suspect's participation in the commission of a specified offence, but this does not have to be the offence for which the suspect was arrested (s36(1)(b)). The suspect must be told this, asked for an explanation and informed in 'ordinary language' what the effects of failure to answer the questions put to them are (the 'special warning', Code C, 10.5B, PACE). The sections are restricted to the condition of the suspect at the time of arrest, and not, for example, as described by an eyewitness to the crime. Section 37 is similarly concerned only with the suspect's location at the scene of the crime at the time of arrest and does not apply to previous visits to the crime scene, or if the suspect escaped from the scene of the crime and was arrested elsewhere. The deficiencies in drafting were set out in scathing terms in *Blackstones*:

> If the intention is to build upon already suspicious circumstances by allowing an additional guilty inference if the accused fails to explain them, it is not clear why the provisions are so restrictive: a suspected rapist may have inferences drawn for failing to explain away stains on his trousers, but not for refusing to explain why he is not wearing any (unless he has discarded them nearby).
>
> (F19.17)

Section 35 allows the prosecution to comment if a defendant does not testify. Section 35(4) preserves the right of the accused not to testify by specifying that failure to do so does not constitute a contempt of court. The court or jury, in determining whether the accused is guilty, may draw such inferences as appear proper from the accused's failure or refusal without good cause to testify or to answer any question. The court must: 'satisfy itself (in the case of proceedings on indictment, in the presence of the jury) that the accused is aware that the stage has been reached at which evidence can be given for the defence...' The parenthesis appears to favour highlighting the accused's failure to testify, rather than a concern for informing defendants of their rights. The initial proposal, based on the CLRC recommendations and the Northern Ireland Order, whereby the accused would be called upon to give evidence, was amended at the report stage in the House of Commons following criticism from Taylor LCJ (1994) that it was 'undesirable and unfair' to call upon the defendant to give evidence and 'does not lie easily with the principle still intact ... that the defendant has a free choice whether to give evidence'. He objected to the inquisitorial element such a requirement would bring to the judge's role.[6] Nonetheless, there is still clearly an element of theatre about this procedure, especially the requirement that this must be done in the presence of the jury.

Section 35(5) creates a presumption that a defendant who refuses to answer questions having been sworn 'shall be taken to do so without good cause' unless there are statutory grounds for not replying, reasons of professional privilege, or through the court's discretion. Inferences may only be avoided in this situation if the physical and mental condition of the accused makes it appear 'undesirable' to the court (s35(1)(b)). Inferences cannot be drawn if the accused's guilt is not in issue, although the purpose of this is obscure. Section 38(6) provides that 'nothing in sections 34, 35, 36 or 37 prejudices any power of a court, in any proceedings, to exclude evidence (whether by preventing questions being put or otherwise) at its discretion', but it is unclear how this exclusionary discretion could be used to prevent inferences under s35.

The CJPOA has been amended and expanded subsequently. When the legislation was first enacted, the defendant had to have reached 14 years of age before s35 applied. This was repealed by s35 of the Crime and Disorder Act 1998. If suspects have been denied access to legal representation under s58 of PACE or Schedule 7 of the Terrorism Act 2000, then inferences cannot be drawn from their silence. They should be given the old caution: 'You do not have to say anything, but anything you do say may be given in evidence' (s58 of the Youth Justice and Criminal Evidence Act 1999; Code C para 6.6(b)). A new procedure was also introduced to allow questioning after the officer has sufficient evidence to charge. Questioning was supposed to stop at the point at which the officer in the case reasonably believed there was sufficient evidence to provide a realistic prospect of conviction for that offence and the suspect had indicated that they had nothing further to say. Further questioning at that stage then becomes merely for the purpose of improving the prosecution case (Walker 2008). Paragraph 11.6 of the 2003 Code C (and subsequent revisions) states that the interview must now stop only when:

> (a) the officer in charge of the investigation is satisfied all the questions they consider relevant to obtaining accurate and reliable information about the offence have been put to the suspect, this includes allowing the suspect an opportunity to give an innocent explanation and asking questions to test if the explanation is accurate and reliable, e.g. to clear up ambiguities or clarify what the suspect said.

---

6 Schedule 10, para 61(3) CJPOA aligned the Northern Irish provisions with those in England and Wales.

This latter development came about as a result of judicial decisions relating to s34 inferences being drawn from questioning after the interviewing officer had sufficient evidence to charge (*Pointer* 1997; *McGuinness* 1999). Cape argued (before the Code was updated) that such an approach would render section 37(1) of PACE otiose. As the custody officer would be permitted to have the suspect interviewed in order to find out whether or not they wish to put forward an explanation, the custody officer would always be justified in authorising detention. This illustrates how the CJPOA has facilitated the introduction of legislation that is detrimental to defendants (discussed in Chapter 6). As Cape (1999:885) argues:

> A high charge threshold, in the context of compulsory detention and an evidentiary regime that permits use of the product of that detention (whether consisting of admissions, lies or 'silence') against the accused, significantly undermines the privilege against self-incrimination. Arguably it also undermines the right to fair trial.

Conclusion

In reviewing the work of the multiple Commissions, associated Parliamentary debates, research, policy and media commentary produced on the right of silence over the years, a number of themes emerge. Those who made the case advocating restrictions on the rights of suspects have used the same techniques repeatedly. The exercise of a right is condemned as manipulation of the system by unpopular groups such as 'professional criminals' or terrorists. Suspects' rights are compared unfavourably to the obligations of the prosecution and the lack of rights for victims, or, in the more emotive terms usually adopted, the inability of the prosecution to bring criminals to justice. This populist strategy increased in use throughout the 1990s and continued into the early twenty-first century. Opposition is countered by the provision of minimal safeguards for 'worthy' or vulnerable suspects (Sanders and Young 1994:197; Easton 1998b:45; Leng 2001c:112) and the canard that the innocent have nothing to hide. Little consideration is given to the presumption of innocence. Notwithstanding the dubious veracity of this claim, the resulting legislation applies to all suspects but it does not affect them all equally. The ostensible targets of the measures are likely to have the wherewithal to defend themselves; it is the 'ordinary' or vulnerable who are most at risk. This focus on individuals, however, is to miss the damage that is done to the system as a whole; in particular to the presumption of innocence.

The effects of these provisions are addressed in the subsequent chapters, incorporating the findings of research conducted with a range of criminal justice practitioners. The utilitarian argument that suspects and defendants should be obliged to cooperate with the investigation and trial process, whilst an arguable one, has not been resolved satisfactorily in the context of an adversarial process, and three Royal Commissions found against it. There was little empirical evidence to suggest that no comment interviews, ambush defences or the refusal of defendants to testify were causing undue difficulties in the administration of justice. As Zander (1996:675) noted, '[t]he government relied on what the police told them more than what the empirical evidence showed, because when one got down to the statistics it did not support the government's position'. The police were a consistent driving force behind these changes. 'Cop culture' and some of the reasons why the police felt so threatened by the right of silence are explored in the next chapter.

Chapter 3

Police custody, cop culture and the caution

The police interview is the initial context in which suspects decide whether or not to exercise their right of silence. It is an encounter which takes place largely hidden from scrutiny, on police territory and on police terms (McConville *et al.* 1994:131; Holdaway 1983). As many defendants have found to their cost, what happens during the interview can effectively determine the outcome of a case. Having examined the arguments made for and against the right of silence in the first section of this book, the following part examines what happened in practice when the right was curtailed in England and Wales by the Criminal Justice and Public Order Act 1994 (CJPOA). The next three chapters explore the impact of the changes on the police interview, the solicitor–client relationship and the trial, respectively. Dramatic claims were made on both sides of the debate as to what would happen following the CJPOA, but there has been little subsequent investigation into what has actually occurred, other than one Home Office report (Bucke *et al.* 2000).[1] After the wealth of criminal justice research in the early 1990s (including McConville *et al.* 1991, 1994; and the RCCJ research reports), no large-scale empirical studies were undertaken between Phillips and Brown (1998) and Kemp (2013). This means that little is known about the effects of the CJPOA on the working cultures of practitioners and the experiences of suspects. This is a problem for criminal justice scholarship more generally as much has changed since these studies were undertaken. The age of the studies means that their findings should be relied upon with caution for contemporary lessons. The data collected for this study offer a snapshot of what occurred in the gap between these studies. Other than where indicated, citations in this chapter are confined to research conducted in England and Wales due to the significant jurisdictional differences in police interrogation procedures. This second part of the book draws upon the findings of a case study that was conducted in one region of England between 1998 and 2001, shortly after the CJPOA came into effect, exploring the experiences and

1 See also Quirk (2013), which draws upon some of the data in this book.

views of a range of criminal justice actors in relation to the right of silence (see Methods for details).

*

This chapter examines the right of silence in relation to the detention and interviewing of suspects at the police station. As discussed in Chapter 2, the police were significant opponents of the right of silence, lobbying over a number of years for political change (Dixon *et al.* 1989; Reiner 1985:169). Chapter 3 explores why the right of silence appeared to assume a disproportionate significance to individual police officers and to the police as an institution when the available evidence showed that it was exercised comparatively rarely. The protections offered by the Police and Criminal Evidence Act 1984 (PACE) are considered, as this provided the main justification for curtailing the right of silence, and it regulates the conditions in which suspects first decide whether to exercise their right. The issues raised by the revised caution that the police are required to give suspects are explored, followed by police interview practices, in particular, when faced with a silent suspect. It goes on to consider how the legislation works in practice, mediated by the occupational culture of the police.

When PACE was enacted in 1984, most of the concern focused on the significant increase in police powers and the greater pressure that suspects would be put under to answer questions (Newburn 2003:64). Whilst the PACE provisions have immeasurably improved the treatment of the 'average suspect', these gains were part of a package of measures recommended by the Royal Commission on Criminal Procedure (RCCP 1981) that were intended to counterbalance the substantial increase in the powers given to the police at the same time. As discussed in Chapter 2, the protections that PACE bestowed – in particular, the right to legal advice – galvanised (or provided a pretext for) opponents of the right of silence. They argued – without waiting to see how the provisions actually worked – that PACE had made it too difficult to prosecute 'criminals' successfully and that accordingly inferences should be allowed from silence.

The exchange abolitionist (Greer 1990) or re-balancing argument assumes that legal representation puts the suspect and police on 'equal terms' (*Chandler* 1976). In reality, the police continue to control almost all aspects of the encounter. They decide everything from what clothing suspects wear, to when they get to smoke a cigarette and, most significantly, when and under what conditions they get to leave custody. The *only* power the suspect has in the 'interactionally restricted setting of the police interview' (Carter 2011:3) is in controlling whether or how to answer police questions. The re-balancing stance failed to consider how effective the PACE measures were when mediated through the occupational culture of the police, the working practices of legal representatives, and by the abilities of suspects to avail themselves of their rights. Increased police powers tend to be exploited to the full (discussed below), whereas many of the protections that suspects receive are under-utilised due to inadequate provision, insufficient awareness or through other pressures. It is insufficient to consider only the formal interview when examining the dynamics of police questioning of suspects; as Maguire and Norris (1992:1) note, 'interviews do not occur in a vacuum'. The interview can be influenced by variables such as the individual and shared experiences of the officer and suspect (Singh 1994), including the exercise of police powers of stop and search and arrest; previous 'conversations', including in the back of the police car on the way to the police station (Box 1987; Loftus 2009); the offence under investigation; the presence or absence of a legal adviser or appropriate adult; and the objectives of the police. The professional skill of the police and legal representatives is crucial, as is the 'performance' of the suspect.

Most police powers are vested in the individual constable (*Metropolitan Police Commissioner, ex parte Blackburn* 1968). As James Q. Wilson observes (1968:7), police work is unusual in that discretionary power increases further down the institutional hierarchy. Much police work takes place without scrutiny (Baldwin and Maloney 1993) or with what McConville *et al.* (1991:16) term 'low visibility discretion'. The police tend to structure their discretion according to 'working rules' based on assumptions about the suspect, the complainant and their individual workloads (McConville *et al.* 1991: Chapter 2). Officers may use the law to enforce their own objectives in addition to the criminal law, such as asserting their authority over certain groups or individuals (Choongh 1997; Singh 1994:169) – for example, using their powers to stop and search, knowing that no criminal proceedings can follow, just to inconvenience or upset the person (Loftus 2009:181). PACE reduced the scope of the 'Ways and Means Act'[2] but could not eliminate it. 'Contempt of cop' (Reiner 2000:517) has been described as another of the core 'unwritten laws' that may be enforced by the police. Suspects who exercise their right of silence present a particular challenge to the police, both in terms of the aims of their investigations and to their authority. As one officer complained in a questionnaire response: 'Suspects were laughing at us – stating no comment just to annoy officers' (Questionnaire 41/PC).

The police were significant lobbyists for the curtailment of the right of silence. This chapter examines some of the reasons for the significance of these changes in terms of police culture. It sets out the PACE regime, challenging the basis of the exchange abolitionist argument. It examines the comprehensibility of the new caution that suspects are given before interview. It considers what is known about police interviews and finally examines what happens in interviews when suspects make no comment.

---

2   What Reiner explains as 'forms of illicit "easing behaviour" ... that involved various ways of distinguishing the "law in action" from the "law in the books"' (1992:442).

'Cop culture' and the right of silence

The police occupy an anomalous position in the criminal justice process. In an adversarial system, they are supposed to play an inquisitorial, fact-finding role, yet, until the Crown Prosecution Service was created in 1986, it was the police who collected evidence, charged and prosecuted offences in what were known colloquially as 'police courts'. The police continue to be perceived, both amongst themselves and by the public, as agents of the prosecution. One officer alluded to this when comparing his role to defence solicitors: 'We're salesmen for jail … it's us against them you know' (PS/A4). Many police officers described their role in combative terms, often using sporting or martial analogies:

> It's almost like a war, if you like. You know, 'I'm not telling you, this is my hand, I'm not going to show you everything [laughs] … It's a game almost, as I say, almost like a game of cards … it's very cat and mouse.
>
> (DC/A5)

> Don't give him any of your ammunition until you've got all his bullets.
>
> (PS/A4)

Such a purposive approach allows little sympathy for arguments about due process or the niceties of the burden of proof, as the following comments make clear:

> Suspect simply would not cooperate and was of the opinion that [the] police had to prove him guilty.
>
> (Questionnaire 95/PS)

> The legal reps play the system of 'if you can't prove it fully then we won't answer questions'.
>
> (Questionnaire 19/CID)

> I believe in truth and justice. Not guilt and innocence, truth and justice, and there's a divide there.
>
> (Custody Sergeant B1)

As discussed in Chapter 2, the police were vociferous opponents of the right of silence. Despite research that showed that it was exercised in only a minority of cases, many of which resulted in convictions, it assumed great importance to them. Over three-quarters of the police officers who completed the questionnaire thought that the changes to the right of silence were necessary. Just 3 per cent thought they were unnecessary. (The remainder either did not know [6 per cent] or were not serving when the changes were introduced [14 per cent]). Of those who elaborated, 60 per cent believed that this was because the guilty had exploited the provisions to escape justice:

> Criminals were given a right to hide from accounting for their actions with no adverse effect.
>
> (Questionnaire 15)

> Too many guilty people were using right to silence to escape justice. Something had to be done to redress the balance.
>
> (Questionnaire 45/DS)

As the following comments demonstrate, the police officers interviewed were overwhelmingly in favour of the changes:

> I thought they were great ... this was going to be a major breakthrough.
>
> (PS/A3)

> It was a push in the back for police and they put pressure on the prisoner, defendant, suspect, suspect is probably a better word, to volunteer any information.
>
> (PC/A8)

Such beliefs may be explained in terms of what has become known as 'cop culture' – what Reiner describes as 'the values, norms, perspectives and craft rules that inform their conduct' (2000:87). It is important to recognise that police culture is neither monolithic nor static (Björk 2008; Chan 2008) and that what officers say does not necessarily reflect their behaviour (Skolnick 2008:39; Waddington 1999). Certainly my own research revealed a diversity of attitudes and opinions, ranging from the reflective and insightful, to the combative and suspicious. Skolnick argues that '[b]eing a police officer is a defining identify, almost like being a priest or a rabbi' (2008:35).[3] Certain broad themes have been characterised as typifying a 'police' outlook, or 'working personality' (Skolnick 1966), including a sense of mission and a general demeanour of suspiciousness, and machismo (Reiner 2000: Chapter 4). Whilst acknowledging the variation between individual officers, my research suggests that certain features of 'the culture of police work' (Dixon et al. 1989:186) meant that suspects making no comment were viewed as challenging officers' sense of authority, wasting their time and frustrating justice. 'These features – identity, danger, authority, the pressure to

3 Skolnick's seminal research focused on American police officers but he notes similarities across continents.

produce, suspicion, the capacity to use force – are enduring aspects of the police occupation' (Skolnick 2008:36; Loftus 2009). Reiner links the need to exercise authority to reducing the danger that officers face:

> Traditional British police organization and tactics have been directed towards minimizing the use of force by converting power into authority, by making the individual constable a symbol of an impersonal and universally accepted law. But in each individual encounter this presentation is liable to be challenged when authority has to be exercised over someone.
>
> (2000:88)

McConville (1992:547) describe the police view of interrogations in which they believe the suspect to be guilty as 'a true moral drama in which right confronts wrong, and the champions of justice take on those bent on attacking the social fabric of society'. Many studies of policing have observed how police officers tend to consign individuals into 'police-relevant' categories (Reiner 2010:123; Norris 1989), and assume that they know who is guilty according to their judgement of their moral character (Chan 2008; Innes 2003; Skolnick 2008). Such officers appeared to regard any measures to protect suspects, or tactics used by the defence – a no comment interview thus being the most provocative example – as unfair or cheating. Conversely, their own 'tactics, or ploys' (Sanders *et al.* 1989:56) were justified in terms of achieving the 'right result'. Brown, however, criticises researchers who conflate 'influences on decisions regarding legal advice' and 'active discouragement' (1997:98–101). Police officers are in the vanguard of the criminal justice system, working in occasionally dangerous situations and seeing the most distressing consequences of crime. A strong sense of responsibility to victims of crime thus develops. This may increase officers' desires to achieve convictions, sometimes by dubious means; what has been termed the 'Dirty Harry' dilemma (Klockars 1980; RCCJ 1993:7; Waddington 1999:112–114), 'pious perjury' (McNee 1983:180–181) or 'noble cause corruption' (Kleining 1996; Woodcock 1992; Mark 1966). This was also illustrated by comments made during the research:

> I still feel disappointed with my length of service that you can't necessarily produce the results that you want to and go back and advise the injured party.
>
> (PS/A2)

> [The police] want to get a conviction ... Nobody sees anything really wrong with that because they always think of that person as guilty and therefore they're doing society a service. They never consider that the

person might be innocent and the prospect that they're doing an injustice.

(Bar/B10)

To be faced with an uncooperative suspect, is no doubt frustrating for officers – and was in part why the RCPPP (1929) had recommended questioning should not be permitted (see Chapter 2). It is undoubtedly difficult for individual officers to act in a disinterested manner. Arguably at a broader level, in the face of a rising crime rate, the silent suspect could epitomise police helplessness. As the then Home Secretary claimed:

> I have lost count of the number of times when ordinary policemen have told me, 'Please do something about the right to silence'. They are sick and tired of professional criminals smirking in the interview room, secure in the knowledge that the jury will never find out that they refused to answer questions that an innocent person would certainly have answered.
>
> (Howard col. 241 HC Debs, 18 November 1994)

Garland (2001) examined how governments reacted to their limited ability to reduce crime by 'acting out' through aggressive law enforcement measures and harsher sentencing policies. In the early 1990s, the police found an equally frustrated government that was looking for some action that could be taken to signal its intent.

PACE: a fair exchange?

PACE (1984) wrought a 'sea-change' (Williamson and Moston 1990:36) in the treatment of suspects in custody and in the more professional conduct of the police (Dixon 1999; Maguire and Norris 1994; Skinns 2011). It is generally acknowledged that the overt abuse or oppression of suspects has become a rarity (Kyle 2004) and 'there have been achievements not matched in other jurisdictions' (Dixon 2010:431). PACE provides miscellaneous requirements to ensure that the conditions in which suspects are held do not become oppressive, such as basic clothing, food and rest breaks. The role of the custody sergeant was created so that a named individual was given responsibility for the welfare of detainees (ss36–39). Suspects are entitled to consult the Codes of Practice, Code C of which governs the 'detention, treatment and questioning of persons by police officers', and they may inform somebody of their detention (s56). Interviews should be tape recorded (s60); and, as is discussed in Chapter 4, there is a right to free legal advice in private, by telephone, in writing or in person (ss58–59). Judges may exclude improperly obtained or excessively prejudicial evidence (ss78 and s82(3)) and must exclude confessions obtained by oppression (s76). PACE did not mention the right of silence expressly but it was implicit in the requirement of the caution ('[y]ou do not have to say anything unless you wish to do so, but what you say may be given in evidence'). The effectiveness of these provisions is examined below. The trope about distinguishing the law in books from the law in action is important in this context. PACE tends to be regarded now as an important safeguard of suspects' rights. At the time it was introduced, it was opposed by many due to the significant expansion in police powers – rights which are now seen as commonplace, or even inadequate.

If the police have insufficient evidence to charge a suspect, then detention may be authorised only in order to 'secure or preserve evidence relating to an offence for which he is under arrest or to obtain such evidence by questioning him' (s37(2) PACE). Suspects did not (*Rice* v *Connolly* 1966), and indeed do not, have to answer police questions, but they are obliged to submit to legitimate questioning. (Unlike under the well-known *Miranda* provisions in the USA where the interviews must cease once suspects indicate that they do not want to answer questions.) From the outset, this created a tension with the right of silence as the power to question can be seen as creating an expectation of an answer (Wigmore, in RCPPP 1929). The police may take arrested suspects into custody in order to increase the likelihood of their answering questions (*Holgate-Mohammed* v *Duke* 1984; PACE Code C, Notes for Guidance 1B). A police officer is 'entitled to question any person from whom he thinks useful information can be obtained ... A person's declaration that he is unwilling to reply does not alter this entitlement' (PACE Code C, note 1K; Home Office Circular 22/1992). The difference since the CJPOA is that what is *not* said by suspects may also now be evidentially significant.

The custody sergeant, who until 2005 had to be a sworn police officer (ss120–121 Serious Organised Crime and Police Act 2005), determines whether or not the statutory criteria regarding arrest, detention, charge and bail have been fulfilled. Custody sergeants are responsible for the well-being of those in custody and for maintaining a record on each detainee. They are both the informer and the gatekeeper of suspects' rights. Whilst the Home Office Working Group on the Right to Silence considered that custody officers ensured that suspects are fully protected (1989:para 37, as did Maguire 1988; Irving and MacKenzie 1989), research available when the CJPOA began its passage through Parliament indicated that custody officers were not just failing to ensure that suspects received their entitlements but, in many cases, were seeking actively to withhold them (McConville 1992; McConville *et al.* 1991; Sanders *et al.* 1989). There were contrasting views among my respondents as to whether this was still a concern:

Custody sergeants just stick things on the sheets without giving it a lot of thought, in fact I've seen that happen. That bit where they're supposed to ask if they want legal advice, they're supposed to indicate why, they're very quickly over that, there's no discussion ... People who've had visits by the officers that are not recorded on the custody sheets. I don't see why they would make this up, and after such visits and promises of bail, things are said ... If it's not on the custody sheet, it didn't happen did it?

(Solicitor/D13/iv)

I think most custody sergeants, certainly in [Town A] are excellent. They look after the defendants properly, they comply with the Codes and you rarely have any complaints over what custody sergeants have done.

(Solicitor/A/v/2)

Custody sergeants are reliant upon, and heavily influenced by, information from the investigating officers. A detective was equivocal about how much needed to be explained to the custody sergeant about the grounds for arrest: 'It's not always practical to explain every minute detail because that could cause an interview some damage if they [the suspect] are made aware at the early stages of what your emphasis is' (DS/A6). It is rare for custody sergeants to question the judgement of fellow officers in front of suspects about whether or not there is sufficient evidence to merit detention. To do so would risk running counter to the prevailing police culture of solidarity and the organisationally imposed achievement of 'results' (Brown 1997; McConville *et al.* 1991:43–44). Indeed, Sanders found a refusal to detain in just 0.05 per cent of cases (2008:54). As a solicitor (Solicitor/A13/iii) explained: '[Rarely] you can say "you shouldn't have him here, you're on a fishing expedition" ... the custody sergeant will invariably say "Well, we're holding him for interview anyway" because they've got to show the end product.'

Detectives in Station A told me that, with CID cases, in practice it is the investigating officers, rather than the custody sergeant, who decide about charge: 'Very rarely would we consult the custody officer and say "well, do you think we ought to charge him or not?" Because that is the sort of process that is decided upon between the [detective sergeant] and the crew' (DC/A5). Thus the activities of custody officers can be little more than presentational, giving the appearance of upholding suspects' rights but in reality merely hiding the status quo behind a veneer of propriety and paperwork. The custody record may be used to validate and legitimise the actions of the police rather than acting as a constraint upon them (Dixon 1991a:133–134; McConville *et al.* 1991:49, 57–60; Skinns 2011). As the official version of events, it is more difficult for suspects to refute if, for example, unauthorised cell visits are omitted (Solicitor/A12/ii) or are recorded as 'welfare visits' (Sanders and Bridges 1990; *Williams* 1992).

The custody sergeant is responsible for identifying those who require the additional protections set out in PACE (Code C 3(b)), such as medical treatment, access to an interpreter or an 'appropriate adult' to support them during interviews. This presents a considerable challenge for the medically unqualified officers, and suspects' needs are usually underestimated (McKinnon and Grubin 2010; Payne-James *et al.* 2010). Whilst those suffering from drug withdrawal symptoms or those unable to understand English are relatively straightforward to identify, less visible conditions such as autism may not be easily recognised by the custody sergeant. Suspects may have an undiagnosed condition, may not acknowledge that they need assistance, or may not want to confide in the police that they have taken illegal drugs or have mental health issues. One custody sergeant explained: 'If they're suicidal I have to get the doctor out – they're drunk, high on drugs, they've got injuries. There's a million and one minefields out there for the Custody Officer … It's a very tough job' (CS/B1).

One third of suspects is 'mentally disadvantaged', with an IQ of below 75. The average IQ score for detainees is 82, compared with a population average of 100. One third of suspects experiences extreme distress or mental disorder at being detained. Fifteen to twenty per cent were assessed by psychologists as being vulnerable enough to require an appropriate adult, compared to the 4 per cent identified by the police (Gudjonsson *et al.* 1993). The Psychiatric Morbidity of Offenders Study (ONS 2010) survey found that 70 per cent of prisoners had a mental disorder. Another study found that 69 per cent of suspects gave a positive result when tested for drug use and one third admitted to dependence upon at least one drug (Bennet 2000). Young *et al.* (2013) found that 6.7 per cent of suspects at a large London police station had intellectual disabilities, 23.5 per cent had attention deficit hyperactivity disorder and 76.3 per cent conduct disorder. Only 4.2 per cent had appropriate adults to support them in interviews – a figure that had remained the same over the last 20 years. Of course if a suspect is vulnerable and does not have support, the answers they give in interview may be compromised.

The PACE protections are of varying benefit and provision is patchy. Suspects may be examined by the forensic medical examiner (usually a general practitioner employed by the police) but this is to determine whether they are fit to be interviewed rather than fit to present their best case (see the discussion of *Condron* 1997 in Chapter 5). The appropriate adult can be a parent, social worker or lay adviser. They are not necessarily qualified or trained and are frequently unable or unwilling to fulfil their protective role (Evans 1993; Medford *et al.* 2003; Pierpoint 2000, 2008). Social workers may experience a conflict between their pastoral or therapeutic role (in which they want to encourage their clients to admit any wrongdoing) and the legal interests of the suspect, which may be served better by making no comment.

One of the biggest flaws in the system relates to juveniles … Duty social worker doesn't give a toss about what goes on … I've actually done training courses for {Town A} Social Services and I've had duty social workers in these sessions saying 'We don't need you'. I said 'You might not, but he does' … And the parents, they either all couldn't care less, in which case they don't look out for the interests of the juvenile anyway, or they're so affronted by the fact that their child may have done something it's 'you tell them the truth or I'll give you a good hiding when you get home'.

(Solicitor/A/v/5)

Reviews of the continued legality of the suspect's detention must take place after six hours and every nine hours thereafter. A senior officer may authorise detention up to 36 hours; a magistrate up to 96 hours. The time limits are up to 28 days for those held under counter-terrorism legislation. These limits have been extended repeatedly. Reviews of the continuing need for detention by senior officers may be routinised, possibly conducted by telephone (s40A PACE). Kemp *et al.* (2012:751) were of the view that the detention reviews conducted by inspectors were no longer effective in encouraging early release. They found the average time spent in detention by all suspects had risen since Phillips and Brown's (1998:109) study from 6 hours and 40 minutes to 8 hours and 55 minutes – although they noted significant variation by police station. Forty-seven per cent of suspects were released within 6 hours; over 5 per cent were held for longer than 24 hours. The wait was much longer for those requesting legal advice (see Chapter 4). Whilst this may be considered reasonably expeditious, and a fixed limit on detention is preferable to none, or one as nebulous as existed before PACE, such a wait can be a great psychological strain on suspects. The police may exploit this discretion as part of the 'softening up process, leaving someone to sit in a cell wondering what on earth's going to happen to them' (Solicitor/J14/i). A study of Crown Court cases (Pleasence and Quirk 2002) found that the median detention time for suspects was 16 hours, of which just 38 minutes was spent in interview.

The power to grant or withhold bail is a powerful negotiating tool (McConville 1992), particularly with those who are especially anxious to be released – for example, in order to fulfil domestic or work commitments, or to satisfy an addiction. Many suspects – in particular, juveniles (Steinberg *et al.* 2009) – are unable to conceptualise the long-term effects of making admissions in interview. They may cooperate with what the police want them to say in order to escape custody, not realising that a confession is not that easy to 'sort out when they get to court'. As one solicitor explained, 'Many of our clients will say "well, I got bail, I was released that night" and that's all they think about, the immediate future' (Solicitor/A5/ii).

The Code of Practice forbids interviewers from indicating whether or how the suspect answers questions might influence the action the police will take. They can, however, respond to a direct question from the detainee. Indeed, 'a strong line of police culture is the view that suspects are manipulative, willing to "deal"' and especially interested in bail (McConville 1992:541).

> I think the police will take advantage. I do believe that a lot of bail bargaining goes on and they say that if you cop for [admit] this, we'll give you bail. I think the police quite often visit the suspect in the cells without the solicitor there, which they're not supposed to do.
>
> (Solicitor/E3/i)

The police were so hostile to the idea of recording interviews that the RCCP tempered its recommendation, for fear that the police would reject its report out of hand (Lustig 1981). Subsequently section 60 PACE required the Home Secretary to issue a Code of Practice for the tape recording of interviews with suspects (Code E). Since 1 January 1992, all interviews with suspects must be tape recorded, except those that take place outside the police station, those relating to offences of terrorism, or those conducted under s1 of the Official Secrets Act 1911. There is, however, a danger of conflating the 'spurious credibility' (Fenwick 1995a:389) of the recording with the veracity of the confession. Tape recordings are listened to in only a minority of even the most serious trials (Zander and Henderson 1993) and the summaries provided are often incomplete (Baldwin 1992b). The difficulties this can cause the prosecution if they are adducing evidence of a no comment interview are discussed in Chapter 5.

The protective benefits of tape recording also cover only one part of the custodial encounter. As McConville (1992:546) has argued, what might appear as signs of guilt or innocence are instead the product of interactions which preceded the interrogation. Leng (1993:18) found that in half of the small number of cases in which silent suspects were re-interviewed, this followed an unrecorded discussion between the interviewer and suspect ('invariably when "off record" the suspect will talk' [Questionnaire 40/DC]). This does not necessarily indicate impropriety, as the suspect may have wanted to say something unofficially; it does, however, reveal a protective 'dead zone'. Police hostility to the recording of interviews declined quickly, however, as they realised it reduced their work in writing up interviews and could be deployed to their advantage (Baldwin 1991). An unintended consequence of tape recording is that it has increased the pressure on suspects. By removing the need for contemporaneous note taking, it has reduced the time they have to consider their responses (Baldwin 1991; Willis et al. 1988) and freed the interviewing officer to concentrate fully on the interview and to scrutinise the suspect's demeanour.

It has been argued that officers can define their actions retrospectively in accordance with the regulations (Holdaway 1983). They can also fulfil the criteria of the statute in such a way that they still achieve their own ends – for example, by re-interviewing suspects once the solicitor has left the police station (Solicitor/E3/ii), or by rushing through the formalities to induce suspects to waive their right to legal advice (McConville *et al.* 1991:48). As Dixon *et al.* (1989:195) cautioned: 'change requires more than the promulgation of new rules. Reform requires a consideration not merely of a specific legal power, but rather of the context of that power in the fundamentals of the mandate, culture, and practice of policing.'

PACE was not given time to be judged before the police campaign against it began. It came into force in 1986 and the Home Office Working Group was announced the following year (see Chapter 2). There was no evidence that PACE was hindering the police – indeed the initial police opposition to it has faded, as it has become normalised, because officers realised they could still do their jobs, and, that protections such as tape recording of interviews could be used to their advantage and to protect their position too. If PACE is seen as a fair exchange, the CJPOA was 'part one of a three-card trick' (Quirk 2013:468) to reduce suspects' protections.

The complex and coercive caution

Since the first iteration of the Judges' Rules in 1912, the police have had to warn or 'caution' suspects that they do not have to answer questions, but that anything they do say may have evidential value. Rule 1 of the Judges' Rules stated: 'When a police officer is trying to discover whether, or by whom, an offence has been committed he is entitled to question any person, whether suspected or not, from whom he thinks that useful information may be obtained.' The Criminal Law Revision Committee (1972) recommended abolishing the caution on the basis that it was illogical for the police to have to warn suspects against answering questions. The CJPOA required an amendment to the caution that the police must give suspects.[4] The caution increased from 22 to 37 words. Suspects are told on arrest, at the start of the interview and following every break in the interview: 'You do not have to say anything. But it may harm your defence if you do not mention when questioned something which you later rely on in court. Anything you do say may be given in evidence'

---

4 Only a late amendment to the Criminal Justice and Public Order Bill ensured that suspects had to be under caution when questioned before inferences could be drawn from their silence (*Hansard* Lords, 7 July 1994 cols 1386–1418; also inserted into the Criminal Evidence (Northern Ireland) Order 1988 by sch. 10, para 61(2)).

(PACE Code C para 10.4). Much controversy attached to this complex re-phrasing of the caution[5]. One police interviewee described it as 'gobbledegook' (PS/B9/i). Attempts to make the caution more 'user friendly' were rejected. Suggestions that the revised caution should include notification of the right to legal advice (Mansfield 1995:30) or a warning that suspects may be subject to covert surveillance in the police station were not accepted. The new caution is 'inappropriate as a concomitant of arrest' (Wolchover and Heaton-Armstrong 1995:366) as, under s34, no inferences can be drawn from failure to mention something when arrested, only 'when questioned or charged'. A sergeant interviewed agreed that the new caution is too confusing on arrest and is also unnecessary, as most suspects are not questioned until they arrive at the police station: 'Unless you're going to conduct some form of interview on the street, why have a caution on the street? You tell somebody they're under arrest, they know what it means – they're coming with you to the police station' (PS/A3).

The wording 'it may harm your defence' is also inappropriate, as suspects do not need a defence before charges are brought (Standing Advisory Commission on Human Rights 1989). Although some legal representatives reported telling the police that they do not need to explain the caution to their clients if this had been done in the consultation, most leave the decision to the police. The police are responsible for ensuring that suspects understand the caution, if necessary explaining it in their own words (PACE Notes for Guidance 10.D; Rock 2010). Clare et al. (1998) argued that this was of limited benefit to suspects as one third of police officers they surveyed were unable to provide an adequate explanation of the crucial middle sentence. The explanation given may be of significance if the prosecution seek inferences under s34 (see Chapter 5). Most legal advisers and police officers follow the same formula for explaining the caution: dividing it into three parts and asking the suspect to explain it back to them. The 'you do not have to say anything' and 'anything you say may be given in evidence' clauses are relatively simple. The extra explanation dwells upon, thereby emphasising, the possibility of adverse inferences. The resonant words 'opportunity' and 'chance' recurred in the explanations given by the police and even many legal advisers. The police had phrased the former caution in such a way as to lead suspects to feel they had no choice about exercising their right of silence (Baldwin and McConville

5 The initial proposal ('You do not have to say anything. But if you do not mention now something which you later use in your defence the court may decide that your failure to mention it now strengthens the case against you. A record will be made of anything you say and it may be given in evidence against you if you are brought to trial') was comprehensible to only 58 per cent of A level students, a level of academic competence few suspects reach (Gudjonsson et al. 1994).

1979:138) and 'the wording seems to assume that the person cautioned will speak ("whatever you say")' (Fisher Report 1977:17). Shepherd *et al.* (1995) found that 59 per cent of suspects perceived the caution as 'threatening' or 'pressuring'. Making the new caution so complex that it needs explanation exacerbates this potential. Officers have been observed 'translating' the caution for suspects with addenda such as 'now is the time to speak' (JUSTICE 1994:4). As a number of my interviewees suggested:

> They read the caution from a set card, set format and they go on to explain it and the explanations that are given are just outrageous. They bear no resemblance to what the law is or what the caution says.
>
> (Solicitor/A5/ii)

> The first bit they understand ... The rest of it they find difficult to comprehend so basically what we turn around to them and say is 'What you say now, if you go away and say something different to the court, what you say now, the court will take no notice of' and that basically is it.
>
> (PS/A4)

Minor deviations from the words of any caution given in accordance with this Code do not constitute a breach of this Code, provided the sense of the relevant caution is preserved (para 10.7 Note 10D). There have been no reported decisions relating to the suspect's understanding of the caution – although some solicitors described, particularly in the early days, calling the police officer at trial and asking them to repeat the caution from memory and to explain its meaning, which they could not do. Several legal representatives thought that the police did not understand the caution and could not explain it, as demonstrated by the following interview transcript examined at CPS Branch A. The interview took place in May 1998, in the presence of a solicitor who made no observation about the explanation:

PC: Do you understand the caution?
SUSPECT: Yes.
PC: Can you explain what you understand by that caution? Can you explain what you understand by what the caution's perception is or do you want me to break it down for you?
SUSPECT: Break it down for me then please.
PC: OK firstly you do not have to say anything at all. Do you understand that?
SUSPECT: OK, yeah.
PC: But basically what we're saying to you is if you have, answer questions tonight and tell us, er, speak to us basically, we're asking you to tell us the truth because if it goes to court then what you say today and what

you say at court the judge may draw inference from that. Basically he may think you are lying at least once or possibly twice.

SUSPECT: I understand that.

PC: OK and anything you do say tonight may be used in evidence in a court if necessary. Do you understand that?

SUSPECT: Yeah.

A solicitor gave a similarly incomprehensible demonstration as to how he explains the caution:

> If they were to be charged and the matter were to go to court, to trial, it could prove to their detriment if they did not put forward an explanation for their behaviour. Now, in as much as the judge could direct the jury that they had time to concoct a story between (I use that sort of language), between the time of their arrest and time at the police station and obviously the trial in court, and the jury could then come to the conclusion in fact he or she didn't have that explanation to give at the court (sic) but now they have it to give.
>
> (Solicitor/E3/iii)

A prosecutor said that she would always listen to the explanation of the caution to make sure the defendant had understood before seeking to rely upon it. In one case, the officers had given such a poor explanation that she had been unable to invite inferences at trial. Suspects may be unwilling to admit that they do not understand the caution; of the general population surveyed, many claimed falsely to understand the caution (Shepherd *et al.* 1995). The increased significance of the caution means that it is more important that suspects understand it fully, which gives greater power to those explaining it, particularly when suspects are unrepresented. Fenner *et al.* (2002) found very limited understanding of the caution among police station suspects and individuals attending a job centre. Clare *et al.* (1998) reported limited understanding of the caution not only among the general population but also a sample of A level students. The majority of police officers who completed my questionnaires thought that first-time suspects (53 per cent) and juveniles (56 per cent) do not understand the caution: 'I still think it's a very complicated language. It's all right for people that have got a modicum of education but a lot of people that we come into contact with will not understand the wording' (PC/B2/1). The majority of legal advisers I interviewed considered that, even though they explain the caution to the suspects before the interview, most do not understand it:

> They say they do ... I don't think they understand what an adverse inference is.
>
> (Solicitor/A7/ii)

I can count on the fingers of one hand the number of clients who have been able to say back to the officer 'I don't have to answer your questions but if I don't etc.' in a nutshell. I think they think, 'Well, the onus is on me to give my version at the earliest opportunity or you're going to think I'm a liar.'

(LE/B8/i)

A quarter of legal representatives were equivocal about suspects' understanding of the caution. One did not always explain it if he was not advising a no comment interview: 'It's not particularly relevant and to dwell on it, I know the theory that one should give the client all options available but sometimes it's just not practical to do that' (Solicitor/E3/iii). Others thought that, 'In general terms, most of them do [understand] but they couldn't explain it' (Solicitor/A13/ii). Such low levels of understanding are of concern, particularly regarding the ability of unrepresented suspects to make an informed choice. This may be exacerbated by the developing perception amongst suspects that they have to answer questions:

More seasoned villains will understand that but youths now, their culture is that you have to speak to the police otherwise you are guilty and that's what they understand and it is very difficult to get them out of that.

(Solicitor/B2/i)

The old lags, the clients who have been around the block, they know that the law has changed and they know that they've got to talk.

(Solicitor/E3/i)

A small minority of legal advisers thought that suspects do understand the caution. One took a particularly bombastic approach to ensuring their comprehension:

The ones that pretend they don't [understand] do and they've got something to hide, and they will object to it or pretend they don't understand and hope they can keep a door open to some half-baked avenue of escape if things go pear-shaped later on. They do understand it – if only because I make them understand it … I also usually get the police not to delve into too much detail during the interview … because asking the average suspect to repeat back what he understands by the caution is meaningless.

(Solicitor/B11/i)

Such views seem unlikely to hold true for all suspects ('You get quite a lot of thickos as you can imagine in the cells' [Solicitor/J14/i]). One solicitor described spending 45 minutes trying to explain the caution to a 13-year-old with a mental age of 7 (Solicitor/B2/i). This may be difficult and frustrating for the adviser; stressful and humiliating for the suspect. Suspects may say they understand the caution when they do not, through bravado or pride (Quinn and Jackson 2003:102). It has been argued that already vulnerable suspects will be made more so by the changes to the right of silence as it increases the complexity of decision making required. Pierpoint (2006:226) described how: 'the young suspect, who was very angry and upset in the interview because of persistent questioning by the police in response to his "no comment" answers, was too distressed to absorb the police's questions until he was comforted'. Vulnerable suspects are also likely to perceive the revised caution as more coercive (Gudjonsson *et al.* 1994:104):

> The more you put the suspect under pressure to have to say some-
> thing, the more you are going to be at risk of them saying things
> either that they don't actually mean, or that they don't realise the
> implications of. And I wouldn't be surprised if in ten or fifteen years'
> time, we have a spate of people saying, 'Well, yeah, I know I said that,
> but I didn't want to stay there, I wanted to go home'.
>
> (LE/B1/i)

Before inferences may be drawn under ss36 and 37 of the CJPOA (failure to account for presence in a place or a substance, object or mark about the person), the police should give a special warning using 'ordinary language' that the suspect is capable of understanding of the consequences of failure to provide a satisfactory answer. There is no set wording but the warning should include: details of the offence being investigated; specific facts which the suspect is being asked to account for; why the investigator thinks these facts may link the suspect to the offence and that a court may draw an inference from failure to account for these facts. The suspect should be told that a record is being made of the interview that may be given in evidence if the suspect is brought to trial (PACE Code C, 10.11 and Note 10D).

The assumption of the legislation, and it appears the courts, is that suspects are in a position to make an informed choice about whether or not to answer police questions. Some may be, but many do not or cannot fully understand the caution. Those who have legal representation may not be helped sufficiently to understand it and the police may use the caution to increase the pressure on suspects to answer questions.

The interview

There are many purposes to a police interview. For a measure seen to be at the heart of policing, officers receive 'remarkably little training in the techniques of questioning' (Moston and Engelberg 1993:223). Common interviewing myths are that a high proportion of suspects require skilled psychological techniques to elicit a confession when very few suspects change their initial decision – to talk, dissemble or remain silent (Baldwin 1992b; 1993). Confessions are becoming less central to interviews (Greer 1994b) and often occur 'despite the officers' efforts to elicit one', not because of it (Baldwin 1992b:14; Carter 2011:13). Most interviews 'involve relatively simple and straightforward interchanges with reasonably compliant suspects' who are 'such co-operative individuals that they should have presented no serious difficulties to a moderately competent interviewer' (Baldwin 1993:331–332). In a summary of the available research, Gudjonsson (1992), found between 42 and 76 per cent of suspects making full confessions, with others making partially incriminating statements. Bryan (1997) found that, pre-PACE, 88.1 per cent made full or partial confessions; post-PACE, it was 87 per cent. Evans (1993) found a confession rate of 76.8 per cent. Moston *et al.* (1992) found 41 per cent of suspects made full admissions and nearly 13 per cent made partial admissions.

Some commentators had suggested that police interviewing was in decline as an investigative technique (Baldwin 1993; Stockdale 1993; Williamson 1992:296). Only six out of ten suspects were interviewed and only 10 per cent of these were interviewed more than once (Bucke and Brown 1997); it nevertheless remains their principal strategy (Ainsworth 2002; Pearse and Gudjonsson 1997a; Reiner 2000; Stephenson and Moston 1994). A confession offers the quickest, cheapest and surest way to secure a conviction and is 'the primary purpose of most interviews' (Hodgson 1994:91). Moston *et al.* (1993) found 80 per cent of officers declared their main purpose of interviewing was to obtain a confession (Plimmer 1997 found a similar result). Holdaway (1988:103) observed: 'Officers require prisoners to admit to their offences, and they employ various strategies to that end … A written statement in which guilt is acknowledged is certainly a priority.' Mortimer (1994) found police officers approached interviews with an accusatory mind-set, believing that the suspect was guilty. Just over 50 per cent had obtaining a confession as their sole or joint aim. Between 64 and 75 per cent of officers reported that they thought the suspect was guilty before the interview started. This presumption can lead officers to put undue pressure on innocent suspects. Despite the high-profile miscarriages of justice in which false or coerced confessions had been made, the RCCJ (1993:68) rejected a proposal that only corroborated confessions should be admissible at trial as this risked excluding valuable admissions. Some evidence emerged from my research that police and CPS practice was moving in this direction anyway. As one officer expressed it, 'a cough [confession] is always nice but you need to nail the coffin shut' (Questionnaire 7/PC). Others recognised that without corroborative evidence '[c] onfessions are a dangerous method of deciding guilt' (Questionnaire

77/DC; Pattenden 1991). McKenzie and Irving (1987:4) thought that: 'The old practice of interviewing for confessions is replaced by one geared to "obtaining truthful confessions by acceptable and non-threatening means"'.

Much of the literature about interviewing, and the focus of this chapter, considers situations in which the accounts of the police and suspects conflict, or where the suspect refuses to comment. The majority of interviews are less antagonistic; 'good-class villains' (Policy Studies Institute 1983: iv 61–64) and the police may have amicable relations that are cultivated by both sides. If the suspect confesses, 'it psychologically becomes less confrontational' (LE/B1/ii). Similarly, if officers have other sources of evidence, they may feel less pressure to obtain a confession.

The police may structure the investigation and interview process in order to 'construct' a case against a suspect, rather than seeking to uncover objective, factual evidence (Edwards 2008; McConville and Baldwin 1982; McConville *et al.* 1991). There may be many competing versions of the event the police are investigating: the suspect may know nothing about it; may deny it happened; may admit the action but not the intention (for example, threw a bottle but did not intend it to hit anybody); may claim to have a full or partial defence (such as duress or diminished responsibility); or seek to excuse or mitigate the actions (through drunkenness or having been provoked). One of the main purposes of the police interview is to articulate and have officially recorded a *particular* version of the criminal event which articulates: 'a certain content (that certain things happened in a certain way), where this content is treated as an objective account of events, and a certain agentic position for the suspect within these events' (Auburn *et al.* 1995:356). If this 'preferred version' cannot be achieved, then an 'intersubjectively agreed account' – a compromise position – may be acceptable (Auburn *et al.* 1995:357). As this process is heavily reliant upon the answers given, any suspect who remains silent is seen as obstructive and, by implication, as having something to hide. Suspicion is a deeply engrained, highly valued policing 'skill' (Chan 2008; Dixon *et al.* 1989). Being 'uncooperative' or evasive is an indicator of suspicious behaviour and refusing to answer police questions is thus the most provocative activity of all (McConville *et al.* 1991:29). I was told repeatedly that 'the innocent have nothing to hide':

> I wouldn't want anybody who is innocent to be found guilty but, to me, the truth has got to be given and if they don't give it to me, or they go no comment, as far as I'm concerned, they are guilty.
>
> (PS/A4)

> They look for the old fashioned cough and that is all they are looking for, instead of trying to gather evidence, which is what should be

doing. They are just looking for a client to admit to an offence, then they've wrapped it up and we can all go home.

(Solicitor/A/v/2)

Police training in interview techniques has historically been criticised. Informal, 'on the job' training provided by more experienced officers, a process described as more akin to an apprenticeship than training (Maguire and Norris 1994:22), made it more difficult to effect changes in behaviours, attitudes and practices. Williamson and Moston (1990:40) found 'the majority of interviewers are surprised by the use of silence [and] are unsure of how to proceed'. Formal training such as the PEACE programme (P – preparation, E – engage and explain, A – account, C – closure, E – evaluate [Shepherd 1990]) was intended to inculcate 'ethical', less aggressive and more 'information gathering' techniques (see Clarke and Milne 2001). It was praised by some but there were flaws in its implementation (Wright and Alison 2004). It could not always be used as not all officers had been trained in it (PS/A3) and interviews were rarely planned, even when the arrest had been (DS/A6). Nevertheless, 'there was clear evidence ... that since the introduction of PEACE an improvement in the ethos and ethical approach to interviewing has taken place' (Clarke and Milne 2001:100).

The police have developed a repertoire of tactics for interviewing suspects, especially the unresponsive, varying in ethics and efficacy and depending upon their individual abilities as questioners. Some improvements in interview techniques were noted in my study (LE(P)/C4/i) and some interviewers, particularly the specialists, such as the child protection teams, were praised. The majority, however, was criticised by legal advisers and Crown Prosecutors for lacking focus or for failing to ask key questions or to establish the necessary elements of offences:

I think interviews are conducted very badly in many cases.

(Judge/B2)

There is a tremendous disparity of abilities.

(Senior Crown Prosecutor/A3)

The worst examples degenerated to pantomimic exchanges:

'You hissed through your teeth at me', that was one of the best ones I've had. 'No, I didn't.' 'Fucking did.' 'Fucking didn't.' I leave you to imagine how that conversation went!

(Solicitor/B10/i)

A lot of interviews are not interviews at all. They are just discursive ramblings from one side, followed by similar discursive ramblings from the other side ... They [the police] confuse knowledge with evidence ... They go for the cough [confession] because they are convinced in their own mind that somebody has done something, rather than doing as the Codes of Practice say, which is conducting the interview for the purposes of obtaining evidence. They are simply looking for confirmation of a pre-conceived idea.

(Solicitor/A5/i)

'Officers regularly employ psychologically manipulative techniques in order to draw suspects into making damaging admissions' (Bryan 1997:229). The police may question in a manner that 'overtly manipulate[s] the suspect's decision making' (McConville *et al.* 1991:69), such as leading or 'statement' questions. Hypothetical questioning was criticised by a number of legal representatives. Such questions are asked most commonly where suspects disagree with witnesses ('Why do you think he would say you did that?') or to satisfy the criteria of a public order offence ('Do you think those around you felt frightened by your shouting?'). They may seek to establish the suspect's personality by asking questions about previous similar incidents ('Have you ever assaulted your previous wife?' [Auburn *et al.* 1995:370]). Officers may use tactics to persuade suspects to confess, such as portraying this as the courageous option, or by implying that there is no other choice. Suggestions may be made about involving other people in the investigation if the suspect does not assist. Officers may allude to, or state expressly, the benefits of cooperation with regard to charge, cautioning, possible sentence or future investigations, even though this is forbidden, unless in response to a direct question from the suspect (Code C, para 11.3). Two solicitors related their experiences:

I'm sure there are inducements when we're not there. Well, we know there are from what we have been told by clients. It's the police looking for the cough.

(Solicitor/A5/ii)

'They told me they'd be' is the favourite one. You come out charged with some horrific series of dwelling house burglaries that'll net them four or five years, and when you say 'You're going down the steps for this one' [going to prison]. 'They told me they'd be TICed.'[6] You can't *have* dwelling house burglaries TICed on a shoplift!

(Solicitor/A5/i)

6 Where a suspect admits to having committed numerous similar offences, such as burglaries or deceptions, and is only charged with the most serious of those offences, the remainder appears on a schedule of offences, which the defendant asks the court to 'take into consideration' when sentence is passed (*Archbold* 2015 Ed 5–160).

'Verballing', or falsely claiming that a suspect had made incriminating remarks when arrested or in interviews before they were tape recorded, was an easy means for the police to strengthen their case (Holdaway 1983). It was suggested that 'non-verballing' or ignoring explanations given by suspects in an attempt to facilitate a s34 inference might be a new police tactic. The police were concerned that such accusations might be made against them.[7] There have been no reports of this. After cautioning the suspect, the interviewer is supposed to put to the suspect any significant statement or silence which occurred in the presence and hearing of the police before the start of the interview, ask them whether they confirm or deny it and if they want to add anything (Code of Practice 11.4).

PACE has transformed police behaviour. A search of the case reports in 2015 revealed no judgments relating to oppression in recent police interviews and only one solicitor in my study reported having encountered physical abuse of suspects (Solicitor/A13/iii).[8] (Although Bridges and Choongh (1998) found that 69 per cent of clients were not asked by their legal advisers how the police had treated them.) 'It totally changed the outlook of the police on people in custody so compared to Judges' Rules, the situation is far supreme' (Legal Exec(P)/C/iv/1). Some prosecutors complained that the balance had swung too far the other way:

> If anything, they are probably too fair ... err on the side of caution ... rather than go for the jugular.
>
> (Executive Officer/A4)

> They're too soft.
>
> (Senior Crown Prosecutor/C5)

The right of silence had been suggested as a contributing factor to 'noble cause corruption' (RCCJ 1993) and the CJPOA is seen by many as having curtailed police malpractice. The police no longer 'need' to obtain a

---

7 The Police Federation (which represents lower-ranking officers) thought the legislation was framed too widely and could apply to all occasions when a suspect is in police custody. They were concerned that they could be accused of 'non-verballing' – falsely claiming that a suspect had said nothing at any point. The Federation supported a Labour amendment modifying the clause and believed that further safeguards were needed for both defendants and police officers (Kirby 1994).

8 We've got stories where the client's been basically made to wet himself, he wasn't allowed to go to the toilet, then he's had to clean it up with his own clothes, or things where the cameras are on the custody desk, nice as pie on camera, get them into the cells, kick shit. So you always read to see where the injuries are and invariably you'll find they are consistent with handcuff injuries, which have been put on too tight or consistent with a struggle where, surprise surprise, they've resisted arrest and the police have been forced to use force.

confession; the pressure on suspects now comes from the law rather than an unauthorised cell visit:

> I think the change in the law has helped somewhat because they think it doesn't really matter to them whether they answer questions or not, that's the point. Because that's the way the culture of the police officers is: if you answer questions, that's fine. If you don't answer questions, that's equally fine, because we've got you anyway because you didn't answer questions. So, for them, instead of it becoming a mission to get you to cough [confess], it just means, well, either way, there's an inference that you're guilty, so there's less pressure.
>
> (Solicitor/B2/i)

'No comment' interviews

Most of the research which preceded the curtailment of the right of silence, focused upon the pre-trial stage. The RCCP (1981:84) summarised the position as 'the research indicates that the privilege not to incriminate oneself is not used by suspects in the great majority of cases and keeping silent altogether is very rare'. The findings of the main surveys published in the 15 years before the CJPOA are detailed in Table 3.1. There is considerable variation in the findings, which show that between 1.7 and 15 per cent of suspects remained silent. Silence may have no effect on the police investigation if, for example, suspects decline to answers questions about other people or questions that are unrelated to the offence under investigation. Brown (1994) reviewed the research to produce a 'best estimate' of the extent of the exercise of the right. He found that 5 per cent of suspects remained completely silent to police questions and between 6 per cent and 10 per cent remained partially silent (14–16 per cent in the Metropolitan Police District). The RCCJ (1993:53–54) summarised the available research findings as follows:

> The right of silence is exercised in only a minority of case. It may tend to be exercised more often in the more serious case and where legal advice is given. There is no evidence which shows conclusively that silence is used disproportionately by professional criminals. Nor is there evidence to support the belief that silence in the police stations leads to improved chances of an acquittal. Most of those who are silent in the police station either plead guilty later or are subsequently found guilty (footnotes omitted).

The data were not decisive, and correlation and causation are difficult to establish. The overall figures mask significant distinctions. It appears that the confession rate had dropped from over 60 per cent to between 40

Table 3.1 Incidence of suspects exercising their right of silence at the police station

Author	Sample	Incidence of silence
Zander (1979)	282 Old Bailey cases	4% silent (75% of these were convicted)
Baldwin and McConville (1979)	1000 Birmingham Crown Court 476 London Crown Courts	3.8% in Birmingham 6.5% in London
Morris (1980)		
Softley (1980)		4% silent to all questions; 8% silent to some
Mitchell (1983)	400 Worcester Crown Court	4.3%
McKenzie and Irving (1988)	68 police interviews (1986) 68 police interviews (1987) 100 files	11% (1986) 15% (1987) 16% silent to some/all questions
Sanders et al. (1989)	527 police interviews	2.4% – complete no comment 5.3% – flat denial, no explanation
Brown (1989)		
Metropolitan Police Study for HOWG (1989)	1558 police interviews	23% overall no comment (6% complete no comment, 6% to questions relevant to offence, 11% to some relevant questions) 42.6% of legally represented made no comment (15.7%, 11.5% and 15.4%)
West Yorkshire Police Study for HOWG (1989)	3095 interviews	12.3% overall no comment (2.3% complete no comment, 2.8% to relevant questions, 7.3% to some relevant questions) 23% legally represented suspects no comment (5%, 5% and 13%)
Moston et al. (1992)	1067 CID interviews	8% complete no comment 8% refused some questions (33% of legally represented, 5% of not)

Baldwin (1993)	600 police interviews (West Midlands, West Mercia, Met.) + 400 video interviews	1.7% complete no comment 18% refused some questions
Zander and Henderson (1993)		11–13% silent to all 9–17% refused some
ACPO (1993)	3600 over eight forces (no methodology published)	22% silent to some or all questions 10% complete no comment 57% of those making no comment were legally advised 47% of those with 5+ convictions made no comment
McConville and Hodgson (1993)	180 police interviews with legal adviser present	2.5% complete no comment 27% refused some questions
Leng (1993)	848 police interviews	4.5% (5% adults, 3.3% juveniles), 1.3% silence not maintained
Phillips and Brown (1998)		10% complete no comment 13% refused some questions Variation from 4–27%

and 50 per cent (Gudjonsson 1992); crime was rising and during the first year PACE was in operation, there was a fall in the number of crimes cleared up (Brown 1989). This was reversed but did not reach pre-PACE levels; whether or not that justified curtailing the right of silence was not a case that had been made empirically.

Table 3.2 shows the results of the data the police interview transcribers in Region X collected, broken down by operational command unit (OCU) or subdivision. Of the interviews that they were asked to summarise, they recorded whether the suspect was legally represented and if there had been a significant refusal to answer questions, as defined by the interviewing officer. It is only the more serious, contested proceedings for which such transcription takes place and the classification is made by the interviewing officer. Both of these factors are likely to lead to an overestimation of the incidence of no comment interviews and legal representation. The overall rate of suspects making no comment was 6.1 per cent. This varied by OCU from 1.2 to 15.1 per cent. The mean rate was 6.2 per cent and the median 4.5 per cent. Eighty-two per cent of suspects making no comment were legally advised (discussed in the next chapter). There did not appear to be any geographical trends in the no comment figures; Areas A1 and F2 were amongst the highest; A2 and F1 the lowest. A sergeant I interviewed from Area A2 thought that the proportion of no comment interviews was lower in his present station than his previous one (F2) because: 'The people are a lot more friendly over here and they'll talk to you more. The [A2] people, they'll come in and they'll admit everything they've done, they don't deny anything!' (PS/A4).

The first study to compare the use of 'no comment' interviews before and after the CJPOA suggested a sharp decline in its use (Bucke et al. 2000). The main findings are summarised in Table 3.3. Data were collected on 3950 suspects from eight police stations across the country, a year before the provisions were introduced (Phillips and Brown 1998) and five to ten months afterwards (Bucke et al. 2000) using the same methodology. The number of suspects who refused to answer all questions fell from 10 to 6 per cent and those refusing to answer some questions fell from 13 to 10 per cent. The reduction occurred across all police stations, by more than 25 per cent in almost every category. The greatest fall occurred amongst those receiving legal advice, black suspects and those charged with serious offences; those groups previously most likely to make no comment. The pre-CJPOA incidence of no comment interviews is twice as high as Brown's (1994) 'best estimate'. The figures for after the changes are also higher than these 'baseline' figures.

Maintaining silence in an interview is psychologically difficult. 'To remain silent in a police interview room in the face of determined questioning by an officer with legitimate authority to carry on this activity requires an abnormal exercise of will' (Irving and Hilgendorf 1980:153).

Table 3.2 Summaries of tape recorded police interviews with suspects transcribed in Region X between Monday 14 June and Sunday 25 July 1999

OCU/%	A1	A2	B1	C1	C2	C3	D1	D2	E1	E2	F1	F2	G1	H1	H2	H3	H4	J1	Mean
Overall legally represented	50.3	43.9	66.5	49.0	66.7	49.2	53.1	45.8	51.0	51.7	54.7	54.8	72.4	82.4	71.9	62.9	62.0	57.0	58.1
Overall no comment	8.7	3.3	15.1	2.6	4.2	7.2	3.7	1.2	4.6	3.4	2.6	7.9	3.7	11.8	10.9	4.3	7.6	8.3	6.2
No comment – represented	6.8	3.3	11.9	1.3	0.0	6.3	3.7	1.2	4.1	3.4	1.7	7.3	3.0	5.9	7.8	4.3	7.6	6.6	4.8
No comment – unrepresented	1.9	0.0	3.2	1.3	4.2	0.9	0.0	0.0	0.5	0.0	0.9	0.6	0.7	5.9	3.1	0.0	0.0	1.7	1.4
Comment – represented	43.5	40.6	54.6	47.7	66.7	42.9	49.4	44.6	46.9	48.3	53.0	47.5	69.0	76.5	64.1	58.6	54.4	50.4	53.3
Comment – unrepresented	47.8	56.1	30.3	49.7	29.2	50.0	46.9	54.2	48.5	48.3	44.4	44.6	26.9	11.8	25.0	37.1	38.0	41.3	40.6
Total no. of interviews	207	239	185	155	48	112	81	83	196	149	117	177	134	17	64	70	79	121	2234

Table 3.3 Summary of the changes in the exercise of the right of silence

Study			Complete no comment		Selective no comment		Total of some/all no comment	
			%	% change	%	% change	%	% change
Area	Metropolitan Police	1998	20	-50	12	-8	32	-34.4
		2000	10		11		21	
	Other forces	1998	7	-28.6	14	-35.7	21	-33.3
		2000	5		9		14	
Legal advice	Represented	1998	20	-35	19	-52.63	39	-43.6
		2000	13		9		22	
	Unrepresented	1998	3	-33	9	-33.3	12	-33.3
		2000	2		6		8	
Ethnicity	White	1998	8	-37.5	14	-35.7	22	-36.4
		2000	5		9		14	
	Asian	1998	13	-53.8	8	0	21	-33.3
		2000	6		8		14	
	Black	1998	21	-66.7	13	-7.7	34	-44.1
		2000	7		12		19	
Overall no comment		1998	10	-40	13	-23.1	23	-30.4
		2000	6		10		16	

Source: compiled from Bucke et al. 2000.

A 'no comment' interview breaches the normal rules of 'turntaking' in conversation (Carter 2011). Linguists often label silence as a 'turn-taking violation' (Heydon 2011:2308). Interviewing officers may exploit an uncomfortable silence to indicate that a suspect's answer is inadequate (Carter 2011:43–46); 'the costs of resistance' (Newbury and Johnson 2006:213). Many suspects are concerned about appearing uncooperative to the police by remaining silent (McConville and Hodgson 1993). Those legal advisers who discuss strategies with their clients tend to advise them to say 'no comment' rather than to maintain absolute silence, as this is more difficult (McConville *et al.* 1994:104). Some legal advisers described 'training' suspects before the interview:

> [I'll say] Put your hands under your legs, sit on your hands and look at the ground and don't make eye contact.
>
> (Solicitor/A13/iii)

> 'Have you got a mum?' 'No comment.' 'Are you wearing a white hat?' 'No comment.'
>
> (Solicitor/D13/ii)

Many legal advisers reported incidents in which they had advised their clients to make no comment but they had been unable to maintain this. It may be that the suspects who are best equipped to make no comment are the 'old lags', those who do not have a good relationship with the police or those who belong to a family or community where cooperation with the police is disapproved of: 'He was the type of person who thinks "I'm big in the area I live" – and he's not! But he thinks he's Mr Al Capone' (LE(P)/F7/i).

> He comes from a family that's well known in the area and they're supposed to be sort of untouchable, the sort of family people are afraid of, and so part of the bravado thing is he'd just sit there and stare throughout the interview and so he chose to say nothing.
>
> (DS/A6)

One interviewee recalled a petty repeat offender who, having read a book about the tactics employed by the IRA to withstand interrogation, would zip up his anorak over his face and face the wall so that the police could not 'break him down' (LE/B8/i). A number of police strategies for dealing with silent suspects have been identified. McConville and Hodgson (1993:ch.8) expanded upon Moston's (1990) typologies to show the different responses that the police employed before the CJPOA: abandoning the interview; downgrading (asking questions about other things, such as their home life); persistence; upgrading (intimating and exaggerating the strength of the case against the suspect); rationalisation (used in almost one third of cases where the investigator tried to dissuade the suspect from their strategy); direct accusations; interpreting non-verbal behaviour; and marginalising the adviser.

The legal advisers I surveyed expressed the view that the most common tactic that they saw was downgrading ('How's the wife?') or repetition of the caution, which emphasises its coercive nature. Some officers sought to undermine the representatives' advice by saying that the Court of Appeal has held that suspects do not have to follow legal advice to remain silent (LE/B1/ii). Even before the CJPOA, detectives in Cambridgeshire and Hampshire were reported to be using extracts from the Law Society's guidance for solicitors in order to persuade suspects to speak, telling them that the Law Society advises its members that 'it may be wise to give an explanation or alibi rather than just remain silent' (Dyer 1990b; Mackenzie 1990). One third of the police questionnaire respondents suggested that they would advise silent suspects that it was in their interests to speak. One interviewee described trying to provoke suspects into reacting:

> You ask something that either upsets them enough or irritates them enough or, just to get them to say something … You might even be a little bit personal, perhaps, without being oppressive or rude or anything. You might just toughen up the questions a little bit. Try and sometimes just make them look a little bit foolish sometimes works … Say or suggest things that you know they're going to disagree with and you know they want to shout at you and say 'That's not true!' or whatever, and if that works, great … perhaps playing a bit dirty and trying to upset them or, you know, just spark them into life, but procedurally, using special warnings and a caution has no effect on someone who doesn't want to talk to you.
>
> (PS/A3)

Most police officers declared that they would continue to put questions to suspects so that the courts would be able to draw adverse inferences from a suspect's refusal to answer questions (71 per cent of questionnaires). They were aware that if they did not, suspects could use this as a 'get out' at court (PS/A4). The police can make a no comment interview a record of their version of events by asking questions to which silence appears a particularly incriminating response, such as 'Are you responsible for this offence?' or by making statements about what they think happened (DS/A6). The suspect has no chance to 'steer' the interview as they could if they were putting forward a version of events (Solicitor/D9/iii). Some officers admitted how discomforting they find silence. Particularly those newer in service are still 'flummoxed' by an unresponsive suspect (LE(P)/C4/i) and abandon the interview (PS/A4; 5 per cent of questionnaires): 'I absolutely love it because they haven't got a clue what to say or do. More often than not, they don't even put half the questions which they should do' (Solicitor/D13/ii).

A police officer from Station B who refused to be interviewed declared, deliberately within my earshot, that if suspects make no comment in his interviews, he refuses to give them a second chance to answer, as though not being allowed to answer his questions were a punishment for their recalcitrance (Solicitor/B2/i agreed). This may, of course, be the case if inferences are drawn subsequently. Other officers are more phlegmatic, believing that they are in a no-lose situation now; either the suspect confesses, or inferences can be drawn from silence (Jackson *et al.* 2000):

> I'm changing from information gathering to giving him an opportunity to say things and if he chooses to give up that opportunity, that's his loss, not mine.
>
> (PC/A7)

> I would thank the offender for not answering my questions and I would explain to him that in my view all he was doing was strengthening my case and then give him another opportunity to talk.
>
> (Questionnaire 7/PC)

There may be further difficulties for suspects relying on an interpreter in interviews. 'Interpreters may relay not only the police officers' questions but also the power of the interrogator to put the suspect under pressure by deciding whether they remain silent or render/paraphrase officers' questions' (Nakane 2011:2328). Interpreters may exceed their role by, for example, not starting to translate the answer if they think it is insufficient (Nakane 2011:2323) so that the silence indicates that the suspect is expected to say more.[9] Interpreters may be concerned that a lack of response or an 'unacceptable' reply from the suspect may reflect badly on the interpreter's ability and may 'repair' or rephrase the police question in order to elicit a reply (Nakane 2011:2320). Unless the solicitor speaks the same language, this is unlike to emerge.

As detailed in Chapter 2, the CJPOA extends beyond a failure to give advance notice of a fact to be relied on in a suspect's defence to the more punitive risk of inferences from failure to account for incriminating objects, marks or substances (s36) about their person, or for their presence at a particular place (s37). This requires, what became known as the 'special warning' – or what the in *Milford* (2001 at 24) described as being 'by way of an ultra-caution'. The force surveyed for this book had produced a flow chart for police officers to follow in deciding whether a special warning was applicable ('Is the interviewee under arrest'?, 'Was the

---

9 This research is based on interpreters in police interviews in Australia.

interviewee found at a place at or about the time of the offence?', etc.). In some instances, the police appeared to use special warnings, asking suspects as another tactic 'really designed to oppress or worry them' (LE(P)/ A12/i) to persuade suspects to speak. PS/A3 admitted that special warnings probably had been used inappropriately at first, as officers had not been trained properly in the use of them. Other solicitors noted:

> Most of them don't have a clue when to use it … They've used it because the IP [injured party] had got a cut, so they said, 'Therefore that mark incriminates your client, special caution.'
>
> (Solicitor/A13/iii)

> Intervening, it's usually on special warnings because the police haven't got a clue on them. 'I'm giving you a special warning because you're not explaining yourself.' 'Officer, he's denying it, he has explained, what else can he explain?'
>
> (Solicitor/B10/i)

Three-quarters of the questionnaire responses suggested that officers would use special warnings if a suspect remained silent, although many added 'only where appropriate'. Seventy-three per cent of police interviewees replied that they used special warnings only rarely; 8 per cent of officers said they never issue them. They may be used in cases that are more serious; one barrister considered that in the cases he sees where a suspect has made no comment, a special warning is 'invariably' given (Bar/B3). Bucke et al. (2000) found that special warnings were given to 39 per cent of suspects exercising either full or selective silence and to 7 per cent of suspects as a whole. In terms of the case law, the sections 'have been largely overlooked' (Owusu-Bempah 2014:126; see Chapter 5). It is not known how often they are raised at trial. It may be that 'although the police make use of the provisions, prosecutors tend not to rely on them at court' (Owusu-Bempah 2014:128).

It appears that special warnings were not particularly persuasive in eliciting admissions. 40 per cent of police questionnaires responded that suspects never gave an explanation after a special warning. Similarly, Bucke et al. (2000) reported that after a s36 special warning, 70 per cent of suspects gave no account of the relevant object, substance or mark, 11 per cent gave an account that was unsatisfactory to the police and 19 per cent gave a satisfactory account. Even fewer suspects yielded to a s37 warning, with 77 per cent giving no account of their presence, 10 per cent an 'unsatisfactory' account and 13 per cent a satisfactory explanation. This may be because those who have reached the stage of getting a special warning have made a deliberate decision to remain silent and are psychologically strong enough to maintain this position (or having been found at the scene of a crime or with something incriminating about their person meant that they were likely to be charged anyway). One police officer lamented that: 'Special warnings are not strong enough, not worded harshly enough to worry suspects' (Questionnaire 96/PC).

Jackson *et al.* (2000) found that special warnings were used in a 'finely tuned' manner in Northern Ireland. Article 3 warnings (the standard caution) were described as 'sledgehammers' that were used in every interview but the detectives would sometimes debate between themselves whether or not a special warning should be given relating to Articles 5 or 6. None in my survey described such deliberations but some did consider the implications of using it selectively to strengthen the prosecution's case:

> It's another tool which you can use in trying to get the true course of events ... It is the sort of 'reasonable man' test, if you like, Mr Joe Average outside would think 'that's ridiculous' ... If they don't give a version we can use the special warning, or if you're not satisfied with their version. That is a little bit of a grey area ... I can't say it is something that I use often because invariably they will give a version. Rather than let them explain that, if you let that run, when it goes to court, it can actually be seen for the ludicrous situation that it is, shall we say, because if you suddenly go 'Hang on, special warning, I don't believe you, what you've just told me, that is a complete fantasy, special warning', they may then change that to a more credible version.
>
> (DC/A5)

Custody sergeants are not supposed to take a suspect's silence into account when deciding whether or not to charge. Two officers thought that it would make no difference; as with confession evidence, it was seen as the 'icing on the cake' (PC/A8). The officers from Station B were more of the view that not answering the reasonable suspicion that the police had when arresting the suspect left a case to answer:

> Remaining silent is sometimes ill-advised as you then have to charge them ... It is the custody sergeant's decision but if allegations and evidence and no comment, then that is a *prima facie* case.
>
> (DS/B4)

> If there is nothing to rebut suspicion, then they have to charge.
>
> (PC/B3)

> If he says 'No comment' I have to take inference from that. If he's innocent or there's an innocent explanation, he'd give it to me ... 'no comment' in itself isn't grounds for charging. We must have evidence.
>
> (Custody Sergeant/BS/B1)

Those in Station A said that, without the evidence, no comment would not make a difference ('I don't think their silence in itself would add any weight from the evidence to consider a charge' [DS/A6]). Following a series of Court of Appeal decisions (see Chapter 5), the PACE Codes of Practice were amended. The test for charging has been raised from sufficient evidence to provide a realistic prospect of a successful prosecution to conviction. This allows the police to put further questions to the suspect which the prosecution can introduce at trial to suggest that it would have been reasonable for the defence to have answered (Cape 2003:364).

The impact of the changes to the right of silence on the progress of interviews has clearly been dramatic but may have diminished as advisers realised that making no comment does not always disadvantage their clients (LE/B1/i). The effect on the outcome of interviews is less clear cut. Bucke et al. (2000) found no change in the 55 per cent of suspects making confessions. Assuming no change in the proportion of guilty suspects arrested, this might indicate that suspects who previously would have remained silent instead simply deny the offence or give a version of events that is either false or inscrutable (of the 'I bought it from a man in a pub' variety). This would support the argument that the most vulnerable suspects, who would be most susceptible to the increased pressure of the new caution, did not use the right before the changes anyway. It was mainly the more robust suspect who could make no comment and they are resourceful enough to be able to give instead an account of themselves that is unlikely to advance police enquiries. The other possibility is that suspects who previously made no comment because they were innocent or against whom the police had insufficient evidence may now answer questions and still be released without charge. The charge rate for suspects making no comment fell from 70 per cent to 64 per cent (Bucke et al. 2000) and there was little difference in the numbers receiving police cautions. The confession rate remained stable during the 1990s, despite the increased protection of tape recording, the greater provision of legal advice and the marked decrease in the number of manipulative and coercive tactics employed by the police (Pearce et al. 1998). The charge rate for suspects answering all questions remained at 50 per cent. This may be due to no comment now only being used tactically in cases where the evidence is weak. The use that is made of these interviews at trial is discussed in Chapter 5.

Conclusion

The safeguards offered to suspects in custody by PACE are undoubtedly an improvement on the common law and the practices that preceded it. They fulfil different purposes to the right of silence, however, and should not be regarded as a substitute for it. This right of silence was not solely a protective measure. It was also a practical expression of the principle that it is for the prosecution to discharge the burden of proof, without assistance from the accused. Research published prior to the CJPOA demonstrated that the protections received by many suspects were either inadequate or easily circumvented. As noted elsewhere, there has been a dearth of English empirical policing research in recent years (Sanders and Young 2008:306), which means that much policing scholarship is based on empirical data that were collected some time ago. This was not the case when the Northern Ireland Order and CJPOA were introduced, which was in many ways the high point for such research. The Act was introduced in direct contradiction to what was known from the existing data at the time. Complaints that the police were unduly hampered by PACE ignored the realities of the custodial experience over which the police have almost total control. The police were and are 'gate-keepers' of suspects' rights, having the ability to circumvent or minimise the effectiveness of many of these protections. As Dixon (1997:92) observed, 'they are never equal exchanges'. The PACE safeguards are tempered by the lack of effective checks on the exercise of police powers or of any effective sanctions against the police for breaches of the regulations. The refusal to answer police questions was hitherto the only effective sanction that suspects and legal advisers had in response to the police either abusing their powers or acting beyond them; this now has evidential risks.

The police are culturally adversarial. They were hostile to the right of silence, perceiving it as a challenge to their authority and as an impediment to the achievement of results – namely detections and convictions. Whilst police conduct in interviews has improved, the CJPOA reinforces the attitudes that PACE was intended to change. The CJPOA accords with prevailing police attitudes about 'appropriate' – that is, compliant and penitent – behaviour from suspects, a presumption that suspects are guilty and the innocent having nothing to hide. The police have been criticised for fulfilling their obligations in a manner which frustrates the spirit of PACE; the CJPOA effectively does the same. The protective benefit of legal advice, a fundamental requirement of a fair trial, is devalued by the quandary in which the legal representative is now placed. Whilst the direct effects of the Act have been limited by the relatively small numbers of suspects making no comment hitherto, it is the effect upon legal representation that has shifted the balance of power in custodial interrogation further in favour of the police. The effects of this are explored further in Chapter 4.

Chapter 4

A 'fundamental dilemma'

The undermining of legal representation at the police station

As discussed in Chapter 3, the police station is a closed environment and historically, the police have expressed mistrust or dislike of 'challengers', those whose role is to scrutinise their work (Holdaway 1983:71–77), in particular legal representatives. There was also a fear that legal representatives would prevent the police from achieving their objectives. As McConville *et al.* argued (1994:102, citing Walkley 1987): '[a]ccording to police mythology, the presence of a solicitor in an interrogation destroys the relationship between the officer and suspect under which a "dominant persuader" is able to exercise pressures on the suspect to conform to police wishes'. The right to legal advice at the police station was the fulcrum of the exchange abolitionist argument to curtail the right of silence. As then Home Secretary Douglas Hurd recognised, the right to legal advice would be difficult to curtail, so attention was focused on the right of silence (HOWG 1989:4). This chapter examines the claims about overly adversarial advocates; levels of legal representation; the effects in terms of disclosure and how the changes to the right of silence have undermined the benefits of legal representation in interview.

The Police and Criminal Evidence Act 1984 (PACE) gives detainees the right to free and independent legal advice, in private, by telephone, in writing or in person (s58 PACE and Code of Practice C). This entitlement has been described as a 'fundamental right of a citizen' (*Samuel* 1988 at 144). The fair trial provision of the European Convention on Human Rights (ECHR) further provides that everyone charged with a criminal offence has the right: 'to defend himself in person or through legal assistance of his own choosing or, if he has not sufficient means to pay for legal assistance, to be given it free when the interests of justice so require' (Article 6(3)(c) ECHR). The European Court of Human Rights (ECtHR) has ruled that the right to legal assistance extends to pre-charge police detention when evidential consequences may attach to the behaviour of the suspect there (*Murray* v *UK* 1996; see also *Imbrioscia* v *Switzerland* 1993). This was extended in *Salduz* v *Turkey* (2008) based on the implied right of the accused not to incriminate themselves, and has become firmly established in the jurisprudence (Lord Hope in *Cadder* v *HM Advocate* 2010).

As discussed in Chapter 2, the additional protections provided by PACE provoked an immediate backlash from the police, some judges and certain politicians, who claimed that the changes, in particular the right to legal representation, had made it too difficult to prosecute and convict 'criminals'. This led to the suggestion that the right of silence should be ceded to restore the equilibrium. The 're-balancing' rationale was flawed for a number of reasons, but particularly in relation to legal advice. When the Royal Commission on Criminal Procedure (RCCP 1981) recommended statutory access to legal representation, it was *alongside* the right of silence, as a counterweight to the proposed increase in police powers. The equation also appeared to rely more on instinct and anecdote than empirical evidence. Whilst there are discrepancies in the methods of collating statistics,[1] the overall trend was that the numbers seeking legal advice rose after the introduction of PACE and after each subsequent revision of the associated Codes of Practice. For a free service, however, it was – and still is – taken up by surprisingly few suspects. Although the right to consult a solicitor existed at common law,[2] very few suspects exercised this right. Estimates of pre-PACE rates of legal advice range from 3 per cent to 20 per cent (Baldwin and McConville 1979), most were under 10 per cent; (Bottomley *et al.* 1989; Brown 1991; Softley 1980; Willis 1984). After PACE this rose to about 25 per cent (Brown 1989; Morgan *et al.* 1991; Sanders *et al.* 1989), and to 32 per cent after the 1991 revisions to Codes of Practice (Brown *et al.* 1992).[3] Not all of those who requested legal advice received it; most requests were denied before PACE (Baldwin and McConville 1979; Softley 1980) and between 25 per cent (Sanders *et al.* 1989) and 33 per cent afterwards (Brown 1989; Dixon *et al.* 1990). Some researchers suggested that there was a greater likelihood of the police refusing or delaying access to a solicitor in more serious cases (e.g. Dixon *et al.* 1990).

There were significant variations in the take-up of legal advice between and within regions. Rates in London were consistently higher than elsewhere. Provision of legal advice differed according to a number of factors, the most significant being the offence type – those suspected of robbery and sexual offences were three times more likely to seek legal representation than those arrested for shoplifting and motoring offences – but this varied considerably by the police station involved (Brown

1 Most of the studies used selective samples (e.g. only those cases that went to trial [Baldwin and McConville 1979] or from a single police force or station rather than the general custody population). Brown's (1989) report is the most comprehensive.

2 The Judges' Rules provided that 'every person at any stage of an investigation should be able to communicate and to consult privately with a solicitor'.

3 These required custody sergeants to read suspects their rights and ask them to sign the custody record indicating whether or not they wanted legal advice.

1989). Local factors, such as the ways in which individual custody ser-geants offered legal advice to suspects, may have been significant (Maguire 1988; discussed in Chapter 3). In addition, Phillips and Brown (1998) have argued that certain interviewing officers would advise sus-pects that they did not need legal representation as they were unlikely to be charged – which, of course, turned out not to be the case once the suspect had made incriminating admissions in interview. The efficiency of the local legal aid provision was also likely to have had an impact, as delays may have deterred suspects from seeking consultations (Brown 1989). Black and Asian suspects, those with previous convictions, the unemployed and those whose appearance gave 'cause for concern' on arrival at the police station, were more likely to seek representation (Philips and Brown 1998).[4]

By the early 1990s, there was clear evidence that, while the numbers of people seeking legal advice had increased, rates varied greatly and were still low overall. Those seeking reform would point out that those accused of serious offences were more likely to be legally represented (Brown 1989; Dixon *et al.* 1990; Maguire 1988); that some suspects would request a lawyer for 'inappropriate reasons: for example, to delay pro-ceedings, to obtain items such as cigarettes and newspapers or to relay messages to family or friends' (Phillips and Brown 1998:59); and that there was a positive association between legal representation and no comment interviews (ACPO 1993; Metropolitan Police 1989; Moston *et al.* 1992; West Yorkshire Police 1989). On the other hand, a wealth of data was emerging at that time that showed that unqualified advisers and acquiescent solicitors were failing to provide adequate advice to suspects or to enforce their clients' rights sufficiently (Baldwin 1992a; Baldwin 1993; Dixon 1991b; Hodgson 1992; McConville and Hodgson 1993; Sanders *et al.* 1989). The Court of Appeal expressed its horror at the bullying and hectoring faced by one appellant, finding the solicitor 'gravely at fault for sitting passively through this travesty of an interview' (*Paris, Abdullahi and Miller* 1993 at 103–104). As discussed in Chapter 2, notwithstanding the available research, there was a stronger political than evidential impetus behind curtailing the right of silence. In par-ticular, the lobbying power of the police was a significant driver and there was considerable police resistance to the presence of legal advisers in the police station.

This chapter assesses the impact of the changes to the right of silence in the context of what was and is known about the quality of legal repres-entation. It explores the interactions between legal representatives, the police and their clients. Many police officers resented the intrusion of

4 Although published after the CJPOA came into effect, the fieldwork was conducted beforehand.

legal representatives into their territory and their interviews (Sir Robert Mark (1973) alleged in the Dimbleby Lecture that a minority of defence solicitors was 'more harmful to society than the clients they represent'). Legal representatives have no formal powers at the police station to monitor or enforce police compliance with PACE. Before the CJPOA, they could advise their clients to make no comment if they thought that the police were on a 'fishing expedition', had acted improperly or were refusing to disclose their case before interview. The CJPOA restricted this means of negotiation, which has circumscribed the benefits of legal advice (Leng 2001c). Cape (1997) went so far as to argue that legal representatives had effectively been 'sidelined' by the legislation. Subsequent developments, explored below, have revealed that the effects of the Act on this critical relationship have, if anything, been even more profound. Legal representatives know that they may have to testify about their advice, which can have detrimental professional and financial consequences. Legal professional privilege (the principle that what is said between lawyer and client must remain confidential) may now have to be waived in an attempt to rebut adverse inferences (Quirk 2013). When the Act was introduced, its opponents' focus on the risk of miscarriages of justice, and misplaced optimism as to how narrowly the courts would interpret the provisions, meant that the potential impact of the Act on custodial legal advice and the nature of the lawyer–client relationship were neglected. Two decades after the CJPOA was introduced, it appears that these have been the most significant effects of the Act.

Active defenders or babysitters?

PACE states that the function of the legal representative is solely 'to protect and advance the legal rights of their client' (Code of Practice C, Note 6D). This specifically includes explaining, and sometimes advising, the exercise of the right of silence. The solicitor may intervene in order to seek clarification; to challenge an improper question or the manner in which it is put; to advise the client not to reply to a particular question; or to request a break if there is a need to give the client further advice. In an adversarial system, this partisan role was essential. The Law Society handbook for legal representatives at the police station was titled *Active Defence* (Ede and Shepherd 1997; Shepherd *et al.* 2007). and there is an extensive legal ethics literature about the duty of lawyers to practise what US lawyers term 'zealous advocacy' (Smith 2012). Principle 4 of the Solicitors' Regulatory Authority Handbook is a duty to 'act in the best interests of each client'. Suspects have been doubly disadvantaged by the fact that few representatives acted according to this ideal and because the CJPOA and subsequent changes in the criminal justice system have compromised lawyers' ability to act in such a manner.

Legal advisers at the police station have what is often a 'disagreeable and solitary calling' (Baldwin 1993:373). They may be regarded as unwelcome by the police, the work is unpredictable and stressful, the environment and the hours uncongenial, and their clients may be awkward or unpleasant to deal with. As Boyle (1993:1279) vividly explained:

> We deal with the lowest level of society at the point of conflict and confrontation with society, in both the police station and in the courtroom. We deal with them shortly after their arrest and usually at their very worst. They are violent, fighting mad, hopelessly intoxicated. At all times of the day or night, weekend or holiday we deal with the sad and the bad. Cells daubed with excrement, clients vomiting copiously, bleeding, head-banging – it is just the norm and comes with the job.

Criminal advice and representation has long been regarded amongst legal professionals as low status or 'distasteful' work (White 1975) that is mundane and lacking in intellectual challenge. This is in part due to a tendency amongst other lawyers to associate criminal practitioners with the poverty and criminality of the majority of their clients (McConville *et al.* 1994:24–26). The lower remuneration rates compared to privately funded and other publicly funded specialisms further reduced its status. In many firms, police station work was accorded the lowest status of all. It was often delegated to the most junior, frequently unqualified, staff, or to agencies, many staffed by retired police officers who were considered inured to the working environment, whilst solicitors concentrated their activities on higher profile and higher paid court work (Bridges *et al.* 1975; Dixon *et al.* 1990; McConville *et al.* 1994:41; McConville and Hodgson 1993; Sanders *et al.* 1989). Recent changes in the legal aid system have made this work more difficult, and the effects of this are discussed below.

There is a 'general non-unitary character of criminal defence solicitors' (McConville *et al.* 1994:17). Whilst some solicitors see their work as political or vocational, in contrast to the combative approach of the police, most legal advisers regard themselves as neutral referees or 'babysitters' (Sol/B2/i; Baldwin 1992a:1764; Hodgson 1994:94). When legal representatives were asked to describe their role for this study, replies included:

> Really the only point of going is to make sure that the interview is conducted fairly.
>
> (Sol/J14/i)

> To make sure the interview is a proper representation of the client's case at that time.
>
> (Sol/E3/i)

This may explain why half of the legal advisers interviewed for this study were diffident about the changes to the right of silence:

> I don't think it's made a great deal of difference, certainly not to our advice. Most clients have got a story to tell, denying it, no matter how ridiculous and, if that is their story, why not tell the police about it?
>
> (Sol/A5/ii)

Almost half had been seriously concerned about the CJPOA, however, and expressed such views with vehemence:

> What that [the CJPOA] effectively did was to shift the burden away from the Crown proving the case, putting that onto the defence to say 'You disprove it'. That, to me, is entirely wrong.
>
> (LE/B1/i)

> They were unpleasant, they were symptomatic of the change in the legal system we've enjoyed since the Conquest, made principally, I felt, to satisfy the rabble of the Conservative Party conference … a back-door method of improving detection and conviction as the police are fairly incompetent of improving it any other way.
>
> (Sol/D9/i)

Several researchers who have conducted observational studies have found a disjuncture between the partisan rhetoric espoused by defence solicitors and their actions (McConville *et al.* 1994; Newman 2013).[5] My interviews too revealed something of a mismatch between theory and reality. Some advisers championed the ideals of the right of silence but qualified it with observations similar to those expressed by the police, such as:

> If the man is an innocent man, he's got nothing to worry about.
>
> (Sol/J14/i)

> How many clients are not guilty anyway? We're not talking about major crime in [Town A]; we're talking about wife beating, shoplifting, theft, burglary, whatever and it doesn't make a great deal of difference at the end of the day because most clients are guilty – unfortunately.
>
> (Sol/A15/i)

---

5 One of my interviewees claimed to go to the police station for all cases. When pressed as to how often this was, he explained that he could not go during the day when in court, and did not want to go out at night, finally conceding that it was probably about once or twice a week.

Only one legal representative, a retired police officer, had supported the changes. He endorsed them in a manner that appeared more in accordance with those of his former colleagues than his current role:

> I think it was a necessary change really ... rights of the victim as well. Your more thinking criminals did it as a matter of course. Into the police station, say nothing ... talk it over with your solicitor, go away, find those witnesses, wait until it comes to court then produce them. That was an absolute travesty of our legal system. A complete waste. Everybody has got to have rights, and everybody has got to be protected, I'd agree 100 per cent because there have been a lot of injustices in the past. But because of injustice in the past, we shouldn't allow criminals to conspire to defeat the system. And that's what they were doing. I don't see any reason at all why, if someone has got proper legal advice at the police station, that he shouldn't have to answer the questions, relative to the evidence.
>
> (LE(P)/A12/i)

Legal representatives have no formal authority at the police station. They are reliant on the police for information and for their safety if they have to go into a cell with a potentially violent client. They are required to be courageous and tenacious if they are to assert their clients' rights. The police have a wide discretion in the exercise of their powers and their personal relationship with the adviser may influence their decisions. Officers may check the status of representatives and try to 'take advantage' of young, female, black and/or inexperienced advisers (LE/B/i/2). Having previously worked as a para-legal, one solicitor noted the improvement in the response he received once he qualified (Sol/B2/i). This absence of authority means that many legal advisers see it as being in the best interests of both themselves and their clients to rely instead on cultivating good relationships with the police. This may mean taking the Utilitarian decision that it is better to be non-adversarial for one client so as not to prejudice future cases (Dixon 1991b:239). As two representatives explained it:

> You've got to be lenient with the police, if you start rocking the boat with the police, then when you want some cooperation, you might not get it and at the end of the day, we're all there for the same thing aren't we – one side or the other side?
>
> (LE(P)/F7/i)

> I like to think I'm moderately objective when I'm dealing with cases. There are solicitors who believe every word their client says and will do absolutely everything and anything to try and thwart the prosecution. Perhaps I'm shooting myself in the foot but, more often than

not, I will need the help of the police in [a] case more than they will ever need my help, so it doesn't pay to be bloody minded, because you get a reputation for that.

(Sol/A12/ii)

Even interventionist legal advisers were aware of the importance of their reputation with the police:

[I am] Chummy, whenever the client's not there and then cold when the client is there and then in interview, put on the other hat and be nasty if they're nasty ... If they expect you to be Mr Chummy, then they're not likely to hold stuff back from you because they think 'Oh this guy's not going to do anything' and when they do pull a few surprises out of the hat and you act like a wanker then they don't know what to do, they're a bit stumped, so it is always best. But it's not good to be bolshy from the word go because you achieve nothing.

(Sol/A13/iii)

Before the CJPOA, many representatives assumed a 'feeble (one might almost say supine) posture' in interviews (Baldwin 1992a:1762), making few interventions to control police behaviour (McConville and Hodgson 1993). Some representatives merely helped the client to understand the questions or to explain their story; others essentially played the role of a third interviewer. Dixon (1991b:242) noted that 'a few advisers had reputations ... both with police and their colleagues, for being too ready to accept the police account of events and to encourage clients to confess'. Despite the common caricature, McConville and Hodgson (1993) found no cases of legal advisers routinely advising suspects to make no comment before the CJPOA; most legal representatives assumed their clients would answer questions and gave either neutral advice or recommended cooperation with the police.[6] Legal advisers commonly gave their working relationship with the police as a reason for not advising silence (McConville and Hodgson 1993:89) which could be seen as a provocative action. Most legal representatives tend to work in the same police stations, with the same officers. The client is a transient figure who needs to be kept reasonably happy to ensure his or her repeat custom, but this can be ensured by negotiations over bail, plea or sentence, without upsetting the police. It may be significant that following the CJPOA changes, public defenders (a salaried defence service) were

6 The most common reason they found for representatives advising silence was lack of knowledge of the police case. Other reasons included: to protect the suspect from self-incrimination; a belief the police case was insufficient to charge; and in response to police hostility (McConville *et al.* 1994:104).

more likely to advise 'no comment' interviews than private practitioners (Bridges *et al.* 2007; see Table 4.1). One solicitor thought that working in the same, more rural, police station gave him some bargaining power as:

> If they're going to bugger me about on one day, they know sure as hell I can do far more damage to them when I come up against them at a later date. On the other hand, that can lead to an incestuous relationship where the solicitor can cleave to the police more than he should, so it's a balancing act.
>
> (Sol/B11/i)

A taxi driver, taking me to an interview, fondly recalled the more lucrative days when solicitors would frequently ask him to drive between police stations as they tried to locate clients they knew had been arrested before they were interviewed. When asked to describe the role of legal advisers in interviews for this study, 13 per cent of police officers defined it as being to 'hinder' the interview. Asked to define 'obstructive' behaviour by legal representatives, one detective cited those who threaten a no comment interview if he refuses to make full disclosure to them (DS/A6). Some officers seemed to find the presence of a legal representative disproportionately threatening:

> Certain legal advisers now appear to be more forthright in opposing what they *suggest* is oppression which in some cases may stretch to seeking to emasculate the interviewer.
>
> (Q25/DS, original emphasis)

> Others are blatant conspirers to pervert the course of justice ... There are those that obstruct interviews and bully junior, inexperienced police interviewers.
>
> (Q36/DS)

A significant minority of police officers remained hostile to legal advisers. Several thought that legal representatives invented defences for their clients – one officer claimed that certain solicitors advise their clients to pretend to be mentally ill in order to receive lenient treatment (PS/B2). Six of the seventeen officers interviewed mentioned this firm; '[t]hey're bandits!' (PS/B2)). Criticisms were made of the 'inducements', such as food, clothing or cigarettes that solicitors offer their clients. Although no question referred to legal aid, almost 10 per cent of questionnaire respondents made some reference to solicitors advising their clients to make no comment in order to inflate their fees. As one detective explained:

Table 4.1 Public defender service (PDO) and private practice (PP) investigation stage file analysis: suspect comments in police interview

		All no comment %	Comment during some interviews	Comment during all interviews	Not clear from file	N
Birmingham	PDO	5	7	74	14	43
	PP	11	–	80	9	45
Cheltenham	PDO	13	4	73	10	48
	PP	7	–	78	15	41
Liverpool	PDO	13	3	79	5	39
	PP	11	3	78	8	36
Middlesbrough	PDO	20	–	80	–	40
	PP	12	9	71	10	42
Pontypridd	PDO	36	–	61	2	44
	PP	14	–	83	2	42
Swansea	PDO	18	–	82	–	38
	PP	13	3	82	3	38
All areas	PDO	17	2	75	6	252
	PP	11	2	79	8	244

Source: Bridges et al. 2007: Table 3.4.

> I don't trust solicitors and legal reps because they are there to earn a lot of money ... They think of it as business proposal. I see it as they are criminals. I get paid whether I prosecute (sic) or not.
>
> (DC/B7)

There may be 'bent solicitors who are protecting their clients in an unfair way' (Bar/B9). McConville *et al.* (1994:99) found this to be 'exceptional' but Bridges and Choong (1998) found legal representatives acting unethically or unprofessionally in 9 per cent of cases, by offering suspects a fabricated defence or protecting them from criminal liability. Such reprehensible conduct should, of course, result in criminal or professional disciplinary proceedings, but reports of any such action are scarce. An essential protection for defence lawyers is that they 'should never be identified with their clients or their clients' causes as a result of discharging their functions' (Principle 18 of the United Nations, *Basic Principles on the Role of Lawyers*). A particularly damaging aspect of the campaign against the right of silence was the insinuation – by some police, politicians and judges – that lawyers were colluding or conspiring with their clients to evade justice. This created a culture in which it became easier to curtail defendants' rights (see Chapters 5 and 6) and which had fatal consequences in the cases of Pat Finucane and Rosemary Nelson in Northern Ireland (see Chapter 2).

Even before the CJPOA there were signs of a change in police attitudes. There was:

> a shift towards greater professionalism amongst investigating officers. This includes a more realistic view of the constraints which law places on police conduct, concern about avoiding complaints and disciplinary action, willingness to work with others in the criminal justice system, and limits on the officer's personal commitment to securing convictions.
>
> (Dixon 1991b:242–243)

Similarly, Irving and McKenzie (1989:160) reported that 'at least where the personal characteristics of the people involved allow, shared professional interests and concerns have gradually loomed larger than the antagonisms'. Reports of police abuse of solicitors, ranging from insults and attacks on the solicitor–client relationship, to planting drugs and campaigns of harassment (Halliburton 1999) are almost unheard of now. Only two solicitors in Baldwin's (1992a) survey had experienced resistance or hostility in interviews and none of the legal advisers I interviewed mentioned any such incidents, although some had experienced obduracy or trickery:

> The police sometimes go out of their way to be rude. They will keep you standing there looking like a spare part just for sport. So, even

though you're the lawyer, you know if you complain, they will do it all the more but find a good reason. If you do nothing that will be deemed to be a sign of weakness so they'll leave you standing in the corner ... As a lawyer, you're an irritation.

(Sol/B11/i)

I get on with [D1] CID but [D2] CID, wouldn't trust them an inch. [Interviewer: 'Why?'] Just things they've done.

(Sol/D13/ii)

One solicitor recalled a series of interviews in which the interviewing officer had lied to him about having statements and evidence (Sol/A13/iii). I was told of local rumours – but no personal experiences – of cases in which the police had bugged the consultation; an allegation of which most lawyers were apparently aware (Wright 1998) and which has, more recently, been admitted by the government (Reprieve 2015).

This thawing of relations that has continued post-CJPOA may be due to increased familiarity; a recognition that scrutiny poses no threat to a properly conducted investigation, even protecting it against challenge at trial or appeal. Other factors might include the lack of adversarialism of most legal representatives; the restrictive effects of the CJPOA upon the impact of legal advice and the effects of the changes introduced following the Human Rights Act 1998. Some officers at Station A2 suggested that they were encouraged to advise suspects accused of serious crimes to seek representation to avoid later allegations of impropriety. Kemp (2013) found several custody sergeants would encourage those accused of serious offences, particularly those who had not been in custody before, to seek legal advice, even though PACE states that they should not seek to influence the decision. Almost two thirds of police officers described the role of solicitors in positive terms, such as ensuring fairness, advising their clients or helping.[7] Most legal representatives considered that overall they had reasonable relationships with at least some of the police:

A lot of arresting officers and interviewing officers don't necessarily want us there, because they see us as a hindrance. But the good officers, the ones who conduct interviews properly, are quite happy to have us there because they know there won't be any question of the

---

7 Some officers thought that legal representatives assisted by calming suspects or by clarifying questions for them (Q11). They can prevent the officer from becoming so embroiled in the interview that their questioning becomes repetitive and thus potentially oppressive (PS/A4). They may be a useful conduit for negotiations that cannot take place directly according to PACE, such as when the police are willing to issue a caution if the suspect confesses (PC/A8), or to suggest the sentence benefits of an early confession (LE/B1/ii).

interview being thrown out at a later stage because of the lack of legal representation.

(Sol/A5/ii)

The service offered by the police station legal adviser varies enormously between the individuals involved. There was a striking disjuncture between the research findings available before the CJPOA was enacted about the quality and combativeness of defence representation and the anxieties expressed about it by the police and other opponents. The curtailment of the right of silence, supposedly a *quid pro quo* for legal advice, of course applies to all suspects, whether represented (effectively) or not.

Provision of pre-interview legal advice

As noted above, while rates of legal representation are increasing, it is still received by only a minority of suspects. Even after the 1995 revisions to the Code of Practice, following the CJPOA, rates have still not yet reached 50 per cent. Not all suspects who request advice receive it. Bucke and Brown (1997) found a request rate of 40 per cent but that a solicitor was not contacted in between 2 per cent and 21 per cent of cases, an average of 11 per cent; Phillips and Brown (1998) found 38 per cent requested legal advice. Kemp (2012) found a request rate of between 40–43 per cent; Pleasence *et al.* (2011) recorded 36.5 per cent receive legal advice (45 per cent having requested it); and Skinns (2009a) reported a 48 per cent advice rate (from a request rate of 60 per cent). The geographical unevenness in representation continued. My study of Region X showed an average rate of legal representation of 55.2 per cent (see Table 3.2) and a median rate of 54.8 per cent.[8]

There are a number of reasons as to why request rates remain so low. As described in Chapter 3, for some suspects the length of detention is of greater immediate concern than whether or not they are charged (Sanders *et al.* 2010:235). Kemp and Balmer (2008:40–41; Kemp 2010:35–41) found that many suspects were unable to make an informed decision about getting advice, and were seemingly unaware of how a solicitor could assist them. Often suspects have little conception of the potential seriousness of their situation – one quarter of those arrested for rape and homicide offences did not request legal advice (Kemp 2013). The police can use such ignorance to their advantage. One solicitor thought that legal advice should be compulsory:

---

8 This figure is likely to be elevated because it counts only those interviewed and only those interviews that were transcribed, so presumably those where a charge was likely to follow.

I'm not saying that to double the amount of work. A lot of people don't appreciate the trouble they are in until ... they come to see you and they say, 'Well, I was told by the police it was only a bit of scrapping'. No, it's called violent disorder and they get three years [imprisonment] in the Crown Court.

(Sol/D9/iii)

Our clients have got no conception of a) what [their rights] are or b) how to go about enforcing them.

(Sol/A5/i)

Previous research suggested that custody sergeants could deter suspects from seeking legal advice by going through their legal rights incompletely and/or incomprehensibly (Sanders *et al.* 1989; Dixon *et al.* 1989, see Chapter 3) – for example, by saying 'sign here and here', indicating the line to decline representation. Kemp (2013) suggests that this is less likely now as there is audio and visual recording in custody suites but that the potential for such manoeuvres still exist. Barring solicitors from the custody suite can give detainees the impression that asking for a solicitor is likely to cause delays. Kemp identified opportunities for dissuasion by the arresting or interviewing officer: telling the suspect that they could be interviewed straight away either *en route* to the police station or as the suspect was booked in by the custody sergeant ('If you don't want a brief I'll take you in for an interview now'); or blaming the solicitor for delays so that the suspect would withdraw the request. The revised PACE Code states that where a suspect requests legal advice but subsequently declines it, an inspector should make enquiries about the reasons why and decide whether the interview can go ahead without a solicitor (PACE Code C para 6.6(d)). Two solicitors in my study mentioned that their clients were sometimes told, falsely, that the solicitor would not come out. Three alleged that, in certain areas, the police actively discourage suspects from requesting representation. One gave the example of a case he was dealing with:

We've got an appointment for a woman ... there's a bastard of a police officer dealing with it. He has told her basically, she has children to look after, if she wants to get in and out of the police station quickly then she shouldn't get a solicitor there, otherwise she'll be kept there all day.

(Sol/E3/iii)

The most common reasons cited by the police in their questionnaire responses for suspects declining legal advice were: time considerations (48 per cent); that the suspect 'knows the system' (31 per cent); or the strength of the case against them (22 per cent). Fifteen per cent of questionnaire respondents, and almost all of the police officers interviewed, disputed the question on the basis that the majority of the suspects they interviewed are legally represented. Such a contention is clearly not borne out by the figures for Station A (see Table 3.2) but this perception may indicate how threatening or inconvenient some officers find having a legal adviser present. Over a quarter of legal advisers thought that time was the main factor for suspects declining legal advice, either the person realising, or the police telling them, that it would take longer if they wanted a solicitor. Kemp *et al.* (2012) observed a common perception among detainees that solicitors were the main cause of delays – a perception that could be reinforced by the police to discourage suspects. When Kemp (2013) questioned custody sergeants about the causes of delay, few blamed the legal representatives. Kemp *et al.* (2012) found that, after controlling for offence seriousness and other factors, suspects who requested a solicitor were held on average for two and a half hours longer; Skinns (2009a) noted a difference of around four and a half hours, an increase from Phillips and Brown (1989:110), who noted a three and a half hour difference). If the police refuse to allow access to a solicitor, which they may do under certain limited circumstances, then no inference may be drawn (s34(2A) of the CJPOA as amended by s58 of the Youth Justice and Criminal Evidence Act 1999).

Suspects who request legal advice do not necessarily receive it in person; some may be advised only by telephone, which may make it difficult for them to talk freely to their adviser if the custody suite lacks a private area (Pattenden and Skinns 2010). One solicitor said that he does not speak to his clients on the telephone as he thinks it is intimidating for them to be brought into a custody area full of police officers (Sol/A13/iii). Others have found that it is difficult to make contact with their clients as telephones are not always answered when the custody suite is busy (Kemp 2010:47–50; Kemp 2013). Legal representatives in this study varied in their views as to whether suspects always required their attendance at the police station. The individual involved may influence the representative's decision about attending. One solicitor had been telephoned shortly before I interviewed him by a regular client who had stolen a pizza. During the advice call, the client said that he was going to admit the offence and that there was no need for the solicitor to visit. The solicitor agreed, but added: 'If he'd been a juvenile or totally new to the criminal justice system, I probably would have gone' (Sol/E3/i). The offence under investigation was also significant to some representatives. Two solicitors suggested they would not always attend suspects accused of shoplifting:

> I'll say, 'Look, you've been arrested for stealing from this shop, just say yes or no, did you do it?' and if they say 'Yes I did it', then I will say 'Look, I'm not sure there's going to be much point in me coming

down'. Because if you admit it, and if they haven't been in trouble before, quite often they'll just be cautioned.

(Sol/J14/i)

Such views demonstrates how some representatives give little thought to the needs of their individual clients (such as the impact of receiving a caution on a person of previous good character) or consideration to the wider benefits and responsibilities of their role (McConville *et al.* 1994). There are many good reasons for the solicitor to attend the police station. In order to fully advance their clients' rights and to safeguard their well-being, solicitors should assess, amongst other things: the suspect's physical and mental state, the circumstances of the arrest, the strength of the evidence and whether the legal criteria of the offence are fulfilled. (To use the example given above, taking goods from a shop and having money would not constitute theft if the suspect had genuinely forgotten to pay.) The advice the representative gives may need to alter if the police change their approach, introduce new material or ask questions about other offences once an interview has begun. These requirements can clearly only be fulfilled if the representative is present.

The right of silence reforms have made custodial legal advice more complex. It appears that many solicitors do not accord the interview such importance, perhaps still holding to the view that 'things can be sorted out at court'. Before the CJPOA, non-solicitor staff were used in between about one third (Sanders *et al.* 1989; Dixon *et al.* 1990) and two thirds of cases (McConville and Hodgson 1993). Only one of the fifteen firms that I visited (B1) had any system for grading cases or specialisation amongst its staff to determine who should attend the police station.[9] Bucke and Brown (1997) found 10 per cent of work being performed by accredited representatives and 6 per cent by unaccredited representatives. I formed the impression that in Region X, legal executives performed the majority of police station work: 'The solicitors don't come out so much now, you get a lot of runners in which, I would say eight out of ten are ex-bobbies [police]' (PS/A4). Half of the firms studied either employed former police officers as representatives or used agencies staffed by them, in part because they were seen to understand the work and to be used to the anti-social hours and environment. Roberts (1995:785) notes that it cannot be assumed that legal advisers who are not legally qualified espouse traditional legal principles or ideologies of adversarialism. Even though solicitors do not always espouse or practise such values, it is even more

---

9 This firm also had '[gold] star' clients; those accused of serious, complex or unusual crimes or who were otherwise considered important. For example, a famous footballer charged with a minor assault would be represented by someone more senior than such an offence otherwise merited (LE/B1/ii).

challenging for those who may have absorbed the occupational police way of working over a long career (see Chapter 3). Two former police officers still referred to their clients in the police vernacular as 'prisoners'. One represented clients in the same police station in which he had previously arrested and questioned them. He saw no difficulties in having 'gone to the other side' but warned his clients to expect 'familiarity' between him and his former colleagues. Thus far, none of his clients had objected. He thought that this was because they knew a solicitor would represent them at court, which they regarded as more important, a view he appeared to share. It was notable that, when asked about police attitudes to the presence of legal advisers, he answered from the viewpoint of the interviewing officer: 'The only time you're going to have a problem with a solicitor present is if you're thinking of doing something you shouldn't' (LE(P)/F7/i). The Law Society introduced an accreditation scheme for non-solicitors to improve the quality of legal advice. Only those registered can be remunerated under the legal aid provisions.[10] This appeared to lead to improvements in the quality of representation (Bridges and Choongh 1998).

The relationship between the legal representative and client is not always a straightforward, hierarchical one. As discussed in Chapter 2, there may be many extraneous influences on a suspect's decision about whether or not to answer police questions. Asking legal representatives how they would advise suspects with whom they disagreed about whether or not to answer questions provoked homilies such as:

> I only advise, I don't direct.
>
> (Sol/E3/i)

> It is their right to conduct the interview as they want. I'll advise them but that's all I'm there for, I'm not there to tell them what to do, because I could end up being criticised by them.
>
> (Sol/A12/ii)

Of course, the decision is ultimately that of the client, but sometimes professionals, of any discipline, have to give advice that the client does not necessarily want to hear – whether that is doctors telling patients to drink less alcohol, accountants recommending a business is wound up or solicitors advising clients whether to answer police questions. This difficulty is discussed below and in Chapter 5, but an experienced legal executive explained the importance of giving directive advice. He described representing a respected authority figure, against whom there was overwhelming

10 Police station legal representation can be provided by a solicitor holding a current practising certificate, or 'an accredited or probationary representative included on the register of representatives maintained by the Legal Aid Agency' (para 6.12 Code C PACE).

evidence of low-level sexual abuse of children. Having sought confirmation from the investigating officer as to the strength of the police case, he advised his client that this was sufficient for him to be charged, convicted and sentenced to three or four years' imprisonment. After a lengthy consultation, the client made full admissions, pleaded guilty and was given a community-based sentence. The representative continued:

> I spent an hour in getting the guy to cross the threshold ... He's got to have the benefit therefore of the experience that we can bring to bear ... It's much easier just to let it carry on and I think that many, many lawyers don't intervene enough in situations like that and it's something that I would criticise many, many of my professional colleagues for.
>
> (LE/B1/ii)

It was clear from the research available at the time the CJPOA was proposed that legal representatives were not obstructing justice, but their presence in a minority of interviews had become a totemic issue for the police and certain politicians.

Pre-interview disclosure

One of the most significant benefits that legal representation offers suspects is in obtaining disclosure of the police case before the interview: 'The usual criminal element, they will always ask for a solicitor. The main reason is they know they will get disclosure of the evidence' (LE(P)/A12/i). Legal representatives have no entitlement to disclosure before the interview but have a better chance of getting it than an unrepresented suspect. Forty three per cent of officers replied in the questionnaires in my study that they would not give unrepresented suspects an outline of the case against them, 56 per cent would not read the main points from statements to suspects and hardly any would let suspects see or have copies of the evidence. Without disclosure, there can be no balance in the interview, as legal representatives have no means of checking the veracity of the police account, of determining the lawfulness of the arrest, or of the legitimacy of the interview. Without knowing the strength of the evidence, legal representatives cannot assess whether to advise suspects to answer questions or not. In the police training manuals on investigative interviewing, officers are advised to use this as a strategy:

> Place yourself in the position of the solicitor. If you had to rely solely on the version of events from the suspect, you would probably advise your client to listen to the police questions without comment to establish the strength of the evidence.

The threat of a no comment interview had been a useful bargaining tool prior to the CJPOA, but this is now a risky strategy. The adviser has to judge whether the danger of adverse inferences from not answering questions outweighs the risk of the suspect providing the evidence that leads to them being charged:

> The difficulty with answering the questions is when half of the case is put together and you then give the opportunity for the police to go round and get the second half of the case together.
>
> (Sol/B10/i)

> We are always, therefore, starting pretty much on the back foot. If we don't see the statements and we are only given a summary, we are working with what they tell us. Whether they are telling us a true and accurate reflection of what the statement says, or whether they are in fact just picking out what they think are the salient points in the statement relevant for the purpose of interview, we know not.
>
> (LE/B1/i)

Several officers suggested that pre-interview disclosure depends on what they are asked for by legal representatives; they will not volunteer anything. Almost 20 per cent of officers replied that they do not give the advisers an outline of the case, only one third read advisers the main points from witness statements and fewer than 20 per cent provided copies of the evidence. Although one solicitor contended that the risk of missing something significant when trying to decipher badly written and photocopied statements made verbal disclosure preferable (Sol/B10/i). Disclosure is at the discretion of the officers; it often relates to how well they know the adviser and their opinion of them:

> It varies because of location and it varies because of who you are. Within [City B] almost no problem at all, it's only a question of degree and it ... literally varies from police officer to police officer ... [Town A is problematic] Now, whether that is because we are a [B] firm going into [A], or whether [A] CID are like this with all solicitors, I know not but I can tell you my own experience is that as an experienced [B] practitioner, if I go into [A], I don't expect to be told the full story ... The impression I get from speaking to [City C] policemen is that they don't have a very good relationship with their solicitors over there. They don't trust the solicitors and vice versa.
>
> (LE/B1/ii)

> Do we know the lawyer and prior dealings (i.e. trust, communication, helpful?) will also have a bearing.
>
> (Q40/DC)

A sergeant saw disclosure as a privilege to which only amenable legal advisers were entitled:

> If there's a solicitor I've had problems with in the past, I'd say no. If they've upset me in the past then, 'No, I'm not going to make your job easier mate, you find out what I've got' ... If the solicitor's there and he's been unhelpful to me in the past, then he's got to earn his corn and he can stop the interview.
>
> (PS/A4)

Such attitudes demonstrate how the contingent nature of disclosure and the importance to defence lawyers of maintaining reasonable relations with the police may make it difficult for advisers to be adversarial. By acting appropriately in one case, they risk getting less disclosure in every other case they have with that officer. The combative approach of many police officers means that they see disclosure of information as weakening their position:

> CID won't let you see any of their statements, they'll just tell you what's in them. Most plods will let you see it ... It's a power game with [CID].
>
> (Sol/A13/iii)

> I wouldn't go out my way to offer information they are not entitled to have. They are as biased as we are!
>
> (Q74/PC)

And, most melodramatically:

> Would you give a country your battle plans if you were about to go to war? No.
>
> (Q100/PS)

This secrecy may be related to the police culture of suspicion of others, described above and in Chapter 3. Several police officers expressed the view that lawyers could not be trusted with full disclosure:

> I'm not saying that solicitors would concoct a story with their clients but I don't know what goes on in their consultation and if I were to say that fingerprints were found on the back of the TV set then he might suddenly have become a TV repairman in a previous life, not, you know, you're just manufacturing a defence on their behalf.
>
> (DS/A6)

It's obvious that when information is disclosed prior to interview the suspect is given get out of jail information that has obviously not come from their own knowledge.

(Q10/PC)

The reluctance of the police to make disclosure accords also with notions of 'case construction' (the idea that the police seek to gather evidence that confirms their view of guilt [McConville *et al.* 1991]). As one solicitor explained:

They believe that it is a legitimate tactic [to withhold evidence] because they will assume that the defendant will lie and therefore, if he tells the truth and it accords with what they've got, you've got a match and therefore he must be telling the truth, but if there's something different and they've held back, they can then introduce that to try to trip the person up or to accuse them of lying.

(Sol/B2/i)

Some officers disclose information incrementally in operations in which a number of offences are being investigated, or if there will be several interviews relating to offences over a long period of time (DS/B6). Edwards (1995) states that 'on advanced interviewing courses officers are advised always to hold some fact back so as to prevent false confessions'.

Since the CJPOA, the tactics used by the police and defence relating to disclosure have changed. Obtaining disclosure remains a problem for legal representatives, but the strategies available to them for eliciting such material are more limited. Because representatives are now wary of advising no comment, if the police refuse to disclose their case, they may advise the client to 'say something and stop the interview if you are not too sure' (Sol/D13/ii) or say that they will intervene if the police introduce undisclosed material. There is a danger, of which officers are aware, that the suspect may have answered before the adviser can respond (DC/A5):

We were having a lot of interviews stopped, 'I need a consultation with my client' and to be honest, I'd rather do that, I'd rather go into an interview and say something and the solicitor knows nothing about it. I mean, it's a particularly selfish way of looking at it, I suppose, the suspect nine times out of ten has answered your question before the solicitor says, 'Oh, hang on a minute'.

(DC/A3)

It was thought initially that the CJPOA had 'transformed the culture of police–legal adviser relations' in terms of disclosure (Bridges and Choongh 1998:xi). One solicitor thought that it had caused: 'a complete re-training ... most officers now understand the reasoning behind the real necessity for disclosure' (Sol/A5/i). Fuller disclosure may indicate a change in police methods, rather than a change in culture, however. Hitherto, 'ambushing' the suspect with evidence was an effective means for the police to achieve their desired 'result'. Now they wish to avoid suspects having any 'get out' from inferences being drawn at trial. One detective said that he provides legal advisers with a copy of all disclosure made, including copies of statements ('it's handy for solicitors') but he said his motivation is to prevent any dispute at court (DS/A6). One legal representative believed that, having opposed the changes to the right of silence, he now felt they had been a reasonable trade-off for the improvements in disclosure (LE/B1/ii).

Another legal executive from the same firm, however, thought that police practice had gone 'full circle back to where we started' (LE/B1/i). When the caution first changed, the police had disclosed everything for fear of losing prosecutions. Once they realised that they were not obliged to make full disclosure, they began withholding statements and giving only verbal summaries of the evidence again. He thought that local police attitudes regarding disclosure may have hardened following an incident in which his colleague had had a statement upon which his advice was based taken forcibly from him after he refused to return it after the interview. A solicitor considered that disclosure had become 'patchy', even from officers who had previously been open, suggesting that such policies are reviewed at a higher level (Sol/E3/iii). A police sergeant agreed:

> [Disclose] as little as possible. There was a point three or four years ago ... the emphasis on disclosure became stronger shall we say. That we were saying, 'Oh, you've got to tell the solicitors everything, disclose, tell them everything, give them the statements'. But I think, as a service, we've stopped that really now, and I don't see that there's any need for that.
>
> (PS/A3)

> It's very cat and mouse.
>
> (DC/A5)

The courts have ruled that inadequate disclosure of the police case will not necessarily avoid inferences being left to the jury from a suspect's silence at the police station (discussed further in Chapter 5). It cannot be fair that evidential significance attaches to the suspect's decision whether or not to reply in interview, when they and their legal representatives must make this decision in the absence of full knowledge of the nature or the strength of the police case.

In 2014, PACE Codes C and H were amended to comply with Articles 3, 4 and 6 of EU Directive 2012/13/EU. This requires that suspects or their legal representatives are provided promptly with sufficient information about the allegation against them 'to safeguard the fairness of the proceedings and the effective exercise of the rights of the defence'. This includes sight of documents and materials which are essential to challenge the lawfulness of the arrest, detention or charge (Code C para 3.4(b)). Before interview, they must be given sufficient information to enable them to understand the nature of any such offence, and why they are suspected of committing it, in order to allow for the effective exercise of the rights of the defence (para 11.1A). There are significant caveats, however. The decision about what materials must be made available rests with the custody officer in consultation with the investigating officer. The PACE Code also includes a limitation, not in the Directive, that this does not require the disclosure of details at a time which might prejudice the criminal investigation. It remains to be seen what effect, if any, this has on proceedings.

The police are now in a much stronger position. Previously, if they refused to make sufficient disclosure, the legal representative might advise a no comment interview. This could frustrate police enquiries if their case was weak. Following the CJPOA, representatives are less willing to advise no comment and the police are in the position of either being able to surprise the suspect in interview or knowing that inferences from a no comment interview may strengthen their case. As one solicitor concluded:

> If you're going to have a watering down of the right of silence, then a person who is being advised or interviewed at a police station has got to be properly advised and you can only properly advise a person when you know what you are advising about and therefore you have got to have disclosure of the Crown's case so that you know. And I'm afraid that I don't think that you always get disclosure or full disclosure, or honest disclosure and so that, if they're cheating, then that defeats the whole idea of it to be honest and it should revert back to the complete right of silence.
>
> (Sol/B1/iii)

Police interviews and the undermining of legal representation

PACE Code of Practice C sets out the responsibilities of the legal representative. It also makes clear that the solicitor may intervene during the interview in order to seek clarification; to challenge an improper question or the manner in which it is put; to advise the client not to reply to a particular question; or to request a break if there is a need to give the client further advice. In exceptional circumstances, the police have the right to exclude a solicitor who is disrupting the interview, but the Code makes clear that merely advising no comment is not a sufficient reason to exclude the representative.

Whilst some legal representatives described the proactive role they play in interviews ('I'm quite prepared to interrupt tactically if my client is about to put his foot in it' [Sol/E3/ii]), legal representatives have been criticised for doing little in interviews other than making notes (Q60/PS). Thirty nine per cent of police questionnaire respondents thought that advisers intervened only rarely. One detective commented:

> A lot don't play a very active role, could do or say a lot more – I would if I was one.
>
> (DS/B5)

> I am constantly surprised how little they challenge my questions. It makes me wonder whether they know what they are doing.
>
> (Q77/DC)

As two very experienced solicitors explained:

> I've lost my rag far more than police officers do with my own clients.
>
> (Sol/B11/i)

> [We intervene] Not to help the police because that's not our job, but not necessarily to hinder them, but to help the cause of justice really.
>
> (Sol/A5/ii)

Following the Law Society's accreditation programme, Bridges and Choong (1998) found that accredited representatives became more interventionist, doing so in 78 per cent of cases in which it was deemed necessary, but they were still more likely to intervene in relation to their clients than to challenge police behaviour. Several police officers had noted a difference in adviser behaviour:

> You seem to get this, more of a confrontation with the younger or newer ones.
>
> (DC/A5)

> I think they try to take control a lot more than what they used to.
>
> (DC/A9)

One officer thought that legal executives try to assert themselves, whereas solicitors 'tend to let interviews roll'. She complained about two legal executives in particular who do not understand that 'interviews aren't battlegrounds' (PC/B3) – an interesting expression, given the combative language many of her colleagues used to describe their own approach to interviews. Amongst my respondents, the recently qualified representatives were more likely to say that they advised no comment interviews than experienced solicitors were.

The cheery legal advice of 'if in doubt, say nowt'[11] became a hazardous strategy after the CJPOA came into force ('Police station work has changed, in my view, out of all proportion' [Sol/B10/i]). Legal representatives have to decide swiftly, often in ignorance of some or all of the facts, whether to advise silence and risk adverse inferences being drawn at trial; or to answer police questions that may provide the additional evidence needed to charge. They have 'to balance what [is] in their clients' interest at the time of the interview with what would be in their interest if the case came to court' (Jackson *et al.* 2000:122). Advisers know that their decision could have negative repercussions for the client and for themselves:

> The imposition on the lawyer is really quite tough, because we are now in a very unenviable position of, if our advice is wrong and we don't give adequate legal protection to our client ... it's an element that can be used to convict them ... There is more thought process required.
>
> (LE/B1/ii)

> At 3 o'clock in the morning you've been dragged out of bed, your pyjamas are sticking out from underneath your jeans and you're trying to write a cogent note about why you've given certain advice which somebody is going to sniff over nine months later.
>
> (Sol/D9/ii)

Only one 'before and after' study explores the effects of the CJPOA (Bucke *et al.* 2000, discussed in Chapter 3). This shows a 35 per cent fall in complete no comment interviews amongst the legally represented. The police data collected in Region X (see Table 3.2 and the discussion in Chapter 3) shows that 82 per cent of suspects making no comment were legally advised. There were, however, areas with high rates of legal advice and a low incidence of no comment (G1) and vice versa (A1). The mean rate of no comment interviews was 6.2 per cent and the median 4.5 per cent. The rate for legally represented suspects was 4.8 per cent. When asked in what situations suspects tended to make 'no comment' since the CJPOA, 70 per cent of police questionnaire respondents considered that it depended on the legal advisers; either that legally advised suspects were

---

11 This maxim suggested that if the adviser or suspect was unsure of his or her position, it was safer to say nothing than to risk making potentially incriminating admissions. Bridges *et al.*'s study showed much higher rates of 'no comment' interviews, ranging from 5 to 36 per cent (see Table 4.1).

more likely to be silent or that certain firms advised silence more frequently, or even routinely (the Area B firm, about which I was told so much, was described by one detective as 'notorious for no comment interviews' [Q45/DS]). Other factors included the individual concerned (39 per cent) or the strength of the police case (37 per cent).

When asked why they might advise a no comment interview now, reasons suggested by legal advisers in this study (although some had never or only rarely done so in practice) included: a weak police case or suspicion they were 'fishing'; insufficient disclosure; or the likelihood of the complainant failing to appear in court. This was often cited in relation to domestic violence or public order incidents – in such cases, if the complainant does attend court, the suspect will usually plead guilty, obviating the question of inferences. Other reasons for advising no comment included: if the suspect was guilty, unfit to answer questions or at risk of incriminating themselves in this or other matters; the overwhelming nature of the evidence; and the complexity of the allegations or age of the incident. Some would advise silence when the police could not prove which individual was responsible for an offence (for example, if two people were in a car in which drugs were found [LE/B8/i]).[12] Some representatives said they have clients who make no comment routinely, regardless of the advice they are given (Sol/D9/i), although another dismissed the professional no-commenter as 'a complete myth' (Sol/B10/i).

Amongst my respondents, only two legal advisers considered that the majority of their interviews had been no comment before the changes. When asked how often they advised no comment interviews now, almost 20 per cent said 'never' and almost a further one third said between 4 and 10 per cent of interviews. Three said that they had 'plenty' (one quarter or one fifth) of no comment interviews. The rest found it difficult to estimate or did not answer directly. Just over one third considered that they advised silence less than before the changes; none advised it more. Bridges and Choongh (1998) observed that advice to remain silent had remained the same, despite almost three-quarters of non-solicitor legal representatives saying that they advised it less often. This advice was given in 19 per cent of cases (11 per cent, 24 per cent and 25 per cent in the three police stations studied). The most commonly cited reasons for advising silence were where the police had insufficient evidence (69 per cent) or had made insufficient disclosure (50 per cent).

---

12 Section 5 of the Domestic Violence, Crime and Victims Act 2004 created the offence of 'causing or allowing the death of a child or vulnerable adult' to circumvent this problem. 'Serious physical harm' was added by s1 of the Domestic Violence, Crime and Victims (Amendment) Act 2012.

In the early days of the legislation, a number of tactics were suggested to avoid inferences from silence. Few of the solicitors I interviewed showed awareness of, or interest in, exploiting such tactical gambits. This may indicate either a lack of strategic awareness or their pragmatism as the Court of Appeal has not been receptive to such practices. The Law Society recommended that solicitors advising clients to remain silent should do so in the present tense at the start of the interview. This meant that the advice would be delivered in a non-privileged situation so referring to it in court would not open the defendant up to cross-examination about other legal advice received (Law Society 1994, 1997, 2006). Such an approach does carry risks, as in *Fitzgerald* (1998), where such a statement was adduced by the prosecution to indicate a prejudicial connection between the suspect and the others in custody. Other strategies included advising suspects to remain silent, then submitting a prepared statement before the interview or at charge. The statement may be used at trial in order to rebut any inference of subsequent fabrication (if, for example, no comment was advised in response to inadequate disclosure). Solicitor B2/i suggested that after a no comment interview he might hand in a statement at charge as some officers only make disclosure during the interview and then refuse the suspect the opportunity to comment later. It may also be useful if it is thought that the suspect would be unable to answer questions precisely enough to avoid saying something incriminating. If the statement gives full details of the defence then no inference should be drawn (Judicial Studies Board 2010). Inferences may be drawn if a more detailed or inconsistent account is given at trial (*R* v *Knight* 2003) and the Court has warned that this 'may prove to be a dangerous course for an innocent person who subsequently discovers at the trial that something significant has been omitted' (*Turner* 2003; *Mohammed* 2009). Some of those interviewed could see a hypothetical benefit in submitting prepared statements, but others could not see the point of such a 'meaningless' action (Sol/B11/i). Some legal representatives were shockingly complacent about the provisions:

> I don't think it harms you if you give a no comment interview. I can't see what inference, if it's a straightforward case where you are going to say x, y and z and you don't say it first time round but you say it at court, I can't see how the magistrates are going to draw an inference.
>
> (Sol/D13/ii)

> I've probably done 500 trials in the magistrate's court, never, ever known it. So much so, I can't remember the law on it, never had to bone up on it because I've never, it's something I needn't concern myself with.
>
> (Sol/B11/i)

Such ignorance is of course self-perpetuating, as he is unlikely to advise a client to remain silent if he is unaware of the provisions.

Most advisers did not stay for charge, even though inferences can be drawn from a suspect's silence at this stage. (One firm had a policy of staying for charge initially, but they stopped doing this once they realised that inferences from silence at this stage were never an issue at trial [LE/B1/ii].) Some claimed that this was due to the exigencies of work; others found waiting boring. One suggested that the police in Region X dislike legal advisers staying for charge, resenting being monitored at this stage (Sol/E3/iii). The decision to stay appeared motivated primarily by whether they would get paid for this time. The changed legal aid arrangements are discussed below (Sol/A13/iii). One solicitor stayed for charge 'because I like to get them signed up for the legal aid and keep the charge sheet then they are less likely to wander off elsewhere' (Sol/A12/ii). His decision was governed by the time of the interview. If it were during the day he would stay; at 4 am, he would go home.

The judiciary has taken a mixed approach to legal representation (discussed in Chapter 5). It held that the presence of a legal representative puts suspects on 'equal terms' with the police (*Chandler* 1976), meaning that a breach of PACE would not necessarily lead to the exclusion of improperly obtained evidence. A poor or inept legal adviser may be more damaging to the suspect than having none as their acquiescence may be interpreted as legitimising inappropriate behaviour, making the exclusion of improperly obtained evidence less likely (*Dunn* 1990). Poor legal advice to make no comment will not protect defendants from adverse inferences (*Condron* 1997; *Roble* 1997). The Court of Appeal has been more supportive of legal representation since PACE (Zuckerman 1989a:340) but courts have not supported suspects' right to legal advice wholeheartedly, particularly for those who have been legally advised in custody previously (*Dunford* 1990). Such reasoning assumes the suspect remembers the previous advice, equates an awareness of rights with an understanding of how they should be exercised and discounts the expertise of the lawyer in advising on the facts of each case (Hodgson 1992). No matter how many times a suspect has been detained and questioned by the police, an adviser may recognise a need to remain silent where suspects cannot be expected to, either through a lack of legal knowledge or because of their physical or mental condition. The judgment fails also to consider the quality of the advice suspects may have received previously: the provision of an adviser does not guarantee the provision of advice, legal advice or competent advice (McConville and Hodgson 1993:193).

The case law is discussed in Chapter 5 but, in summary, it has made the work of legal representatives much harder and the courts have shown little sympathy for, or understanding of, the legal representatives' role. There is an irreconcilable tension between s58 PACE, which provides the right to legal advice at the police station, and the CJPOA. Implicit in the right to legal representation is the assumption that the professional offers expert advice to the lay client. The court considered that: 'It is not so much the advice given by the solicitor, as the reason why the defendant chose not to answer questions that is important' (*Condron* 1997 at 833). Contrary to early expectations, and indications from the Court of Appeal (*Roble* 1997), inadequate police disclosure does not justify the exclusion of a no-comment interview; rather it should be left to the jury to consider the reasonableness of the advice (*Argent* 1997; *Kavanagh* 1997; *Imran and Hussein* 1997).[13] Judge B/2 was 'fairly unsympathetic' to defence claims that no comment was advised due to inadequate police disclosure: 'The suspect is told at the time "the reason we want to know where you were on such-and-such a day is because we suspect that you were responsible for this crime". It seems to me, that's quite good enough.' Such limited detail is, however, insufficient for the legal representative to assess the merits of the police case – whether it is adequate to justify the arrest, or sufficiently strong for the police to charge immediately.

In *Hoare and Pierce* (2004), their solicitors advised them not to answer police questions on the basis that Pierce's continued detention and interview were unlawful as the custody time period had expired and it was not clear what evidence the police had to suggest Hoare had committed an offence. The trial judge rejected the submission that the detention was unlawful, accordingly evidence of the no comment interview went before the jury. This seems unfair. If the solicitor had a reasonable and genuine belief that the police were acting beyond their powers, then this advice offers the only immediate sanction or disincentive for the police to stop acting in this way. That these interviews were not excluded demonstrates the expectation that defendants must cooperate with the process and makes the job of legal representative much more difficult.

The Court has given examples of situations which may 'justify' (*Howell* 2003:para 24) a legal representative advising a no comment interview. (The significance of its choice of verb is explored in Chapter 5.) The illustrations included the suspect's condition (ill-health, in particular mental disability, confusion, intoxication or shock) or genuine inability to recollect events without reference to documents, or communicating with others, but its judgments are insufficiently consistent for legal representatives to have any confidence when advising clients at the police station. Inferences were allowed in *Condron* (1997) where the solicitor thought that the defendants were unfit to be interviewed due to the effects of heroin withdrawal. Inferences were also allowed in *Roble* (1997), a case in which the solicitor advised no comment because she considered his understanding of English to be

13 Birch (1999) suggests that the severity of the judgments is mitigated by the weakness of these cases and the unrealistic requests for disclosure.

insufficient to deal with difficult legal concepts and she was unclear as to what his instructions were. As Cape (1997:402) has argued:

> If defendants can never be sure that they are acting reasonably in relying on the advice of their lawyer, then they can never be sure that they should accept their lawyer's advice. If they cannot be sure about that, then it raises the fundamental question of the utility of legal advice at the police station. Custodial legal advice may be guaranteed by the European Convention on Human Rights, but its value as such is in danger of being seriously eroded.

The Court gave examples of what would not be considered reasonable grounds for advice: the absence of a written statement from the complainant; the likelihood that the complainant will withdraw; or the solicitor's belief that the suspect will be charged anyway:

> There must always be soundly based objective reasons for silence, sufficiently cogent and telling to weigh in the balance against the clear public interest in an account being given by the suspect to the police. Solicitors bearing the important responsibility of giving advice to suspects at police stations must always have this in mind.
>
> (*Howell* 2003 at para 24)

This echoes the wording of the JUSTICE Report in 1967 that if the privilege against self-incrimination were abolished, 'it will become contrary to public policy and to professional etiquette for a solicitor to encourage his client not to answer questions' (JUSTICE 1967:5). These judgments inhibit the defence from testing the police case and allow the police to question the suspect no matter how tenuous the evidence. This effectively puts the onus upon the suspect to answer questions. In *Howell* (2003), the Court of Appeal deprecated the idea that defendants could avoid adverse comment by remaining silent on legal advice. One of the reasons it gave was that 'it may encourage solicitors to advise silence for other than good objective reasons'. As noted above, the legal representative's role at the police station is solely to protect and advance the suspect's legal rights (Code C, *Notes* 6D, PACE), not to advise 'for good objective reasons'. The Court has approved the protective function but advice relating to the presumption of innocence or putting the prosecution to proof is regarded as tactical or 'bad' advice rather than a proper response in an adversarial context. This puts the lawyer in a quandary as: 'Since the lawyer is an officer of the court, the question is raised as to whether they should deliberately do something they know will, or is highly likely to, be disapproved of by the court' (Cape 2006:68).

The potential evidential importance of legal advice has affected the nature of the solicitor–client relationship as advisers now consider the ramifications for themselves as well as, or perhaps instead of, the client (Cape 1997; Leng 2001c:127).

> They're thinking I'm there to advise them. I say 'it's got to be your decision at the end of the day'. I don't want to get the blame ... I'm fearful of that. That's why I try to put the guilt trip on the client as it were. I let him decide. More often than not, I get him to sign something.
>
> (Sol/D13/ii)

> It's so rare that you advise them to remain silent, that you make sure you've got concrete reasons for doing it, because you always think 'I may have to take the stand about this one day'.
>
> (Sol/A13/iii)

Even before it became standard practice, four of the firms I visited insisted that clients signed their attendance notes or a specially produced document or to say that the decision to make no comment was entirely their own. One of the disclaimers I was shown was so all-encompassing as to be meaningless to suspects but covered the adviser against any eventuality:

> I [name] have been advised by my Solicitors, [name and address of firm], that an adverse inference may be drawn if I make no comment in an interview. Nevertheless I wish to have a 'no comment' interview and fully understand the consequences that may subsequently arise. Signed ___ Name (please print) ____ Date ___.
>
> (Firm J14)

Communication between the solicitor and client is covered by the concept of legal professional privilege. Once it is established, the lawyer's mouth is 'shut for ever'. This was justified on the public interest ground that communications between clients and lawyers should be uninhibited. 'Candour cannot be expected if disclosure of communications between client and lawyer may be compelled, to a client's prejudice and contrary to his wishes' (*Rondel* v *Worsley* 1969). The House of Lords described legal professional privilege as a fundamental right, protected by the ECHR and held:

> a man must be able to consult his lawyer in confidence, since otherwise he might hold back half the truth. The client must be sure that what he tells his lawyer in confidence will never be revealed without his consent. Legal professional privilege is thus much more than an ordinary rule of evidence, limited in its application to the facts of a

particular case. *It is a fundamental condition on which the administration of justice as a whole rests.*

(*R v Derby Magistrates' Court ex parte B* 1996 at 507, emphasis added)

Whilst acknowledging that the right was not absolute, their Lordships declined to undertake a balancing exercise, reasoning that 'once any exception to the general rule is allowed, the client's confidence is necessarily lost'. The bare assertion that a suspect remained silent on legal advice does not constitute waiver of privilege but, unadorned, such an explanation is unlikely to avert inferences (*Condron* 1997). Legal privilege is waived if the defendant or lawyer gives or elicits evidence of the grounds for advising a no comment interview. Once privilege is waived, the reasons may be explored and exploited by the prosecution to encourage the jury to draw inferences. The legal representative can be asked about any other reasons for the advice, including whether it was for tactical reasons, the nature of the advice and the factual premise upon which it was based (*Bowden* 1999). This was held not to contravene Article 6 as the suspect experiences only the 'indirect compulsion' to waive privilege of being able to offer merely a bare explanation as a defence (*Condron* v *UK* 2001). Even the CLRC had been alert to the potential harm this could cause:

> Obviously if the accused's solicitor had to give evidence of what the accused told him when he consulted him about the charge, this would help the jury to make up their minds about his guilt; but equally obviously justice could not be properly administered unless people could speak freely when seeking legal advice .
>
> (CLRC 1972:para 19)

Only one of the legal representatives I interviewed had given evidence as to why he had advised a no comment interview. Three-quarters of the representatives who expressed an opinion said that they would not be troubled by having to give evidence. The others were concerned, through fear ('It scared the living daylights out of me' [Sol/A12/ii]), a belief that solicitors should not have to justify their advice (Sol/A13/iii), because of the financial implications of losing a client; or having to appear unpaid as a witness (Sol/B2/i). (A solicitor cannot represent a client and be called as a witness in their cause so, in magistrates' court cases, they would have to pass the case to somebody else.) Such attitudes are wholly contrary to the protective function of legal representation and construct a risk that 'a barrier will be created between suspect and adviser: the whole purpose of independent legal advice and the basic principles of adversarialism will be undermined' (see also Sharpe 1998b:563).

Conclusion

Following the CJPOA, the decision as to whether or not a suspect should answer questions is more complex, but the entitlement to legal representation has become more restricted. It has been argued that the commitment shown during most of the 1990s by the government and legal aid authorities to increase the take-up and quality of custodial legal advice has been replaced by a focus on containing costs (Bridges and Cape 2008:4–5). A centralised contracting system was introduced in 2001 that led to a sharp decline in the number of firms undertaking criminal work and legal aid rates have been cut repeatedly. If a suspect requests legal advice, the police now telephone the Defence Solicitor Call Centre (DSCC) for a decision as to whether the suspect should receive only telephone advice from CDS Direct (Criminal Defence Service) or whether the suspect should speak to a solicitor – either their own solicitor or the duty solicitor. Non-imprisonable offences (such as minor public order offences) and drink-driving related offences are now generally limited to telephone advice. Since 2008, defence practitioners have been paid a fixed fee for police station advice (Kemp 2010:110–117; Kemp 2012:41–42). This means that solicitors tend to get involved in cases at the time of the police interview, which can be many hours after the initial request for legal advice' (Kemp 2013:202). In March 2014, there were approximately 1,600 legal aid firms. The government sought to reduce this to 527. Following legal challenges, this has been suspended (Ministry of Justice and Gove 2016). Nevertheless, many firms have gone out of business and there are now large areas of the country with no firms undertaking criminal work (Baksi 2014).

The direct effects of the CJPOA have been limited by the relatively small numbers of suspects making no comment hitherto, but its effect upon legal representation has shifted the balance of power in custodial interrogation further in favour of the police. Representatives were never as adversarial as they were portrayed by the abolitionists. In many cases, the service provided continues to fall short of the protective function it is supposed to offer, leaving suspects further disadvantaged by the CJPOA. Although the accreditation requirements appear to have improved the performance of para-legal staff, the CJPOA provisions have made it much more difficult for legal representatives to act in an adversarial manner.

The ECtHR has acknowledged that the provisions place the accused in a 'fundamental dilemma' and emphasises the 'paramount importance' (*Murray* v *UK* 1996 at 60) of legal advice to suspects at the police station in ensuring fairness. This fails to recognise the dilemma that the legal adviser now faces. The courts have expressed their expectation that suspects will cooperate with the police when at the police station. There is, however, no reciprocal obligation on the police to disclose their case. Legal representatives have never had any formal authority at the police station to enforce their clients' rights; a no comment interview was one of the few sanctions or negotiating ploys they could use. Cape notes the 'signs of a growing antipathy towards adversarial principles and the adversarial role of defence lawyers'. It cannot be said that the role of legal representatives has been reduced to ensuring procedural compliance, for without a right to know the police case, this is impossible. It appears that the Court considers the role of the adviser should be merely to facilitate the expeditious processing of their clients. Its approach to this in deciding about adverse inferences, together with its interpretation of the CJPOA provisions generally, are discussed in the following chapter.

The Court fails also to recognise that the safeguards provided at trial, such as allowing inferences to be drawn only once the prosecution has established a *prima facie* case, do not apply when the suspect and solicitor actually make their decision. The protective benefit of legal advice, a fundamental requirement of a fair trial, is devalued by the quandary in which the legal representative is now placed. By making custodial legal advice of potential evidential significance, perhaps requiring representatives to testify at the trial of their clients, the Act has compromised the lawyer–client relationship, thus eroding the protective benefits of legal advice and tipping the balance even further against suspects.

Chapter 5

Silence in court

The police were vocal opponents of the right of silence but many of the senior judiciary were instrumental in supporting its curtailment Roberts and Zuckerman (2010), both in their judgments and in a personal capacity (see Chapter 2). Their interpretation of the CJPOA provisions, much speculated upon beforehand, has developed in unanticipated ways. The CJPOA provisions operate in two ways at trial: inferences being drawn from a defendant's failure to mention facts relied upon at trial when questioned or charged (ss34, 36 and 37); and from a failure or refusal to testify (s35). As discussed in Chapter 2, the ostensible rationales for the changes were to combat the 'ambush defence' (whereby the defendant could wrong-foot the prosecution by offering an exculpatory version of events for the first time at trial), and to avoid a defendant being able to refuse to testify with impunity. There was little evidence that either was causing a significant problem to the prosecution. There was some ebb and flow in the decision making after the CJPOA came into force (both the Judicial Studies Board specimen directions and the Law Society guidance for police station representatives had to be rewritten repeatedly), but the case law is now relatively settled.

This chapter sketches out the overall developments in relation to silence at the police station (ss34, 36 and 37), then silence at trial (s35).[1] It is generally agreed that defendants are now more likely to answer police questions (see Chapter 3), and to testify, but this has not made a noticeable difference in terms of increasing charge, plea or conviction rates. Contrary to the arguments on both sides of the right of silence debate, the legislation appears to have been evidentially decisive in very few cases and has not been identified as a direct cause of miscarriages of justice; if anything, in the early days, some otherwise apparently robust convictions were quashed due to inadequacies in the directions to jurors. From the outset, the Court

---

1 For more detailed analysis of the case law, see the practitioner handbooks, *Archbold* and *Blackstones*, and criminal evidence textbooks such as Choo (2015), Glover (2015) and Roberts and Zuckerman (2010).

made it clear that it would not permit a 'coach and horses' to be driven through the provisions (*Cowan* 1995 at 380) and the decisions of the European Court of Human Rights (ECtHR) have had a more limited influence than many expected. Lord Bingham stated that, since the provisions 'restrict rights recognised at common law as appropriate to protect defendants against the risk of injustice they should not be construed more widely than the statutory language requires' (*Bowden* 1999:para 181). The parameters of permissible inferences have nevertheless widened significantly and have had unforeseen consequences, most significantly on legal professional privilege, as discussed in Chapter 4. Academic commentary about the legislation has questioned its evidential value and criticised the complexity of the case law (Birch 1999; Dennis 2002; Easton 2014; Leng 2001b; Owusu-Bempah 2011, 2014). Even some judges have questioned whether a more straightforward approach might be preferable (Phillips 2007), as legislation that was supposed to simplify matters has left jurors and magistrates to grapple with highly complex directions, and the evidential dangers of this 'common sense' reasoning are considered below. Judicial interpretation of the law has developed a presumption that defendants should cooperate fully in the investigation and trial process, and that those who do not cooperate have something to hide. It is argued that the police station interview has effectively become part of the trial process (Jackson 2001c) and the language used by the Court of Appeal suggests that judges 'have imported to the courtroom the traditional police suspicion of defendants and their legal representatives' (Quirk 2013:468) described in Chapter 3.

The widening application of section 34

If a defendant relies at trial upon any fact that was not, but could reasonably have been, mentioned during questioning or charge, a court or jury may draw such inferences as appear proper from this (s34). An inference from pre-trial silence[2] can be used by the judge in deciding whether the prosecution has established a case to answer, and again by the jury to convert that case into a finding of guilt.[3] Whilst s38(6) of the CJPOA preserves the right of the court 'to exclude evidence (whether by preventing questions being put or otherwise) at its discretion', the courts are unlikely to exclude evidence of police interviews other than in 'the most exceptional case' (*Condron* 1997 at 196). Examples suggested by the Court where inferences should not be left to the jury include: following insufficient disclosure of the police

---

2 To reiterate, s34 extends beyond a no comment interview to failure to mention any fact, but for ease of writing, 'silence' and 'no comment' are used as a shorthand.

3 The CJPOA applies in the magistrates' court and Crown Court. The discussion of the case law mostly refers to Crown Court appeals but the same principles apply to magistrates, whose work is considered below.

case; where the nature of the offence or the material involved is so complex, or relates to matters so long ago, that no sensible immediate response is feasible (*Roble* 1997); if the arrest was unlawful; or where the prejudice caused would outweigh the probative value (*Argent* 1997). The probative value of silence is debatable, however – '[s]ilence at interview has no intrinsic weight' (Birch 1999:774) – and it will almost always be prejudicial to the defendant. Even if evidence of the interview is excluded so that no inference can be drawn from silence when questioned, inferences may still be drawn from silence when charged, as long as this is not unfair (*Dervish* 2002).

Section 34 has been described as 'a notorious minefield' (*B (Kenneth James)* 2003:para 20). It is essential to a fair trial (*Condron* v *UK* 2001) that the judge should direct the jury carefully as to the drawing of inferences. The specimen direction for judges went through several iterations but now appears stable. In summing-up, the fact(s) which the accused failed to mention but now relies upon should be identified. The jury should be directed that it may only draw an inference if, apart from the defendant's failure to mention these facts, the prosecution case is so strong that it clearly calls for an answer. It must also be satisfied before drawing inferences that there is no sensible explanation for the defendant's failure, other than that he or she had no answer at that time, or none that would stand up to scrutiny. An inference should be drawn only if the jury think it is fair and proper to draw such a conclusion, and a defendant must not be convicted wholly or mainly on the strength of the inference. The judge should identify the inferences which might be drawn beyond the standard one of late fabrication, and remind the jury of any evidence which the defence argues means that no inference should be drawn (see below). When the judge rules that a s34 inference should not be drawn, a pre-CJPOA (*Bathurst* 1968) direction should be given (*McGarry* 1999) but there is no requirement for judges to direct the jury not to draw inferences if they accept a suspect's reasons for not answering questions (*Karapetyan* 2013). These protections have been undermined in practice as neither a defective direction (*Adetoro* v *UK* 2010; *Chivers* 2011) nor the absence of a *Bathurst* direction (*Collins* 2014; *Francom and Others* 2000) will necessarily render a conviction unsafe.

Following some conflicting interpretations, it has been established that the jury must consider both the *reasons* for the suspect's silence and the *reasonableness* of this decision (*Beckles* 2005:para 46). What is reasonable is a matter for the jury 'in the exercise of their collective common-sense' – an objective test, but by reference to the circumstances of the case, including those known to the defendant (*Hoare and Pierce* 2004:para 52). In deciding what is reasonable, a court is to consider 'the actual accused with such qualities, apprehensions, knowledge and advice as he is shown to have had at the time' (*Argent* 1997 at 33). Matters such as the time of day, the defendant's age, experience, mental capacity, state of health, sobriety, tiredness, personality and legal advice are all relevant in principle. Again, in practice, this has not necessarily been the case, and the reference to legal advice has been qualified, as discussed below. A simpler test has been established for magistrates: (1) Has the defendant relied in his defence on a fact which he could reasonably have been expected to mention in his interview, but did not? If so, what is it? (2) What is his explanation for not having mentioned it? (3) If that explanation is not a reasonable one, is the proper inference to be drawn that he is guilty? (*T* v *DPP* 2007).

The risk of invoking a s34 inference may hamper the presentation of the defence case both at the police station and at trial. It was recognised in *Knight* (2003:para 11), a case in which a statement was submitted before a no comment interview, that, whilst s34 was intended to encourage a suspect to give a full account to the police, it does not require suspects to subject this account to scrutiny by the police as this would be 'a significantly greater intrusion into a suspect's general right of silence than is a requirement, or encouragement, upon the suspect to disclose his factual defence'. Again, this rhetorical commitment does not appear to have been followed in practice. A number of judgments seem to penalise the suspect for failing to cooperate with the investigation and also to hinder the legitimate testing of the police case. Inferences can be drawn from a suspect's failure to mention a fact, even where no relevant question was put in interview. The Court of Appeal rejected the argument that a 'proper' inference is one that is relevant in determining whether the accused is guilty and not one that is simply adverse to the defendant, as such a limited construction would thwart the intention of the Act (*Beckles and Montague* 1999, in which the defendants remained silent until they were selected at an identification parade). The Court has failed also to recognise that the safeguards provided at trial, such as allowing inferences to be drawn only once the prosecution has established a *prima facie* case, do not apply when the suspect and solicitor actually make their decision. The judgment in *Hoare and Pierce* (2004:paras 53–54) makes clear that defendants can now be penalised for exercising their right of silence. It was held that the basis of s34 'is an assumption that an innocent defendant – as distinct from one who is entitled to require the prosecution to prove its case – would give an early explanation to demonstrate his innocence'. The Court continued, with an extraordinary turn of phrase:

> The s34 inference is concerned with *flushing out innocence* at an early stage or supporting other evidence of guilt at a later stage, not simply with whether a guilty defendant is entitled, or genuinely or reasonably believes that he is entitled, to rely on legal rights of which his solicitor has advised him. Legal entitlement is one thing. An accused's reason for exercising it is another. His belief in his entitlement may be genuine, but it does not follow that his reason for exercising it is...
>
> (Emphasis added)

To suggest that innocence needs to be 'flushed out' – another term with connotations of concealment and evasiveness – rather than presumed is astonishing. Suspects are entitled to the presumption of innocence (*Woolmington* v *DPP* 1935).

Section 34 can be triggered even if no evidence is given or called at trial (*Bowers and Others* 1998). 'A fact relied upon' may be established by the defendant submitting a written statement to the police, a pre-trial defence case statement or cross-examining witnesses. Even a suggestion put to a witness by the defence that is not adopted can fall within the section (*Webber* 2004), as can evidence given by a co-defendant that is adopted by counsel. Relevant facts are not restricted to establishing simply what happened, but may involve any explanations or supporting detail. In *Argent* (1997), the prosecution alleged that the defendant had stabbed fatally a man who had asked his wife to dance. Argent gave a no comment interview, then testified that he had not been drunk, that no one had asked his wife to dance and that they had left the club, without being involved in violence, to walk home via a restaurant that was closed. They had talked to the babysitter and he knew nothing of the man's death until the police visited his house. Other than talking to the babysitter, these points merely rebutted the prosecution's case; they 'were non-facts effectively' (Pupil to Bar/B5, describing a similar case) yet inferences were left to the jury. Whilst effectively they add nothing more to the defence than 'I didn't do it', a detailed rebuttal is likely to be more persuasive, but this now risks invoking inferences.

Mirfield (1997:239–240) identified the three main forms of evidential significance of a suspect's pre-trial failure to mention a fact as: 'silence as guilt'; 'silence as corroboration'; and 'silence as ambush'. Whilst s34 gives no guidance as to what inferences may be 'proper', there is a presumption that any inference drawn will be adverse (*Condron* 1997; *Napper* 1997). The inference drawn need not be about specific facts; it may just be a general inference of guilt (Pattenden 1995:606). The inference that the prosecution could invite was restricted initially to subsequent fabrication; that the suspect's silence could only sensibly be attributed to the suspect having no answer or none that would stand up to cross-examination (*Condron* 1997). Permissible inferences were then expanded to include that the defendant: was unwilling to be subjected to further questioning; had no innocent explanation to give, or none that would stand up to scrutiny; or had tailored the explanation to fit the prosecution case (*Argent* 1997; *Daniel* 1998; *Milford* 2001:para 33; approved in *Webber* 2004:para 30). It does not matter whether the defendant could not mention the facts because they were invented after the interview, or would not mention them having fabricated them beforehand, the issue for the jury is whether the defence is more likely to be false for having not been disclosed immediately (*Daniel* 1998). This test, adopted from *Cowan* (1995) in relation to inferences under s35, is inappropriate to apply to questioning in the police station. As the prosecution is not expected to provide a complete case against suspects at this stage, suspects should not have to respond to preliminary police enquiries with their finished defence. Whilst an account that will not withstand cross-examination at court may be rejected, an account in interview may appear similarly feeble, but its veracity cannot be deduced in the same way. The defendant may be unwilling to be subjected to further questioning for any number of reasons, not necessarily consistent with, or indicative of, guilt (see Chapter 2). The Crown Court Bench Book (Judicial Studies Board 2010:258), a reference source for judges preparing summings-up for juries, explains that 'the object of section 34 is 'to deter late fabrication of defences and to encourage early disclosure of genuine defences'. This goes beyond merely combating the 'mischief' of ambush defences and, of course, is less of an encouragement than a penalty. It identifies permissible inferences (or 'conclusions' as it describes them) as: that the fact now relied on is true but the defendant chose not to reveal it earlier; the fact is irrelevant; the fact is of more recent invention; the fact is fabricated; or that the defendant is guilty (Judicial Studies Board 2010:261).

Lies and silence both 'derive their evidential force, if any, from the motive behind the accused's evasive behaviour' (Pattenden 1998:154), yet the Court of Appeal treats these behaviours differently (*Morgan* 2001). Defendants receive greater protection if it is established that they have lied and the judge has to give a *Lucas* (1981) direction than if the jury infers from the late mention of a fact that the defence is false and draws inferences under s34. It was suggested that the warning that s34 inferences could be drawn only if there is no other sensible explanation for the failure is 'analogous to the essence of a direction on lies' (*Petkar* 2004: para 51), but this overstates the similarity. The more restrictive *Lucas* direction allows jurors to draw an adverse conclusion only if they are sure that a lie has been given for a non-innocent reason (*Burge and Pegg* 1996; *Randall* 1998). The jury should be directed to consider reasons why the defendant may have lied such as to bolster a true defence, to protect someone else, or through embarrassment, panic or confusion. A *Lucas* direction should be given wherever lies relied upon by the Crown might be used to support evidence of guilt rather than merely reflecting on the appellant's credibility (*Goodway* 1994). Both a s34 direction and a *Lucas* direction may be required if a suspect gives an interview that contains both no comment and lies, then advances new facts at trial (as in *Friend* 1997). This is likely to be unnecessarily taxing for the jury (as discussed below).

Legal advice is 'a very relevant' circumstance to be taken into account by a court in deciding whether the defendant could reasonably have been expected to mention the fact relied on at that time (*Argent* 1997). It was argued in *Condron* (1997) that if a legal representative had advised a suspect to make no comment, evidence of that interview should be excluded. Defence counsel 'resiled from this extreme position, recognising that, if it was correct, it would render section 34 wholly nugatory' (*Condron* 1997 at 191), as any competent solicitor would then advise silence. Leng (2001c:127) describes this as a 'policy driven' decision that ignores the evidence of the low rates of legal advice and silence before the changes, but accords with the rhetoric about wily lawyers abetting criminals in abusing their rights. The court considered that: 'It is not so much the advice given by the solicitor, as the reason why the defendant chose not to answer questions that is important' (*Condron* 1997 at 192). As Wolchover (2002) noted:

> Such inferences are justified by the supposed axiom of common sense that it is human nature for the innocent accused to declare the basis of their innocence. Equally, however, it is an article of common sense that if suspects are given the inalienable right to take advice from a lawyer at the police station it is not unreasonable to expect them to follow that advice.

The jury is not concerned with the correctness of the solicitor's advice, nor with whether it complies with the Law Society's guidelines, but with the reasonableness of the defendant's conduct in all the circumstances and whether the accused 'genuinely and reasonably' relied on legal advice to remain silent (*Argent* 1997 at 35–36). A reliance on legal advice 'does not give a licence to a guilty person to shield behind the advice of his solicitor' (*Betts and Hall* 2001:para 54). The Court approved the trial judge's direction to the jury on this matter: 'You should consider whether or not he is able to decide for himself what he should do or having asked for a solicitor to advise him he would not challenge that advice' (*Howell* 2003: para 10). This seems contrary to the purpose of offering legal advice. It is hard to think of another situation in which a lay person is expected to reject the advice of a professional. It was stated in *Sakyi* (2014) that following the advice of a solicitor was very different to accepting the advice of a doctor or an accountant, but it was not explained how or why. Such a view appears to show a lack of understanding of the circumstances of the majority of defendants, discussed in Chapter 3. As one Senior Crown Prosecutor said:

> With the more inexperienced or vulnerable defendants, particularly the younger ones, it's not unreasonable to expect them, if they're told by a chap in a suit to say 'no comment', then they are going to do that without question really.

(SCP/A5)

The Court of Appeal was unmoved by the claims of a suspect who was advised to make no comment as his solicitor was unclear as to what his instructions were and considered his understanding of English to be insufficient to deal with difficult legal concepts (*Roble* 1997). It held that, as the solicitor did not give evidence of all the facts her client had told her, it did not know the basis upon which she had formulated her advice. Such analysis demonstrates further the application of double standards by the courts; reasons for the legal representative's advice are deemed irrelevant when they are adduced to avoid inferences or to support excluding the interview (it is the defendant's reasons for silence that are significant), but the lack of reasons may be used as justification for drawing inferences (Cape 1997:402). Once privilege is waived, the reasons may be explored and exploited by the prosecution to encourage the jury to draw inferences (see chapter 4).

The European jurisprudence concerning the privilege against self-incrimination is 'somewhat inconsistent and problematic' (Dennis 2002:27). In the judgment of *Funke* v *France* (1993) '[t]he Court expresses itself in terms which might be thought Delphic' (Leigh 1997:660). The Strasbourg jurisprudence on self-incrimination to date has been somewhat enigmatic – or, to borrow Lord Steyn's turn of phrase, 'unsatisfactory and less than clear' (*Brown* v *Stott* (2003) [2003] 711G). The ECtHR had emphasised that the privilege against self-incrimination and the closely allied principle of the presumption of innocence reflect the expectation that the State bears the general burden of establishing the guilt of an accused (*Saunders* v *UK* 1997). Contrary to the expectations of many commentators, however, the ECtHR declared that the drawing of inferences from the failure of suspects to answer police questions or from their refusal to testify does not breach Article 6 per se (*Murray* v *UK* 1996; *Condron* v *UK* 2001). No explanation was given as to why it should be 'obvious' that: 'These immunities cannot and should not prevent that the accused's silence, in situations which clearly call for an explanation from him, be taken into account in assessing the persuasiveness of the evidence adduced by the prosecution' (*Murray* v *UK* 1996 at 60). The distinguishing feature appears to be the degree of compulsion to which suspects are exposed, which must not be sufficient to destroy the essence of the right (*Funke* v *France* 1993). The CJPOA/Northern Ireland provisions place the suspect under only 'indirect compulsion' (*Murray* v *UK* 1996:65) and are not, therefore, considered unfair. The application of criminal sanctions for failure to answer questions does, however, breach suspects' right to a fair trial (*Heaney and McGuiness* v *Ireland* 2001) – even in a situation where the questions related to accounting for the suspects' movements under counter-terrorism legislation.

A statutory requirement to answer questions does not, of itself, contravene Article 6; the use of such responses in criminal proceedings can do (*Funke* v *France* 1993; *Saunders* v *UK* 1997; *IJL, GMR and AKP* v *UK* 2001). It may be argued that suspects questioned under the other statutory schemes are presented with an explicit imperative to answer questions and a defined penalty for any such failure. Under the CJPOA, they are obliged to make a decision based upon a variety of unknowns, faced with the hypothetical compulsion of an unknown and evidential sanction. Department of Trade and Industry inspectors questioned Mr Saunders under s436 of the Companies Act 1985 (*Saunders* v *UK* 1997). This meant that a refusal to answer questions could be treated as though it were a contempt of court. The answers that Mr Saunders gave the inspectors were then used in criminal proceedings against him. The ECtHR held that: 'The public interest cannot be invoked to justify the use of answers compulsorily obtained in a non-judicial investigation to incriminate the accused during trial proceedings' (1997 at 340).

'Where the reason put forward by a defendant for not answering questions is that he is acting on legal advice, the position is singularly delicate' (*Beckles* 2004: para 43). The ECtHR held that it is essential to a fair trial, rather than merely 'desirable' as the Court of Appeal had found, for the judge to direct the jury not to draw an inference if they are satisfied that the applicants remained silent on legal advice (*Condron* v *UK* 2001:para 62). The fact that an accused has remained silent on legal advice must be given 'appropriate weight' by the domestic court as there may have been a good reason for such advice (*Condron* v *UK* 2001: para 60). To which the obvious response would be, in the absence of professional misfeasance, what other kind of reason is there? Lord Phillips (2007) observed euphemistically that: 'The Court of Appeal has had some difficulty in giving effect to this ruling.' *Betts and Hall* (2001), which followed *Condron* v *UK* (2001) in holding that adverse comment was disallowed if the suspect has genuinely relied upon legal advice, was rejected emphatically in *Howell* (2003). This has been described as 'dangerous' (Birch 2003:408) and 'a mischievous decision which has created inconsistent case law ... It is clearly *per incuriam*'[4] (Choo and Jennings 2003:189). Nevertheless, it remains the current position. The Court held that: 'The premise of such a position is that in such circumstances it is in principle not reasonable to expect the suspect to mention the facts in question. We do not believe that is so' (*Howell* 2003 at para 24). It continued that an innocent person will generally be expected to seize the chance of denying the allegations. The only 'good' reasons for remaining silent will be those approved of by the Court. It considered the purpose behind the legislation, in a judgment that has received surprisingly little attention, given its abrupt reinterpretation of the adversarial system:

> [Section 34] ... is one of several enacted in recent years which has served to counteract a culture, or belief, which had been long established

---

4 Through or characterised by lack of due regard to the law or the facts.

in the practice of criminal cases, namely that in principle a defendant may without criticism withhold any disclosure of his defence until the trial. Now the police interview and the trial are to be seen as part of a continuous process in which the suspect is engaged from the beginning ... This benign *continuum* from interview to trial, the public interest that inheres in reasonable disclosure by a suspected person of what he has to say when faced with a set of facts which accuse him, is thwarted if currency is given to the belief that if a suspect remains silent on legal advice he may systematically avoid adverse comment at his trial. And it may encourage solicitors to advise silence for other than good objective reasons.

There is even less evidential value in speculating why a client accepted legal advice than in inferring guilt from silence. Asking jurors to add another tier of speculation to their assessment of the evidence risks multiplying the negative effects of silence and 'short-circuits' the deductive reasoning that leads from silence to guilt. A jury might accept that a suspect remained silent on legal advice, yet convict upon other evidence; it is unlikely to assume a suspect accepted the lawyer's advice because he or she was guilty and then acquit. In deciding if the defendant's claim of reliance on legal advice is genuine, an objective test is to be followed; that is:

> even where a solicitor has in good faith advised silence and a defendant has genuinely relied on it in the sense that he accepted it and believed that he was entitled to follow it, a jury may still draw an adverse inference if it is sure that the *true* reason for his silence is that he had no or no satisfactory explanation consistent with evidence to give.
>
> (*Hoare and Pierce* 2004 at para 51, emphasis in original)

As discussed in Chapter 4, the risk of invoking inferences undermines legal representatives' bargaining power to ensure the fair treatment of suspects at the police station and inhibits the adversarial testing of the police case. Advisers now have to assess not only the current strength of the police case – whether or not the investigating officers are willing to disclose it – but also its potential strength should the case come to trial. Advising a suspect to answer questions may provide the police with sufficient information to charge; whereas recommending no comment may result in inferences being drawn that strengthen a weak prosecution case to the required standard of proof. The Court of Appeal dismissed a suggestion that non-tactical motives (such as where advice cannot be given because of inadequate disclosure of the police case or the solicitor believes the client could not give a fair account in interview because of a physical or mental vulnerability) should not attract inferences. This was rejected as the advice may not be *bona fide*; there may be more than one reason for giving it; and 'it is not so much the advice given by the solicitor, as the reason why the defendant chose not to answer questions that is important and this is a question of fact which may be very much in issue' (*Condron* 1997 at 192). The repeated reference to *bona fide* advice by lawyers (including by the ECtHR) is troubling as it suggests by implication that lawyers may advise in bad faith – a suggestion that accords with the pre-CJPOA rhetoric by politicians and the police (see Chapter 2 and discussion in Chapter 6).

The Court has re-interpreted the role of the legal representative's role at the police station in a manner that is incompatible with the duty under PACE 'solely to protect and advance the suspect's legal rights' (Code C, *Notes* 6D, PACE, see Chapter 4). Whilst recognising the need to protect the vulnerable, the priority, as in court procedures, now appears to be the expeditious processing of cases. Before the Codes of Practice were changed, the Court allowed inferences to be drawn from failure to mention a fact during an interview that should have been stopped once the police had sufficient evidence to charge. (This expanding of the boundaries is discussed in Chapter 6.) The presence of the lawyer may perversely disadvantage suspects who remain silent, as it may be reasoned that few legal advisers will recommend silence now. One magistrate was of the view that: 'Any lawyer worth his salt is going to say "if you've got an alibi, you've got to declare it now" … if there was a lawyer present, it would probably look a bit more suspicious' (JP/B). If the solicitor has to testify, this is likely to attract a disproportionate amount of the jury's attention compared to its evidential value (Birch 1999:786). The Court of Appeal has previously held legal professional privilege to be almost sacrosanct. In *Bowden* (1999 at 827) it indicated that 'there is nothing in any of these sections [34–37 CJPOA] to suggest that Parliament intended in any way to modify the existing law on legal professional privilege'. In *Webber* (2004: para 27), Lord Bingham stated: 'We would not wish to modify that statement in any way.' Yet, in its desire to ensure that suspects do not evade inferences, it has done exactly that (*Seaton* 2010; Quirk 2013). The giving of evidence at a *voir dire* as to the reasons for legal advice for silence operates as a waiver of privilege at trial even if the evidence is not repeated before the jury: 'The defendant cannot at any stage have his cake and eat it; he either withdraws the veil and waives privilege or he does not withdraw the veil and his privilege remains intact. But he cannot have it both ways' (*Bowden* 1999 at 51). It would appear, however, that the courts have decided that the prosecution can enjoy the best of both worlds, as suspects either have an unexplained silence from which inferences may be drawn, or they seek to explain this, have to waive privilege and risk exposure of everything said in consultation – as well as perhaps an adverse inference.

'Special warnings' for failure to account for facts in interview

Sections 36 and 37 (allowing inferences to be drawn from suspects' failure when questioned to account for suspicious objects, substances or marks or their suspicious presence in the vicinity of offences) 'have escaped serious academic and judicial scrutiny' (Owusu-Bempah 2014:135). Almost 40 per cent of suspects making no comment were given a special warning, the majority of which yielded little that was satisfactory to the police (Bucke *et al.* 2000:39). It is not known how often these inferences are raised at trial; my respondents had little experience of them. Despite concerns about their inappropriate use at the police station (see Chapter 3), practical difficulties may be experienced when seeking to draw inferences under ss36 and 37 because 'as often as not, the police have cocked up the special warning in the first place' (Sol/A5/i). These sections have rarely been raised on appeal; a search on Westlaw yielded just 11 cases relating to s36, the most recent in 2010, and two cases regarding s37 (*Bowden* 1999 and *Webber* 2004).[5] It may be that the sections are unnecessary – if a suspect is caught at the scene of a crime, holding a weapon or covered in blood, for example, the prosecution case is likely to be strong, a guilty plea more likely and any additional inference unnecessary.

The legislation has been interpreted in a way that is largely less favourable to the defence. The reasonableness of the officer's belief that the suspect has been involved in the commission of a specified offence has been challenged only in *Milford* (2001: para 36) and was dismissed in a way that suggests 'that there is a presumption that the investigator's belief is a reasonable one' (Marks 2013:824). A defence submission that inferences could not be drawn where the interviewing officer had given a special warning stating that he was investigating the wrong offence (in this case, drug trafficking rather than conspiracy to supply heroin and cannabis) was rejected 'out of hand' (*Compton* 2002:para 33) despite the clear requirement in s36(1)(b) that this should be done. The judicial directions for ss36 and 37 are modelled on the direction for inferences under s34. If it is decided that no direction under s36 is appropriate, an adapted version of the s34 direction should be given (*Milford* 2002).

The legislation does not specify how detailed an account must be following a special warning and the Court has interpreted this broadly. In *Compton* (2002), one suspect told the police that the large sum of heroin-contaminated money found in his home came from his father and the sale of a vehicle, adding that his wife was a heroin addict. Whilst this was neither a failure nor refusal to account, it was held that inferences favourable to the prosecution

---

5 2 December 2015. There were 117 re s35 (including four practice directions) and 216 domestic criminal appeals involving s34.

could not be avoided if a suspect merely referred to facts from which an account favourable to the defence might be surmised. The ECtHR held that an inference under the corresponding Northern Ireland provision was permissible only 'if the evidence against the accused "calls" for an explanation *which the accused ought to be in a position to give*' (*Murray* v *UK* 1996 at 51, emphasis added). This is certainly arguable in cases in which the prosecution relies on expert evidence of drug traces to establish the provenance of the drugs (Marks 2013). This was the central issue in *Compton*, in which the prosecution expert was unable to identify the source of drug contamination on banknotes. Marks (2013:822) asks rhetorically, 'what, other than an admission of guilty, would be capable of amounting to an "account" in these circumstances?' Redmayne (2008–09:1084) argues that drawing inferences from a failure to provide an account that it was not reasonable to expect the accused to give could breach the privilege against self-incrimination because it could not be justified rationally and amounts to a penalty, but this has not yet been tested.

'The purpose of s36 [and 37] is opaque' (Marks 2013:821). Since reasonableness 'is not a concept which finds place in s36' (*Roble* 1997 at 3), the sole question is whether the suspect accounted for the relevant substance. In this way, the sections are more akin to s35, drawing a direct line between silence and guilt, rather than the credibility of any account advanced at trial (*Compton* 2002:para 32). The lack of a reasonableness requirement in s36 or s37 means that inferences may be drawn even where no inference under s34 is allowed or appropriate (*Milford* 2002). The courts have not specified, as under s34, that the defendant's characteristics should be considered. This adds another complication for legal representatives at the police station where both s34 and s36 or s37 are at issue. To use the example in *Roble*, there may be a judicially acceptable reason for advising a client who claims to have been acting in self-defence to make no comment at interview that will avert s34 inferences. The representative will have to be alert, however, to the risk that inferences could still be allowed from the resulting failure to account for why the suspect had a knife. Birch (1997:450) laments that 'it is a shame that section 36, which overlaps shamefully with section 34, ever came into being'.

Section 35 – 'Hobson's choice'[6] and inferences from not testifying

> Where this subsection applies, the court or jury, in determining whether the accused is guilty of the offence charged, may draw such

---

6 'Thus the suspect is faced with Hobson's choice – he either testifies or, if he chooses to remain silent, he has to risk the consequences, thereby automatically losing his protection against self-incrimination' (*Murray* v *UK* 1996 at 51, partly dissenting opinion of Mr E. Busuttil).

inferences as appear proper from the failure of the accused to give evidence or his refusal, without good cause, to answer any question.

(s35(3) CJPOA)

The submission that 's35 is so at variance with established principle that its use should be reduced and marginalised as far as possible' was rejected in the first appeal to test the provisions (*Cowan* 1995 at 943) and later by the House of Lords (*Becouarn* 2006 at 2597). It was held that, as s35 contains no scope for limiting its interpretation other than 'where the mental or physical condition of the accused makes it undesirable for him to give evidence' (s35(1)(b)), the provisions should be of otherwise general application. The Court did, however, read s35(3) ('may draw such inferences as appear proper') broadly enough to leave judges a discretion to withdraw inferences from the jury if it would not be proper to draw them. In practice, few appeals have succeeded on this point. The Court has occasionally appeared sympathetic to the defence perspective and warned that the routine application of s35 'can lead to unnecessary problems, whilst not necessarily contributing to the achievement of justice' (*Lancaster* 2001:para 17). Overall, however, its interpretation of 'undesirable' for the purpose of excluding inferences has been 'for the most part, restrictive' (Owusu-Bempah 2011:691). The only other statutory ground for withdrawing inferences from the jury was that the defendant should be over 14 years of age at the time of the trial (s35(1)). This was interpreted as the defendant's actual rather than mental age (*Friend* 1997; a case in which inferences were allowed from the failure to testify of a highly distractible, virtually illiterate 15-year-old with a mental age of 9 and IQ of 56 who was on trial for murder on the basis of joint enterprise with his older brother). This subsection was repealed when *doli incapax* (the presumption that a child between the ages of 10 and 14 is incapable of committing an offence) was abolished (sch. 10, para 1 of the Crime and Disorder Act 1998, SI 1998/2327). The Court later rejected a submission that the statute should be applied more generously in the case of those who are 'young or who have mental difficulties' (*Dixon* 2013:para 57). Youth, of itself, is an insufficient reason for withdrawing inferences from the jury; there needs to be some additional evidence or exceptional factors to justify so doing (*AC* 2001:paras 40–41 – a defendant aged 13 years and 10 months). The consideration that is supposed to apply to young defendants in the wake of *V* v *UK* (1999) to ensure their rights to a fair trial, including steps to assist their understanding and participate in proceedings and to prevent their avoidable intimidation, humiliation or distress, does not seem to have been applied regarding s35 (Owusu-Bempah 2011:697; Practice Direction 2000).

The Court considered it impossible to anticipate all the circumstances in which judicial discretion might be exercised to withdraw inferences from the jury '[n]or would it be wise even to give examples as each case must turn on its own facts' (*Cowan* 1995 at 945), and it is not a decision with which the appeal courts will interfere lightly (*Cowan* 1995 at 946). The decision can only be challenged on the basis that it was *Wednesbury* unreasonable (*Friend* 1997 at 239); that is, that no reasonable court could have come to the same conclusion. Given how widely the provisions have been interpreted, it is hard to envisage a situation where such a challenge could succeed. In the case of *Gledhill* (2007), the defendant, who was suffering from Battered Women's Syndrome, did not give evidence, as this would inculpate her abusive co-accused. The reasoning of the trial judge and Court of Appeal is worth examining for the determination it shows not to allow any concessions to the overriding principle that defendants should testify. The Recorder concluded:

> one returns to the position time and time again that her position is a difficult one, not an impossible one ... One has a degree of personal sympathy with anybody in those circumstances, but the fact that she would find it undesirable, it seems to me, is not the test at all and I have to take a much more objective view. The Act is designed to prevent those who, by reason of their physical or mental condition, would not do themselves justice from going into the witness box. It does not extend, in my judgment, to excuse those who would find it difficult and would rather not face cross-examination and the ordeal of giving evidence.

This, to reiterate, was a woman who would not tell the police her partner's name 'due to the violence that I may suffer. If you arrest him and then tell him what I've been saying then he will just beat me up and I could be at the bottom of the block tomorrow morning' (*Gledhill* 2007: para 6). The Court of Appeal reaffirmed that it would only interfere with the broad discretion of the judge if the decision was 'obviously wrong', and it did not think that this was such a case. It did, however, quash the conviction due to flaws in the directions given to the jury, coupled with its general sense of unease about the conviction.

There should be some evidential basis or exceptional factors before the jury can be directed not to draw inferences (*Cowan* 1995 at 944). Defence counsel cannot suggest reasons for the defendant's silence at trial without supporting evidence; the 'rule against advocates giving evidence dressed up as a submission' was emphasised in *Cowan* (1995 at 946). The court did not 'think it incumbent on a judge or appropriate for him to embark or invite the jury to embark on possible speculative reasons consistent with innocence which might theoretically prompt a defendant to remain silent' (*Cowan* 1995 at 949). No explanation was given for the distinction between inadmissible speculation as to innocent reasons for not testifying, and permissible inferences which operate to the detriment of defendants. Leng (2001c:132) argues that such a restriction 'runs counter to the adversarial tradition' and illustrates the punitive use of the provisions. He contends that, since there will almost always be a possible innocent explanation for silence, allowing jurors to speculate might lead to adverse inferences being drawn only rarely, thus reducing their effectiveness as a sanction. The House of Lords rejected the submission that the jury should be directed, as they are when a defendant is found to have lied (*Lucas* 1981), that there might be innocent reasons for the defendant not testifying. Again, the vocabulary used is revealing:

> There does not appear to be any good reason why a defendant should *shelter behind* the suggestion that there may be some compelling reason for his failure to give evidence other than fear of cross-examination, when that may be quite misleading.
>
> (*Becouarn* 2006 at 2597, emphasis added)

A relatively common reason for defendants not testifying prior to the CJPOA was to avoid having their previous convictions revealed to the jury. Before s101 of the Criminal Justice Act 2003 made the admission of bad character evidence easier, s35 could disadvantage those with previous convictions if their defence involved challenging the character of prosecution witnesses, as their antecedents could then be put before the jury (s1(f) of the Criminal Evidence Act 1898). First the Court of Appeal (*Cowan* 1995 at 944), then the House of Lords (*Becouarn* 2006) refused to accept that inferences should not be left to the jury if defendants did not testify for this reason, as this would give them an unfair advantage over those with unblemished records and might mislead the jury. Inferences were left to the jury in *Fell* (1996), even though there were strong suggestions that the defendant had been threatened the night before he was due to testify. The judge ruled that, if defendants are involved with serious criminals, they should receive no benefit from this. It might be argued that neither should this be a disadvantage, as associating with criminals, or being threatened by them, does not necessarily make the defendant a criminal or, more specifically, guilty of the crime being tried. Duress may thus offer a defence to the crime of which the defendant is accused but no protection from the penalties of failing to cooperate with the court (*Rafik* 2014).

The test for withdrawing inferences from the jury because of a defendant's health is a separate one from that of whether the defendant is fit to plead. Fitness to plead relates to the cognitive ability of the defendant to understand proceedings and to instruct legal representatives (*Pritchard* 1836). It can include whether a defendant has sufficient intellect to give evidence but '[t]hat, of course, is a very different matter from whether it is "undesirable" for a defendant to give evidence' (*Dixon* 2013:para 56). The trial judge in *Friend* (2004:para 14) thought that the wording of s35 created 'some undefined area, between unfitness to plead and in effect normality, in which area, by reason of an accused's physical or mental condition, it was undesirable for him to give evidence'. The Court thought that the 'clear purpose [of s35(1)(b)] is to mitigate any injustice to a person who is physically or mentally handicapped' (*Friend* 1997 at 240), but this does not appear to have been the overriding concern of the courts. Whilst acknowledging that the trial court has a wide discretion in deciding the issue (*DPP* v *Kavanagh* 2005), judges have expressed anxiety that this subsection 'should not be operated to give too wide a loophole' (*Lee* 1998), and should be activated only in exceptional circumstances (*Friend* 1997). Inferences were permitted from the silence of a drug addict, whose solicitor thought he was suffering withdrawal symptoms, because to decide otherwise would create a loophole which addicts could exploit (*Kavanagh* 1997). A reasoning which Leng (2001c:131) argues speaks to a focus on the broad policy rather than the individual circumstances of the case. Again, the language used addresses the implied duplicity of defendants rather than showing any understanding that defendants may be trying to avoid doing something frightening, seeking to avoid damaging their defences or wanting to put the prosecution to proof – something that judges are still obliged to remind jurors is the defendant's right.

Where the defence seeks to rely on the health exception, a *voir dire* (a 'trial within a trial') may be held in the absence of the jury. The judge may then direct the jury not to draw inferences. If, as is more common, the judge declines to make an advance ruling, the defence must present the expert evidence again before the jury. This can be problematic if the evidence supporting the defendant not testifying also reveals unhelpful personal characteristics. The defence in *Dixon* (2013, discussed below) made the tactical decision to withhold some of its expert evidence because it also reported the defendant's antisocial personality disorder, bizarre thinking processes, poor impulse control and weak anger management skills. Understandably it was thought that the effects of revealing this could be more detrimental in a joint enterprise murder trial than any adverse inference from not testifying.

The test is 'if it appears to the court' that it is undesirable for the defendant to give evidence. The court may have very different views to the defendant as to what is desirable. The Criminal Procedure Rules 2005 (SI 2005/384) have effected a 'sea change' in the way in which criminal cases should be conducted (*DPP* v *Chorley Magistrates' Court* 2006:para 24; see Chapter 6). Judges are under a duty to manage cases actively and to ensure that evidence is presented in the shortest and clearest way. The judge in *Anwoir* (2009) would not allow medical evidence explaining the defendant's failure to testify to be put before the jury because it was submitted late (a punitive approach, discussed further below). The conviction was quashed in this case but was distinguished in *Ensor* (2009), which appeared to endorse the punitive approach. Redmayne (2008) contends that the vagueness of the Court of Appeal's approach has been deliberate.

It might be questioned whether a judge or magistrate is equipped to make a determination on medical grounds as to the effects on the defendant of testifying. Where conflicting expert evidence has been presented, inferences have been left to the jury on the basis that the defence has not proved the undesirability of the defendant testifying with 'any degree of certainty' (*Ensor* 2009 at 262). It was held that: 'To talk in terms of the burden of proof being on either party once the issue is effectively raised seems to us to be inappropriate and unhelpful' (*LH* 2001:para 19). This appears to be a higher standard of proof than the civil standard (balance of probabilities) which usually applies when a defendant raises an issue in a trial. The judge may also look beyond any expert evidence, to factors including the conduct of the accused before and after the offence (*Friend* 1997). A judge is entitled to take account of the potential significance of the defendant's evidence; counterintuitively, the less its significance, the less severe the physical or mental condition has to be for it to be undesirable for the defendant to give evidence (*Tabbakh* 2009). In *Tabbakh* (2009), the Court balanced explicitly the well-being of the defendant and the importance of establishing whether he had been involved in the preparation of terrorist acts. The defendant had been granted asylum in the UK following his arrest and torture in Syria. He had an unchallenged diagnosis of post-traumatic stress disorder and a history of self-harm, which continued during the trial. The judge said, and the Court of Appeal accepted, that:

> in an ideal world, with no other factors to be considered, one would want to avoid a situation arising where anyone was put under stress to self-harm. But his own health and welfare is not the only issue, in my judgment, which I should take into account in reaching a judgment as to whether it is undesirable for him to give evidence...
>
> (At para 8)

It is not sufficient that the defendant merely suffers from some physical or mental condition, nor that the condition may cause some difficulty in giving evidence. 'Extreme difficulty in giving evidence is quite common among defendants and other witnesses who give evidence in criminal trials. That does not in itself make it "undesirable" that that person should give evidence' (*Ensor* 2009 at 262). Difficulties in giving evidence are matters to be taken into account by the jury: 'It does not *justify* a comprehensive failure to give evidence. It may go as to the weight of evidence, not as to the decision whether or not it is undesirable for him to give evidence' (*DPP* v *Kavanagh* 2005: para 18, emphasis added). Most of the examples given where inferences should not be drawn, such as triggering an epileptic fit or a florid episode of schizophrenia (*Friend* 1997), relate to the effects of testifying on the defendant rather than on the fairness of the trial. The condition has to be such that 'if he gives evidence it will have a significantly adverse effect on him, such as to make it "undesirable" for him to give evidence' (*Ensor* 2009 at 260). A defendant may become unwell by having to give evidence but be able to provide coherent testimony. Giving evidence, conversely, may have a minimal impact on the defendant's well-being but create injustice.

It was conceded in the second, successful appeal of *Friend* (2004) that, because s35(3) allows the jury to draw 'such inferences as appear proper', judges can go beyond a mere 'damage to health' test and they retain a discretion to withdraw evidence from the jury if they think that no proper inferences can be drawn. In this case, the appellant's, previously undiagnosed, attention deficit hyperactivity disorder (ADHD) made it undesirable for him to testify and thus 'it is clear that the judge would not have ruled in favour of drawing any adverse inference' (at para 30). This seems to be one of the Court's more sympathetic judgments as it is not apparent that the ADHD finding added significantly to what was known about the accused at his trial and first appeal – and in the light of subsequent judgments, it is far from certain that the trial judge would have excluded inferences. The Court has reiterated that a variety of circumstances, unrelated to damage to health (such as the defendant lacking self-control or being unable to remember parts of the evidence), might mean that it would be unjust and, therefore, undesirable to leave inferences to the jury (*Dixon* 2013; *Tabakh* 2009). As discussed below, although the Court has not resiled from this position, when the judgments are read, it has been honoured more in the breach than observance. Inferences have been permitted where the defendant has profound intellectual disabilities (*Dixon* 2013), has subsequently been sentenced under the Mental Health Act 1983 (*Charisma* 2009), and when the defendant was arguing diminished responsibility and had no recollection of the crime (*Barry* 2010), although it was conceded that the direction would need to be 'careful'.

The judgment in *Dixon* (2013) is illustrative of both reasons why a defendant might not testify and of the Court of Appeal's scepticism. Dixon was convicted of murder on the basis of joint enterprise. He was aged 17 and a half at the time of the offence. The court received evidence that he had a combination of difficulties, including: hyperkinetic conduct disorder; an IQ of around 70; dyslexia; low non-verbal abilities; and a poor working memory. He had language levels of a seven or eight-year-old child – he did not understand words such as 'jury', 'defence', 'evidence', 'oath' or 'alleged'. He was unable to follow information given at normal speed but would often pretend to do so. He had high levels of suggestibility and compliance and a severe stammer that could render him unable to speak. An expert report stated that the stresses associated with a trial would heighten his vulnerability and communication difficulties and he could become challenging, suspicious, confused and deceitful when put under pressure. Nevertheless, the Court held that, having given the defendant the help of a trained intermediary, it was permissible to leave inferences to the jury. The prosecution case was fairly strong ('The impression of all members of the court was that what was captured on the CCTV placed the primary defence of this appellant of self-defence in considerable difficulty' [*Dixon* 2013:para 89]). To allow inferences to be drawn from the failure to testify of such a defendant who, however unappealing, is also so clearly disadvantaged may create a sense of unfairness in the proceedings.

The strength of the presumption that defendants will now testify is exemplified by the refusal to withdraw inferences from the jury in the extraordinary circumstances of *Cameron* (2001). In this case, the 14-year-old complainant refused to answer further questions from defence counsel, having been pressed on some of the inconsistencies in her account of rape and indecent assault. Rather than stop the case, the judge took the unprecedented measure of putting questions to the witness on behalf of the defence but in a 'non-adversarial and non-searching' manner. The Court rejected a submission that, as the complainant had escaped cross-examination, the defendant should not have been exposed to adverse inferences for doing the same. In a high-profile Crown Court case (*D (R)* 2013), the defendant refused to remove her niqab. It was held that 'the right to give evidence involves a corresponding duty to submit that evidence to the scrutiny of the jury'. Judges have since been told that if a Muslim woman refuses to remove her niqab, she should not be allowed to give evidence and the judge should direct the jury about her failure to do so, but with appropriate modifications.

Only one of the legal representatives I interviewed described making any tactical efforts to avoid inferences being drawn against defendants for not testifying ('We've tried to pull all sorts of stunts!' [LE/B8/i]). He had sought a psychiatrist's opinion for one of his clients as to whether being held in prison in solitary confinement, without a light, and being allowed only one hour of exercise a week would justify him not testifying. The report concluded, unhelpfully for the defendant, merely that: 'Mr [X] has an inordinate fear of the witness box.' In another complex trial, the client had Crohn's disease and the representative was considering obtaining expert reports about how testifying might aggravate this condition, but he acknowledged that 'Fact of the matter is, he'll be a bloody awful witness and that's why we're trying to avoid calling him!'

At the close of the prosecution's case, the court must satisfy itself, in the presence of the jury, that defendants who have not indicated that they intend to give evidence understand the consequences of not doing so (s35(2) of the CJPOA). The judge must ask the defence representative:

Have you advised your client that the stage has now been reached at which he may give evidence and, if he chooses not to do so or, having been sworn, without good cause refuses to answer any question, the jury may draw such inferences as appear proper from his failure to do so?
(Practice Direction 2015, 26P.2)

This cannot be overlooked even where the accused has absconded (*Gough* 2002). This means that inferences cannot be drawn against the absentee but they can be drawn against a co-defendant who does not testify, as the absconder's 'manipulation of the legal system to his own advantage was no basis for *bestowing a similar advantage* on his co-accused' (*Hamidi and Cherazi* 2010:para 24, emphasis added). If defendants are unrepresented, the judge (or magistrate) must warn them, before the jury:

You have heard the evidence against you. *Now is the time for you to make your defence.* You may give evidence on oath, and be cross-examined like any other witness. If you do not give evidence or, having been sworn, without good cause refuse to answer any question the jury may draw such inferences as appear proper. That means *they may hold it against you.* You may also call any witness or witnesses whom you have arranged to attend court or lead any agreed evidence. Afterwards you may also, if you wish, address the jury. But you cannot at that stage give evidence. *Do you now intend to give evidence?*
(Practice Direction 2015 26P.5, emphasis added)

The judge or magistrate may remind the accused of his or her 'duty' to answer all proper questions or risk the drawing of inferences, although this should not be done in an oppressive manner (*Ackinclose* 1996). Just as the police have been criticised for amplifying the caution at the police station to increase the pressure on suspects (see Chapter 3), the wording approved by the Court goes beyond what is required by the statute. The warning that is used for unrepresented defendants is more than twice as long and is in much more coercive terms than for those who are represented. This seems likely to have an effect on the jury as well as the defendant.

Whilst it may require adaptation, the judge must direct the jury to consider five essential elements. The burden of proof remains upon the prosecution throughout and the jury must be sure of the defendant's guilt; the defendant is entitled to remain silent; an inference from failure to testify cannot on its own prove guilt; the prosecution must have established a case to answer before any inferences can be drawn; and the jury must have concluded the silence can only sensibly be attributed to the defendant's having no answer, or none that would stand up to cross-examination (*Cowan* 1995 at 945). The courts have emphasised that the burden of proof, far from being altered or watered down, remains on the prosecution; the effect of s35 is simply to add a further evidential factor in support of the prosecution case (*Cowan* 1995). This has been asserted rather than explained. Whilst technically this is true, it must make it easier for the prosecution to discharge the burden. Inferences under s35 can elevate a *prima facie* case to a finding of guilt. Unlike sections 34 there are no triggering conditions for s35:

> Consequently, the inferences may go straight to the issue of guilt rather than the likelihood of any specific facts ... Nonetheless, s35 as a whole promotes the assumption that an innocent defendant would be prepared to assert his innocence. This link which s35 maintains between silence and guilt has been exacerbated by an expansive interpretation of the provision in the Court of Appeal and a judicial reluctance to interfere with its operation by reference to asserted excuses. The result is a potentially pervasive use of inferences connecting in-court silence to guilt, creating a danger that some of these inferences might be incorrect.
>
> (Owusu-Bempah 2011:691, footnotes omitted)

'Common sense' inferences and lay tribunals

One of the main objections to the right of silence was that it offended against common sense (*Sullivan* 1966 at 105; *Gilbert* 1977 at 243), in particular by denying the assumption that an innocent suspect would want to give an explanation. '[T]he object of section 34 is to bring the law back into line with common sense' (*Webber* 2004:para 33). As set out in Chapter 1, there are many reasons why a suspect may choose to remain silent and why that silence may be of no evidential significance, in particular that assumptions about a 'natural' response to being accused do not necessarily apply in the police station or courtroom. As Easton (1998a:114) notes, '[c]ommon sense may be unreliable, impressionistic and unsystematic. It is because of the weaknesses of common-sense thinking that clear judicial guidance is so important'. Inferences from silence is one of the few types of evidence to require specific judicial directions (Birch 1999:772). The judges in *Birchall* (1999 at 312), whilst 'reluctant to countenance the view that direction of a jury called for the mouthing of a number of mandatory formulae', recognised the risk of injustice unless the CJPOA provisions were the subject of carefully framed directions to the jury. '[H]ow these nuances of meaning and interpretative potential are communicated to the lay people of the jury, who are neither legally nor linguistically expert' (Cotterill 2005:15). Wolchover (2005:5) notes the 'status and rhetorical virtuosity of judges in influencing juries'.

Section 34 has been condemned as 'a headache for the conscientious jury, and a tool with which the slapdash, incompetent jury may wreak injustice' (Birch 1999:772). Jurors may be ill equipped or unwilling to perform the intellectual contortions required by the direction. Allowing jurors to draw inferences from speculation about the absence of evidence or the defendant's refusal to participate in the process 'may result in inconsistent, unreasoned and unappealable decision making' (Sharpe 1997:153). Lord Phillips:

> expressed some general disquiet at the prolixity of directions that are given to the jury ... Most judges that I have spoken to are familiar with seeing the jurors' eyes glaze over as they give a series of directions the object and effect of which is not to simplify the jurors' task, but to render the summing-up proof against an appeal on the ground of misdirection.

Clear directions are particularly important given the inscrutability of the jury's verdict (*Condron* v *UK* 2001). As juries do not give reasons for their verdicts, and much research into their decision making is prohibited, it is not known to what extent jurors are drawing inferences, nor indeed to what extent they did before the CJPOA. As Lord Diplock said when speaking in favour of the CLRC Report, 'Thank God!, a jury generally has enough common sense to ignore the mumbo-jumbo which I, as a judge, had to say to them at the early stages of a case so that they forgot about it when they went into the jury room' (338 Parl.Deb., H.L. [1973] at 1650).

The Home Office study into the effects of curtailing the right of silence called for further research into this (Bucke *et al.* 2000:76). Cheryl Thomas (2010:35) noted that no empirical research had been conducted in England and Wales on jurors' understanding of judicial directions, a concern shared by Lord Chief Justices (Judge, 2008) and Phillips (2007). Thomas's ground-breaking study of juror comprehension of judicial directions examined a direction on self-defence, a much more straightforward instruction than those on adverse inferences ((1) Did the defendant believe it was necessary to defend himself and (2) Did he use reasonable force?). Between 49 and 69 per cent of jurors at different courts claimed to find the directions easy to understand. Jurors at one court centre were then asked to identify the two questions the judge had explicitly directed them to answer. Whilst 68 per cent of this group had said that the directions were easy to understand, only 31 per cent accurately identified both questions and 20 per cent did not correctly identify either question. If fewer than a third understood the self-defence direction, the figures for silence (particularly when coupled with all the other directions the jurors receive) are likely to be much lower. Jurors may also have to perform a demanding intellectual process if the judge decides at the close of the case to direct the jury that they must not draw inferences as they 'will have heard the prosecution milk the accused's silence in interview for all its worth in cross-examination and will then have to undergo the gymnastic self-manoeuvre of expurgating those questions and answers from their collective mind' (Tregilgas-Davey 1997:501). (Magistrates, of course, have to perform even greater 'mental gymnastics', as there is no separation of responsibilities in summary trials.) Those I interviewed expressed their concerns about how juries decide:

> It worries me a little bit with juries ... I do wonder whether they understand the directions given to them by the judge.
>
> (PCP/A14)

> Juries make up their own law without us knowing it.
>
> (Bar/B2)

> I don't think [CJPOA] had that much effect with juries because I don't think they understand it.
>
> (LE/B8/i)

Whilst many of those who opposed the CJPOA also defend the right to jury trial, it may be that juries are unsympathetic to the right of silence:

> People over here don't understand the right of silence, it hasn't become a part of popular culture like it has in the States. People speculate in the States as much as they do here but they've got the Fifth Amendment and that is such a holy object.... It has always been the common view, right back to the 17th Century witch-hunts 'you will speak out in your defence if you've got a defence and if you haven't, keep your mouth shut'.
>
> (Bar/A1)

The 1994 British Social Attitudes Survey revealed that only 31 per cent of respondents thought that someone should have a right to remain silent under police questioning; a decline from 42 per cent in the 1990 survey (Social and Community Planning Research 1996). Cotterill (2005:22) states it is perhaps an 'inevitable consequence of human reasoning' that silence is interpreted as guilt. As the Court of Appeal noted in *Sparrow* (1973 at 493), 'In our experience of trials, juries seldom acquit persons who do not give evidence when there is a clear case for them to answer and they do not answer it.'

Judges have made other, more problematic, unfounded assumptions about juries' decision making. In *Dixon* (2013:para 55), it was held that in deciding whether to leave inferences to the jury, the judge was entitled to consider 'the anticipated approach of a fair-minded jury' who would take account of the defendant's physical and learning difficulties. In *Charisma* (2009), it was held that, rather than not testifying, the defendant could have given evidence explaining that he had lost his memory as a consequence of his drug taking and head injuries. The Court seemed to take no account of the potential effect on a jury of such an admission during a trial for sexual offences against a 16-year-old. It continued:

> If genuine, that would have been taken very much into account. *The jury would not have held it against him* that he was unable to say anything about events on the night in question. A genuine loss of memory would have precluded him from doing so. They would have evaluated the evidence of the complainant in the light of what the appellant had said in his police interview.

Two points emerge from this: first, the jury had no way of knowing whether or not the memory loss was genuine, particularly as two highly qualified psychiatrists had come to different conclusions; and second, the judges have no way of knowing what that, or indeed any other, jury would have done. A barrister explained that 'physical disabilities sometimes don't attract the sympathy of the jury' (Bar/A1). A report by Scope (2014) detailed that 67 per cent of the British public feel uncomfortable talking to people with disabilities – more so with less visible conditions (mental health conditions or learning disabilities) than with visible physical or sensory impairments. Jurors may misinterpret the defendant's demeanour – assuming slurred speech is a result of intoxication rather than tiredness, for example (Scope 2014:9).

Magistrates now have to give reasons for their verdicts in order to comply with the Human Rights Act 1998 (following *Condron* v *UK* 2001), but there has been no study of this. There was a general sense among my respondents that magistrates do not like defendants not giving evidence and that they drew inferences prior to the CJPOA anyway, making the effects of s35 less marked in summary trials (see also Bucke *et al.* 2000:53).

> Magistrates think you're an awkward sod if you don't give evidence ... Your advice would vary depending on where the case is to be heard.
>
> (Sol/A15/i)

> [Lay magistrates] think 'no comment: guilty'.
>
> (Clerk/F)

The lay and stipendiary magistrates had differing views about the changes. The lay magistrates had all been in favour of the changes ('A step in the right direction' [JP/F]; 'Fairly relaxed' [JP/J]), whereas, the stipendiaries were divided about the changes:

> I was as concerned as most people were.
>
> (Stipe/C)

> I felt quite comfortable about them ... [After PACE] the safeguards for the defendant were at the expense of the considerations one ought to give to society at large and the victims of crime.
>
> (Stipe/A)

Previous research has highlighted the risk of magistrates becoming 'case hardened' (Wasik 1996), and using 'schemata, prototypes or categories to make decisions quickly and routinely' (Lloyd-Bostock 2006). Concerns were expressed about the varied standards of justice at the magistrates' courts. 'Magistrates vary so much from bench to bench. You cannot generalise, it's impossible. You can't even generalise about the likelihood of a conviction or not because they do vary so much' (SCP/A11). Some said that it felt on occasions as though they needed to disprove the prosecution case, and that magistrates appeared to have become more sceptical towards silent defendants after the CJPOA (Bucke *et al.* 2000:47). Prosecution and defence lawyers thought it was 'much harder in the magistrates' court to have any kind of legal argument' (Bar/B12). A Senior Crown Prosecutor explained:

> The general rule is, you keep as much law out of the magistrates' court as you possibly can, unless you've got a stipe. A lay bench you see, you want to avoid that sort of thing [legal argument about inferences] if you possibly can.
>
> (SCP/A3)

The complexity of the provisions means that some magistrates want to avoid the issue altogether (Clerk/F). One clerk believed that some magistrates prefer to be told what inference to draw, with a risk that, in busy courts, some clerks do 'overstep the mark' (Clerk/C). Few magistrates had much experience of the provisions. This might indicate that their support for the changes was based on a sympathy with the prosecutorial values of the changes rather than personal experience. Those who are not legally qualified may have little sympathy with traditional legal principles or ideologies such as the presumption of innocence (Roberts 1995:785), although it should be noted that the greatest incursions into the right of silence have been made by the legally qualified Court of Appeal. Without an understanding of or sympathy towards such values, however, there is a danger that 'common sense' assumptions about silence provide a short cut to determinations of guilt. A magistrate told me that, where previously the late production of an alibi might have prevented a case from being proved beyond reasonable doubt, now the inference could be drawn to prove their guilt because 'any normal person' would have put it forward earlier (JP/B). One solicitor thought that if defendants do not testify after a submission of no case to answer fails, they are very unlikely to be acquitted:

> The standard that gets applied by most magistrates in most trials is in fact little more than the balance of probabilities ... My clients very often are put in the position of having to prove their innocence rather than the other way round.
>
> (Sol/E3/i)

There are many problems with a 'common sense' approach but the post-CJPOA system is possibly a more dangerous hybrid. Juries and magistrates are not left to exercise their common sense unfettered but are potentially confused by complex legal directions.

The impact of the CJPOA

When the CJPOA was going through Parliament, the Home Secretary was asked about the effect of the corresponding Northern Ireland provisions. He replied, 'A number of other things have changed in that period. How can one possibly seek to test the influence of one isolated change?' (Michael Howard, HC Debs, 11 January 1994, vol 235, col 27). It is curious that such a contentious measure, with such extravagant claims made on its behalf, has been the subject of so little empirical analysis. The limited extent of the 'problems' the CJPOA was introduced to tackle has meant that it has had a less dramatic direct impact than had been predicted by either side of the debate. The proportion of contested trials, particularly at the magistrates' court, is small; most defendants testify (which is not a significant change) and a high proportion of cases are motoring offences, in which there will not usually have been a police interview. Silence issues arising at the magistrates' courts tend to be relatively straightforward (Bucke *et al.* 2000:46–47). Some were of the view that jurors and magistrates had always drawn inferences anyway from late mention of a fact or failure to testify and that the changes merely 'legitimated what was already in practice happening, particularly in the magistrates' court' (SCP/C8). The requirement that a *prima facie* case must have been established before inferences can become an issue reduces the impact: if a case is weak, an inference is unlikely to carry it over the threshold; if it is strong, the inference will make little difference. As discussed in Chapter 3, there has been an increase in suspects answering police questions. The Home Office 'before and after' study of the effects of the CJPOA reported the overall rate of convictions remained constant at the magistrates' court and declined slightly in the Crown Court, which seemed more likely to be due to other procedural changes (Bucke *et al.* 2000:66).

Bucke *et al.* (2000:45) found most Crown Prosecutors considered that silence would play only a marginal role (if any) in the decision to prosecute. Amongst my respondents, the testing of s34 in court was relatively rare. Reasons for the low numbers included that: prosecutors were content merely to cross-examine defendants on their silence; the prosecution accepting that the advice was reasonable or that the questions had not been put fairly; or appropriate advice meaning that no charges are brought (Bar/B5). Another said he rarely had 'no comment' interviews but that s34 inferences from late mention of facts was something that happens 'quite a lot' (Bar/B8). In most cases, the prosecutor may refer to the defendant's failure to comment in the opening speech, and then cross-examine the defendant once the relevant fact has been introduced. According to one barrister, interviewed by Bucke *et al.* (2000:48) this can have the effect of planting a 'landmine', with the court left waiting for the defendant's testimony (if forthcoming) and an explanation for the silence.

Some Crown Prosecutors highlighted not only the value of any adverse inferences but also the pressure that talk of inferences could put on defendants which could be increased by cross-examination. The advantages to the prosecution of being able to put these points may be outweighed by the difficulty, delay and expense involved in obtaining an accurate transcript of the police interview (Bar/B5 and Bar/B10). In *Hoare and Pierce* (2004: para 34), it was held that a summary of the interview constituted sufficient evidence to leave the issue to the jury. Several solicitors and prosecutors criticised these summaries prepared by the police as 'wholly misleading' (LE/B1/i). In *Webber* (2004:para 6), the edited summary presented to the Court omitted the appellant's denial of having been present.

Bucke *et al.* (2000:43) noted that 'respondents' opinions of the provisions depended upon their particular professional viewpoint'. Barristers had been generally hostile to the CJPOA (RCCJ 1993:Ch. 4, para 13). Most of those I interviewed condemned the changes made to the right of silence:

> Wrong against principles of English law, wholly undermining the Golden Rule.
>
> (Bar/B7)

> An unnecessary and, I thought, retrograde step.
>
> (Bar/B13)

Others said that, having worked under the new provisions, the effects had not been as bad as they had feared:

> I was quite concerned about it, I think, now it's been in operation for some time, I'm not that bothered about it.
>
> (Sol/A12/ii)

> Sounding cynical, you just tend to find them making up their stories at an earlier stage.
>
> (LE/B8/i)

In *Brizzalari* (2004:para 57), the Court cautioned prosecutors against seeking to activate s34 too readily. Amongst my respondents, whether prosecuting barristers invited jurors to draw inferences from a no comment interview depended in part upon the age, experience and mental agility of the individual defendant, whether legal advice had been given, the strength of the prosecution case and whether relevant questions had been put in interview. Some would just challenge defendants about their (lack of) response in cross-examination (Bar/B3). Bucke *et al.* (2000:48–49) identified three types of reasons why barristers might not exploit the provisions: presentational (preferring to focus on more probative or persuasive evidence and not over-complicate issues); tactical (to avoid appearing unfair towards the defendant) and personal (a sense that the provisions were unfair or not 'jurisprudentially proper', although this was fading). When I asked barristers whether they would always invite inferences from a no comment interview or a defendant's failure to testify if prosecuting, a minority said that the CPS would expect them to. Opinion was evenly divided amongst the other barristers who expressed a definite view about inviting inferences: 'The trouble is, when you are prosecuting, you tend to see it with a different hat on, don't you? So you just grasp at any help you might have to prosecute' (Bar/B6). Others regarded automatic use of the provisions as breaching the barristers' unwritten code of conduct:

> It may also smack of seeking to get the prosecution at any cost ... Although the prosecution may appear to be there to hatchet everybody, I don't concede that to be our role. At the Bar, you have the privilege, in a way, of being independent. You get to prosecute and you get to defend. It doesn't do, or it never looks good, to be some kind of over the top advocate taking every point.
>
> (Bar/B12)

Bucke *et al.* (2000:46) noted that some prosecutors were concerned that making an issue of a defendant's silence when the prosecution case was already strong risked 'overkill'. An analogy was drawn with the cautious use of the right of prosecutors to put a defendant's previous convictions before the court in certain circumstances (another restriction that was subsequently liberalised; see Chapter 6):

> It might be different in the magistrates' court because you get some quite zealous, professional CPS prosecutors but when it comes down to counsel, they rarely get involved with that ... they don't feel it makes the game fair, it feels as though they are taking advantage of a defendant's background and also the result is almost a foregone conclusion ... It's so easy to do, it's almost unprofessional to do it, unless you feel that it is absolutely necessary ... Most barristers defend and prosecute and they look at it from both angles.
>
> (Bar/A1)

The majority of Crown Prosecutors felt that the changes had been of some benefit to them:

> It's marginally more helpful. It's not an enormous thing in the prosecution's favour, it's just the common sense moves really.
>
> (SCP/A11)

> It's helped level the playing field which was stacked against us.
>
> (EO/A4)

Crown Prosecutors were much readier to seek inferences from no comment interviews, in principle at least, than barristers (Bucke *et al.* [2000:49] found the same). There were striking differences between the two branches – those at Branch C were much readier to use the provisions, whereas most at Branch A qualified their use of the provisions as depending on the circumstances and the other evidence:

> Having got past the half way stage, I think it would be remiss of me, as a prosecutor, not to draw attention to the fact that they can draw that inference. I think it is incumbent upon me to do so.
>
> (SCP/C1)

> If you've got a case and you've got victims to consider, you've got witnesses to consider and you're satisfied the case is there, then you're going to do your damnedest to make sure you get the conviction and that is a perfectly correct way of proceeding.
>
> (PCP/C9)

Those at Branch C were more sceptical as to whether the changes had made any real difference:

I don't think that the effect has been as extensive as those who introduced it thought it would be. Simply because I don't think the problem was as great as those people perceived it to be.

(SCP/A5)

Politically probably a show for the public, in real terms, no big difference ... There are so many let outs to the use of the right of silence that it effectively has no teeth. Waste of time.

(PCP/C9)

A minority of barristers felt uncomfortable about cross-examining a fellow professional and the tension that this could introduce between solicitor and client (Bar/B3 and B4). Some Branch C prosecutors thought that if a local solicitor was called to give evidence, the case would be transferred out of the area. Whilst a stipendiary magistrate (C) said that he would 'find it very difficult to visit the sins of the lawyer on the defendant', one barrister thought that the likeliest source of miscarriages of justice following this legislation was from suspects being poorly advised to make no comment in interview. Poor legal advice is not, of itself, a reasonable ground of appeal; the appellant has to identify how the error rendered the conviction unsafe (*Day* 2003).

Whilst the direct effects on the outcomes of cases have been limited, it would appear that the provisions have effected a significant change in the conduct of defendants at trial. Section 35 is generally considered to have reduced dramatically the number of defendants not testifying (Bucke *et al.* 2000; Phillips 2007:7). As there are no centrally collected statistics as to the number of defendants giving evidence, it is difficult to assess the impact of the provisions. Amongst those I interviewed, refusal to give evidence was considered rare. The court clerks said that inferences from silence were so rare that they would have to look up the procedure for directing the magistrates.

There are many other reasons why the direct impact of the CJPOA has been less than its supporters anticipated. As Lord Carswell noted 'the ability to give evidence conferred by the 1898 Act was a not unmixed blessing' (*Becouarn* 2006 at 2591). Advocates have always had to consider carefully whether or not to call their clients to give evidence. Some thought that the provisions had not made a significant difference as magistrates and jurors had always drawn inferences against defendants who did not give evidence (Bucke *et al.* 2000).

Human nature being what it is, I think any individual ... cannot avoid drawing a certain inference when a person flatly refuses to speak in their own defence ... it all adds up to a rather devious character.

(JP/F)

I'm absolutely certain that juries would often say to themselves, although told not to, 'well, why didn't he tell us what happened? He's probably guilty, that's why'.

(Judge/B1)

A minority of barristers said that s35 had not made a great difference to them when defending because they had tended to call their clients before the law changed anyway:

Most people want to get in front of a jury and say 'I didn't do it' ... I like calling my clients because I think if my client is an innocent man, I think he ought to get in that box and tell the jury that he's innocent.

(Bar/B8)

I've always been a fairly robust cross-examiner and it's always seemed to me that a jury who's seen prosecution witnesses knocked about a bit would feel a sense of unfairness if the defendant didn't open himself up to the same thing.

(Bar/B13)

Certain types of defences, particularly those depending upon the character or intention of the accused, are more difficult to present if the accused does not testify:

[The jury] want to sum up the kind of person he is, particularly if it's a case of dishonesty, for instance, where they want to make their own evaluation about whether that man, to their estimation is dishonest or not. Then it would be stupid in many respects and it would probably be indicative of guilt if they didn't give evidence.

(Bar/B6)

Such difficulties must be balanced against the risk that testifying will reveal characteristics that undermine the credibility of the defendant or may antagonise the jury or magistrates:

The last thing you need is your obnoxious client losing his temper with the prosecution and proving exactly why he was guilty of a Section 4 [public order offence]!

(Sol/B10/i)

[If] the person was such a personality that they would give entirely the wrong impression. Visually as well as auditory, and that may be a value judgment ... You'd have to look at the jury.

(Bar/B2)

The damage that defendants can wreak upon their cases was the main reason for not calling them before the CJPOA. Some practitioners remained of the view that defendants remained more likely to be acquitted by testing the prosecution case without testifying:

> The defence case is usually at its best at the end of the prosecution case; it's downhill thereon ... they go in the witness box, they will start saying things which will take the whole thing totally off course and they'll be open to cross-examination and they are just going to come across as a complete arsehole.
>
> (Sol/A5/i)

> You see people sometimes these days giving evidence and you think 'that was a grave mistake, you'd be better off [not doing so]', despite the fact that an adverse inference can be drawn.
>
> (Judge/B2)

> I've lost count of the number of trials I've won where I've won it on cross-examination of the defendant ... Whereas at the end of the prosecution case I've felt, 'Well, there was a certain doubt there, if the trial ended here and now, they'd have to acquit'.
>
> (SCP/A5)

Some interviewees recognised the difficulties in changing the behaviour of repeat offenders; what might be characterised as the 'occupational culture' of defendants. As one district judge explained:

> When you get the old lag ... who possibly in the past has kept his mouth shut and got away with it ... it takes a great deal for him to come across with a change of lifestyle at this time of life.
>
> (Stipe/C)

Defendants can, of course, still be acquitted, despite not having testified. Examples included: if a full account had been given in interview; if supporting witnesses or third party evidence were called; or if the defendant was 'a bit simple or slow-witted' (Bar/B6). No comment was reported to still be an effective strategy in domestic assaults. Before the CJPOA, it was said that 'no comment' interviews caused greatest difficulties in cases in which police and prosecutors have to establish *mens rea* ('it's very difficult establishing a mental element when someone doesn't tell you what's in their mind' [SCP/C2]). In the most common example I was given, handling stolen goods, the change in the law makes little difference to the chances of a successful prosecution as silence can still 'stymie it fatally' (SCP/A5). If the complainant does not attend court, charges will be dropped if there is no other evidence. If the complainant does attend, the defendant will plead guilty, meaning that inferences are not at issue. Others still relied on putting the prosecution to proof:

> This is the beauty of the art, it may not be justice necessarily, but this is the way it works … the more witnesses the prosecution rolls in, the better as far as I'm concerned because you've got more chance of driving a wedge between them. And if you've got five or six conflicting accounts in respect of important points, then there's no inference in the world can put that right.
>
> (Sol/A5/i)

A minority of barristers thought that s35 had had a significant impact:

> As a prosecutor, it's helped in a substantial way … You can deal with many people who aren't *au fait* with the witness box, they have difficulties with questions, you can make a fool of them quite easily by just the very nature of the questions which you are going to put to them and invariably all those good points which the defence make go down the tubes … Invariably the defendant goes in the box and invariably, if you are prosecuting, you have a field day!
>
> (Bar/B3)

> The rules are now slanted such that it is almost always advisable for them to go into the box and give their side of the story.
>
> (Bar/B4)

Advocates now face a similar dilemma to police station legal representatives whereby calling the client might undermine their case but the inferences from not calling them may be enough to secure their conviction. The decision whether or not to testify is ultimately for the defendant to take, as several advocates emphasised. Even before the CJPOA, barristers were supposed to ensure that clients who chose not to give evidence signed a memorandum stating that their decision had been taken voluntarily having received advice (*Bevan* 1993). This should now be the invariable practice, whether the decision is contrary to or follows the advice that has been given (*Chatroodi* 2001). Whilst pragmatic, it assumes a wiliness on the part of defendants and a desire to 'appeal proof' any convictions. Similar objections may be expressed about this as against legal representatives asking clients to endorse their notes before a no comment interview at the police station (see Chapter 4) and to sign defence statements (Quirk 2006, discussed in Chapter 6).

My respondents had mixed experiences of how judges were utilising the provisions. 'I'm not so worried about the magistrates, the Crown Court

I'm a bit more concerned about ... A lot of the judges are very pro-prosecution' (Sol/A7/ii). Some thought that judges were reluctant always to invite inferences or to exercise their powers as far as they might (BCP/A10) due to the risk of giving guilty defendants an escape route on appeal (Bar/A1), or from a sense of fair play: 'Bad laws ... shouldn't be sustained by good judges ... one depends on the decency of the judge and so you can have a different result, with the same crime in front of different judges' (Bar/B6).

The rhetoric employed in support of the changes described the benefits for tackling serious crimes. Few of my respondents thought that the CJPOA had made much difference in such cases:

> Professional criminals have either covered their tracks so well, or give interviews which are well prepared ... They would probably still not give evidence.
>
> (Judge/B1)

> Professional villains, if they're there, they will remain silent come what may, unless they see some advantage to it. By and large, professional villains don't get caught if they're professional villains. On the occasions that they do get caught out, they've been caught red-handed and they know they are going to go down for a long period of time ... [so] why sit in a police station having to answer some copper's questions?
>
> (Sol/B2/i)

None of my respondents told me of cases in which they thought an innocent person had been wrongfully convicted due to inferences from their silence. A few gave examples where they thought a conviction would not have been achieved without inferences:

> The prosecution evidence was so thin, that if it had been a stipendiary magistrate and not a lay bench in [Town J], I'm sure he would have been acquitted and I don't think I would have needed to call him.
>
> (Sol/J14/i)

One solicitor was considering appealing a case, having called his client after a failed submission of no case to answer: 'The consequences of the direction were pretty potent because he had a lively and attractive defence ... I think, pre-Act, the verdict would have been different' (Bar/B13).

Conclusion

The CJPOA provisions have reduced markedly the number of defendants who refuse to testify as well as those making no comment at the police station, as described in Chapter 3. The limited nature of the mischief that the provisions sought to address and their evidential application, however, means that they appear to have been decisive in only a limited number of cases. As Leng (2001c:110) notes: 'In the great majority of cases in which an inference may be drawn it will ultimately be irrelevant to the issue of guilt or innocence.' Elks' (2008:42) review of the first ten years of the Criminal Cases Review Commission identified eight referrals based on judicial directions relating to ss34 and 35: two were quashed, six upheld.

The ECtHR has had a restrictive effect on the development of the provisions (Dennis 2002). This includes the requirements that convictions must not be based 'solely or mainly' on silence (*Murray* v *UK* 1996) and that juries should be directed specifically to take legal advice to remain silent into account (*Condron* v *UK* 2001). As with the 'Instrumental' endorsement of the right of silence given by the RCCJ, the 'common sense' judgments of the ECtHR in determining the fairness of proceedings fails to explore how suspects experience, and criminal justice practitioners implement, these provisions. This equivocation has facilitated further encroachment upon the right of silence by the domestic courts (such as *Howell* 2003). Jackson notes that the European Court of Human Rights has addressed the right as 'primarily a procedural right attached to the right to a fair trial rather than a substantive right expressing the principle that individuals generally should not have to account to the State for their actions or activities' (2009:841). The Court of Appeal has interpreted the provisions boldly. Notwithstanding the restraining influence of the ECtHR, the courts have widened the parameters of the Act.

> The larger picture that emerges from the [CJPOA] cases is of a Court of Appeal so committed to crime control that at almost every turn – even when an interpretation favourable to the defence is plausible – the legislation has been construed in the prosecution's favour.
>
> (Pattenden 1998:164)

Complaints have been made that the CJPOA is unfairly testing jurors and magistrates, has lengthened legal consultations at the police station and has led to more legal argument, more complex summings-up and directions, and unnecessary and otherwise unmeritorious appeals. The provisions have 'made life more complicated' (Judge/B1) and 'have contributed more to the complexity and cost of the criminal process than to justice' (Leng 2001c:125). Some judges have expressed concern that the complex directions 'promotes the adverse inference question to a height it does not merit' (*Bresa* 2005:para 4). This has led to calls for the repeal of the Act for pragmatic reasons (Birch 1999:770), or as 'a matter of principle' (Dennis 2013:208). In political terms, such a development appears unlikely.[7]

The provisions have been used to create a culture of expectation that suspects should cooperate with their investigation and trial and that failure to do so is indicative of guilt. The judgment in *Howell* (2003) suggests a shift from the presumption of innocence to an assumption that the innocent have nothing to hide. There has been little judicial sympathy for the impact of this move on the solicitor–client relationship. The provisions have been interpreted widely by the courts and have altered fundamentally the climate in which the accused is questioned and tried (Jackson *et al.* 2000; Leng 2001c). 'These provisions do seem to change the climate – as they were intended to – such that *in law*, the suspect is recruited as an active part of the investigation process' (Mirfield 1995:616). The legislation is revealing in terms of a changed judicial attitude towards defendants and their legal representatives. This should be considered cumulatively with the presumptions relating to the conduct of suspects at the police station under s34 CJPOA, and to submit defence statements under the Criminal Procedure and Investigations Act 1996 (CPIA), discussed in Chapter 6. Together with changes such as the credit given for early guilty pleas and case management procedures, the provisions have forced defences to be produced earlier:

> The 'rabbit out of the hat' defence, which was so amusing and exciting, has gone ... a lot of the fun has gone out of it now.
>
> (Stipe/C)

> It has changed the whole way that everybody approaches cases ... It makes them actually put forward a case from the word go.
>
> (Bar/B5)

Whilst in administrative terms this may be convenient, such an expectation inhibits the defence in testing the strength of the evidence of the police before deciding whether or not to answer questions. There is no corresponding requirement upon the police to disclose their case and the prosecution is entitled to change its case without censure. This disciplinary approach is illustrated by the refusal of some judges to refund legal aid contribution orders to acquitted defendants who made no comment at interview (*The London Advocate* October 1999; Sol/E2/ii).

---

7 Cl 11 of the Liberal Democrats' draft Freedom Bill 2009 proposed the 'repeal of provisions which restrict the right to silence'. The coalition government decided not to include it in the Protection of Freedoms Bill 2010–11 because the current arrangements 'strike the right balance' (email correspondence between the author and the Ministry of Justice, dated 1 August 2011).

The CJPOA has created a 'normative expectation' (Leng 2001a:246) that the accused will cooperate in the investigation and trial process. Section 34 inferences are no longer restricted to subsequent fabrication but can now be used, in effect if not explicitly, for punitive as well as 'evidential' purposes to sanction recalcitrant defendants for not cooperating with the police at the earliest opportunity. The Court of Appeal has described the police interview and trial as a 'benign *continuum*' in which the suspect is engaged from the beginning (*Howell* 2003); a characterisation few suspects are likely to recognise. The provisions have been interpreted boldly and in accordance with earlier judicial notions of deserving[8] and undeserving defendants (*Alladice* 1988; *Goldenberg* 1988; *Crampton* 1991). This 'defendant-centred subjectivity' (Sharpe 1997:155) is dangerous as it is easiest to erode the rights of unpopular groups. The character of the defendant is considered in such cases in order to assess the effects of the breach of provisions on the suspect and the reliability of the evidence thereby obtained. To apply such judgments when considering whether evidential sanctions should be applied to the failure of the accused to cooperate, however, is to short-circuit the process of determining guilt. The expectation of cooperation is incompatible with principles of adversarialism, sits uneasily with the presumption of innocence and assists the prosecution in discharging the burden of proof. This 'disciplinary' attitude contrasts with the reluctance of the courts to exclude evidence in order to punish improper police conduct (*Sang* 1980). Parallels may be drawn with how the police may use their powers not merely for law enforcement but also to enforce their authority and command respect (Singh 1994; Choongh 1997).

Judicial decisions affect the climate in which defendants are tried, and what happens earlier in the criminal justice process (*Howell* 2003). This has effectively made the police interview a part of the trial but without the benefit of the safeguards or the rules of natural justice that attend a fair trial (Jackson 2001a:147; Leng 2001c). The interpretation by the courts of the CJPOA provisions hinders the adversarial preparation of the defence and is part of the armoury of increasingly inquisitorial powers given to the police, evidence from which may then be deployed in an adversarial context (Cape 2003:369). The arguments of principle that were made against the provisions, set out in Chapter 1, of themselves, proved insufficient to resist the changes. It is still, however, instructive to consider the

---

8 In a markedly different judicial approach, former paratroopers wanted for questioning in relation to Bloody Sunday won a High Court case against being detained and transferred to Northern Ireland for interview by police. One of the reasons given was that the claimants intended to exercise their right to silence in the interviews. 'It is, in our view, almost impossible to foresee that any will depart from that position. The interviews are therefore likely to be short and straightforward.' www.belfasttelegraph.co.uk/news/bloody-sunday/bloody-sunday-paras-win-court-battle-against-detention-and-transfer-to-northern-ireland-34295430.html.

effects of the CJPOA against these claims. Despite the repeated insistence of the Court of Appeal, that the provisions do not affect the burden of proof, it is argued that the CJPOA provisions sit uneasily with the presumption of innocence, in some cases making it easier for the Crown to discharge the burden of proof.

Chapter 6

Conclusion

The transformed landscape of the criminal trial

The right of silence in England and Wales has never been of merely local interest. For largely historical reasons, English legal decision making carries a disproportionate global influence (Karstedt 2002). Most common law[1] systems are based upon the English system, English case law is at least persuasive in many of these courts and most recognise the right of silence. The right of silence was seen as the 'keystone of criminal justice' so it is unsurprising that the proposals to curtail the right recommended by the Criminal Law Revision Committee (1972) and enacted by the Criminal Justice and Public Order Act (1994) attracted worldwide attention, condemnation and emulation – in unequal measure. At the time of the CLRC Report, Damaška (1973:507) wrote, 'Comparative research of criminal justice systems is still in its infancy.' When the right of silence was curtailed in England and Wales, policy transfer had still not been explored extensively in relation to criminal justice. As late as 2002, Jones and Newburn (2002:179) noted that, whilst there had been significant and influential studies of the interests and ideologies involved in the politics of crime control, 'we still know remarkably little about how and why criminal justice policy changes, particularly in the UK'. So despite being 'one of the great criminal justice controversies of the twentieth century', the influences on and of the English policy on the right of silence were not tracked contemporaneously, and have received surprisingly little attention since.

Since the early twenty-first century, an extensive scholarship has emerged about the 'growing homogenization of criminal justice across western societies, driven in particular by the spread of punitive policies from the USA' (Muncie 2005:38). This has focused in particular on developments in crime prevention, prison management and sentencing policy (Christie 2000; Garland 2001; Nellis 2000; Newburn 2002; Newburn and Jones 2007) and specific elements of criminal procedure such as the

---

1 Silence is regarded as a 'rare event' in the inquisitorial European systems (van Kessel 1998:833). In the interests of completing this book, this chapter examines only English-based common law systems.

'Americanization Thesis' in plea bargaining (Langer 2004). Much has been written about the creation of international criminal courts and tribunals, a convergence between inquisitorial and adversarial systems (Jörg *et al.* 1995; Jackson 2005), and the European Union principle of mutual recognition. Less attention has been given to the transfer of criminal evidence provisions, and none to the movement of the right of silence.

Just as Chapter 1 shows how, by the late twentieth century, the right of silence had become a prerequisite for any credible domestic or international criminal justice system, this concluding chapter considers how the English experience has influenced policy in other jurisdictions, and examines how its effects continue to reverberate both domestically and across the common law world. As discussed below, every country that considered curtailing the right of silence referred directly to the CLRC or CJPOA. The right of silence could, therefore, be looked at in direct policy transfer terms ('a process by which knowledge of policies, administrative arrangements, institutions and ideas in one political system (past or present)' is used in the development of similar features in another [Dolowitz 2000:3]). Just to map the 'transmission' of the right of silence, however, is to miss what is interesting and perhaps unique about it. A range of metaphors has been applied to the movement of policies between countries. Twining (2009:271) examines 'reception', 'transplants', 'spread', 'expansion', 'transfer', 'exports and imports', 'imposition', 'circulation', 'transmigration' and 'transposition' before settling on 'diffusion'. Langer (2004:5) criticises the widely used 'legal transplant' metaphor for its failure to account for the transformation that legal ideas and institutions may undergo when they travel between legal systems, preferring 'legal translation'. Yet none of these terms fully captures the effects of the right of silence debate, which had much broader ramifications which were felt even in countries that ultimately decided not to follow England. As discussed below, this was neither a one-off nor a one-way transfer. I argue rather that the curtailment of the right of silence was a legal *tremor* – a build-up of pressure (rising crime rates, influential lobbyists and political sensitivities) that led to a shift in the tectonic plates of the criminal justice system in England and Wales. The protests that followed the recommendation of the CLRC to curtail the right of silence in 1972 suppressed the debate in England, but the fissures spread to Australia, and found an outlet in Singapore, Malaysia and then Ireland. The issue then returned with much greater effect in first the Criminal Evidence (Northern Ireland) Order 1988, then the quake of the CJPOA 1994 (see Chapter 2). This sent shockwaves around the world, including in Ireland and Australia again, India and New Zealand, leading to further curtailment of the right in countries with fewer protections for suspects than England. Even where it was decided to retain the right of silence, previously solid fixtures of the criminal justice system had been destabilised and the boundaries of acceptable ideas for reform had moved.

The detailed examination of the effects of curtailing the right of silence in this book shows that criminal evidence rules have played a significant and under-examined role in the spread of the more punitive, expressive and populist justice system, detailed in David Garland's *The Culture of Control* (2001). Garland has explored how, in both the United Kingdom and the United States of America, governments reacted to their limited ability to reduce crime by 'acting out' through aggressive law enforcement measures and harsher sentencing policies, accompanied by strident, punitive rhetoric. The object of such policies is primarily expressive, 'to denounce the crime and reassure the public' (Garland 2001:133), rather than an instrumental effort to reduce crime. There has been little application of this criminal justice policy literature to evidential changes such as the right of silence, but the parallels are striking. For example, the decision to reverse Conservative Party policy and introduce privatised prisons was taken by then Prime Minister Margaret Thatcher 'because of her conviction of the need for radical reform outside the prevailing consensus; not for any reasons of penological principle or administrative practice' (Windlesham 1993:421–422). The decision 'was a symbol as well as an experiment' (Windlesham 1993:307). In every country where the right of silence has been curtailed, the abolitionist case has rested on questionable or non-existent evidence that it was helping the guilty 'get away with it'. Exemptions from, or erosion of, the right of silence have most commonly been justified on the basis of the need for exceptional measures to combat different variants of guilty offenders, all of whom could be viewed as having committed different types of 'signal crime' (Innes 2014); thus, terrorism or organised crime (England and Ireland), 'bikie' gangs (Australia), financial crime, the deaths of children when the parents blame each other or say nothing (England) and sexual abuse (Northern Territory). In some instances, targeted legislation has been introduced, but in most cases the legislation applied to even the most trivial offences and the exception has swiftly become the norm.

The CJPOA also coincided with the increased surveillance of the 'risk society', which in many cases has reduced the need for confessions or adverse inferences. During the 1990s, 78 per cent of the Home Office crime prevention budget was spent on implementing CCTV, and a further £500 million was spent on CCTV between 2000 and 2006 (House of Lords 2009). Forensic methods have developed (McCartney 2013). Mobile telephones, automated systems for public transport or payments in shops mean that it is much easier for the police to identify and track a suspect's movements. The police have also been given greater powers of surveillance – if they can access communications, bug legal consultations or use 'covert human intelligence sources' then confession evidence and the right of silence is rendered almost redundant. This makes it harder to isolate the effects of the CJPOA on the outcome of cases.

The CJPOA marked 'the start of the modern law and order arms race' in England and Wales (Chakrabarti 2008:369). The Act began a new departure in the prosecution of crime; an assertion that 'criminals' were benefitting unfairly from the safeguards in the Police and Criminal Evidence Act 1984 (PACE) – in particular, the right to legal advice at the police station – and should cede some of them in order to restore equilibrium. This was a significant difference from how the right of silence argument was framed in other jurisdictions. This campaign of 're-balancing' the criminal justice system involved the police, politicians and senior members of the judiciary. It chimed with other 'populist punitive' changes that valorised common sense over empirical or theoretical considerations regarding suspects' rights and prosecuting crime. Each iconoclastic act – whether criminal justice or criminal evidence – added to the febrile political atmosphere regarding law and order and, when it did not have the desired effect, required another bold gesture. The danger of such an approach is that, in the face of a continued need of governments to be seen to be tackling crime, subsequent gestures have to be bolder. Each development pushes further the boundaries of what is acceptable. The effects of such a reactive and apparently ad hoc approach to justice set out in the preceding chapters offer lessons that can be applied more widely.

The right of silence had come to be seen as a prerequisite for a fair trial. In Chapter 1, I characterise the CJPOA provisions as 'symbolic abolitionism'; a term which applies equally to the changes in other countries. As Tonry (2010:388) argues, 'Symbols matter, however, not only from the short-term perspective of whether they will play well on the evening news but also from the long-term perspective of whether the values they embody or undermine will affect prevailing ways of thinking.'

Chapter 2 locates the backlash against the right of silence in the political context of rising crime and the effective lobbying of the police. A distinction is often made in common law systems between rules regarding the obtaining and the admissibility of evidence (Jackson and Summers 2012:12); the CJPOA, whilst ostensibly relating to how the evidence is used at trial, has had an influence on how such evidence is gathered. It is generally agreed that defendants are now more likely to answer police questions and to testify (see Chapters 3 and 5), but this has not made a noticeable difference in terms of increasing charge, plea or conviction rates. Nor has it had the dire effect that others feared it might – police conduct of interviews is rarely questioned nowadays and there has been no direct evidence of wrongful convictions as a result of the changes. It was perhaps the failure of both sets of predictions that meant that discussion of the right of silence seemed to stop for some years. Leng (2001c:112) suggests the almost exclusive focus on these polarised positions meant that insufficient attention was paid to other theoretical and practical problems which might result from the CJPOA. The greatest impact of the CJPOA has had been on the practices of lawyers and their relationships with their clients (Chapter 4). As their bargaining power at the police station has been reduced, they have to make more difficult calculations about answering questions and know that they may have to give evidence as to their advice. An aspect of the CJPOA that has not been considered widely is the significant influence it has had on judges (Chapter 5 and below). At first, the evidential effects of the changes were of only 'marginal' significance (Dennis 2002) but, as time has gone on, the courts have drawn the parameters of the legislation more widely, something which has largely passed without comment (Quirk 2013).

Further crime control developments followed and these changes were rapidly normalised. It is only in retrospect that the damage to other due process protections can be traced back to this seismic legislation and it can be seen more clearly how the Act has 'transformed the landscape of a criminal trial' (*Chief Constable of the RUC ex parte Begley* 1997 at 1479). Of course the CJPOA did not re-balance the system, but it was a disingenuous calculation to attempt. In an adversarial system, the disparity in power and resources between the individual and the State makes such compensatory measures necessary in order to ensure a fair contest. The argument was difficult to counter in populist terms even though there was little evidence that the right of silence was causing undue difficulties in the administration of justice. The legislation applies to all suspects but it does not affect them all equally. 'Hardened criminals' are unlikely to be affected by the provisions (the greatest problem the authorities face is in detecting them), but to focus on the 'ordinary' or vulnerable who are most at risk is to miss the more insidious damage that is done to the system as a whole. As I have argued elsewhere:

> suspects have been trebly disadvantaged by the CJPOA. The right of silence has been diminished, legal representation has been devalued, and the encroachment on such 'a "bench mark" of British justice' facilitated further statutory and common law restrictions on evidential protections for defendants.
>
> (Quirk 2013:467)

This final chapter examines the spread of the policy around the world and concludes by drawing upon the lessons that can be learnt from this policy: the respective roles of the legislature and judiciary and the effects on legal representation. Despite the complexity of the case law and its limited evidential utility, repeal of the CJPOA appears unlikely, but there is much to be learned, in England and elsewhere, from its enactment and the after-effects.

The warning signs

By the late 1960s and early 1970s 'practically every law reform body in the common law world was studying evidence' (Brooks 1978:245–246). As Gooderson (1968:64) observed:

> No expert long range forecast is needed to predict that in the near future a wind of change of a velocity and a turbulence hitherto unknown is going to sweep away many common law principles of the law of evidence regarded in the past as fundamental.

Following a decade of rising crime and social upheaval in England, the first 'foreshock' that the right of silence should be curtailed came from the JUSTICE (1967) report. It was noted in America that: 'what the Supreme Court has just embedded in American criminal law by constitutional construction [the landmark *Miranda* v *Arizona* (1966) decision], the British Justice Commission is trying to abolish altogether' (Tierney 1968:28).[2] These two events marked a significant divergence in approach.

The *Miranda* decision requires that the police must inform suspects of their right to remain silent, stop questioning if the suspect wishes to exercise that right and tell suspects of the entitlement to have a lawyer during interrogation. 'The Supreme Court's most famous criminal law decision' (Cassell 1999–2000) features in every list of the most significant US Supreme Court decisions. It attracted great controversy and, two years later, the US Congress passed 18 US Code § 3501, which sought to revert to the previous 'voluntariness' test. The Supreme Court eventually ruled the legislation unconstitutional, holding that *Miranda* has become 'embedded in routine police practice to the point where the warnings have become part of our national culture' (*Dickerson* v *US* 2000). It has been argued that the *Miranda* decision 'has been upheld by the USSC more for reasons of *stare decisis* than it would out of any deep-seated commitment to uphold it on its merits' (Jackson and Summers 2012:244) and its scope has been reduced. The right of silence nevertheless remains an important part of American law and cultural life in a way that it has never been in England: to 'plead the Fifth' is a common expression for avoiding a difficult question and the late night television programme *Watch What Happens Live* has a segment of the same name in which guests are asked three questions, and get to 'plead the fifth' to only one of them.

2 There is an immense literature relating to the Fifth Amendment (Levy 1968). Even though *Miranda* was influenced by English history (two of the Justices referred to English law and the historical reasons behind the Fifth Amendment), there has been little interaction between the two systems since on this topic. The specific constitutional arguments are difficult to apply elsewhere, so the USA is referred to only in passing.

The first significant tremor in England was the Report of the Criminal Law Revision Committee in 1972 that recommended curtailing the right of silence on utilitarian grounds (see Chapter 2). There was an immediate and ferocious backlash that stymied reform in England and Wales, but the CLRC Report has offered enduring intellectual and judicial credibility to the proposition. The Report provoked shock across the world. The American military establishment expressed concern about potential prosecutions of its troops based in England; the Chairman of the American Bar Association gave a lecture entitled 'Is Due Process Fleeing Its English Home?' (Thoresby 1973); and an academic conference was held in Australia to discuss the CLRC findings (University of Sydney 1973). In a letter to *The Times* (5 October 1972), Manfred Simon (a retired French judge who had been consulted by the CLRC) described its proposals as:

> the first timid step to dismantle the venerable fortress built by many generations of British lawyers to protect the innocent and to challenge the arbitrary action of Government. It is a sad illustration of the insidious process whereby standards of even the most civilised countries can under modern pressures subtly but irresistibly be eroded.

Lord Ritchie-Calder (*Hansard HL Debs*, 14 February 1973, vol 338, cols 1617–1618) reminded their Lordships that their debate about the CLRC would resonate far beyond the Chamber:

> The effect on my international colleagues [at the Centre for the Study of Democratic Institutions in California], who included visiting Fellows from Eastern Europe and distinguished members of the American legal profession ... was traumatic. To see the underpinning of the traditional standards of British justice being deliberately removed shook them...

Following the CLRC Report, other countries immediately launched enquiries as to whether such measures were feasible or appropriate for their own systems. This was not coincidental – they referred explicitly to the findings of the CLRC and some found its proposals persuasive. One of the contributors to the Law Reform Commission of Canada explained that: 'It was reassuring to find that much of the thinking underlying the [English CLRC] Report paralleled that underlying the Commission's Evidence Code' (Brooks 1978:285) – a wording that again suggests how other countries looked to Britain as an example. The South Australian Criminal Law and Penal Methods Reform Committee (1974) also recommended allowing inferences from pre-trial silence. Neither of these reform bodies were successful in their proposed reforms at this stage. Singapore (The Criminal Procedure Code [Amendment] Act No 10 of 1976) and Malaysia (the

Criminal Procedure Code [Amendment and Extension] Act 1976) were persuaded by the CLRC Report and its draft bill and promptly enacted the 'silence' elements (Yeo 1983; Singh 1974, 1975) to allow inferences to be drawn from silence 'on being charged or officially informed' of the possibility of a charge and at-trial, and the effects of this are examined below.

India revised its Code of Criminal Procedure in 1973 to specify that comment should not be made from an accused's silence, preferring the American reasoning in *Adamson* v *California* (1947). What is interesting in terms of policy transfer – and I have found no reference to this in the literature – is that s342(2) of the previous Indian Code of Criminal Procedure 1898 contained a very similar wording to that in the CLRC Report:

> The accused shall not render himself liable to punishment by refusing to answer questions or by giving false answers to them; *but the court and the jury (if any) may draw such inference from such refusal or answers as it thinks fit.*

> (Emphasis added)

The Thomson Committee in Scotland briefly considered the CLRC findings (1975 starting at para 50.08). It recommended preserving the right of silence and that no inferences should be drawn from silence under police questioning (para 7.12), but that inferences should be allowed from a defendant's refusal to testify (50.12). The Thomson Committee expressly disagreed with the CLRC finding that refusal to answer questions or to testify should amount to corroboration. The Criminal Justice (Scotland) Act 1980 re-introduced the quasi-inquisitorial procedure of judicial examination whereby an accused can be questioned in the presence of a sheriff at the early stages of an investigation. If the accused fails to answer and then gives an explanation at trial which could have been given at the judicial examination, this can be drawn to the jury's attention.

The Australian Law Reform Commission (1975) took a diametrically opposing view to the CLRC. It concluded that any diminution of the pre-trial right of silence 'would undermine one of the most fundamental tenets of the present criminal' (paras 107 and 150). It observed that exercise of the right was 'illusory in practice' (para 140) and recommended more rigorous enforceable rights for suspects, including access to legal advice and the recording of interviews (McNicol 1984:276). The New South Wales government, having considered the report of its own CLRC and the debate in England, proposed only the abolition of the unsworn statement from the dock. The Queensland Law Reform Commission (Australian Law Reform Commission 1975:2) decided against making any recommendation about the right of the judge or prosecutor to comment on the failure of an accused to give evidence because '[t]he course of the recent debate in England on this and related matters leads us to believe that it would be difficult to devise a legislative formula dealing with the right to comment that would win widespread acceptance'.

The idea re-emerged in Ireland in a different form via sections 18–19 of the Criminal Justice Act 1984. This Act also created a general power of arrest for questioning and required advance notice of alibi evidence. As was the case in England, it followed extensive lobbying from the police about the (unsubstantiated) difficulties they faced in overcoming a 'wall of silence' erected by terrorist suspects. The State already had far-reaching powers under s52 of the Offences against the State Act 1939, which obliges suspects to answer certain questions concerning their movements. The Criminal Justice Act 1984 provides that such inferences as appear proper could be drawn from a failure or refusal to account for: any object, substance or mark on the suspect's person, clothing or footwear or possession, or place where arrested; or from a failure or refusal to account for his or her presence at a particular place around the time the offence was committed. If evidence of these matters is given at trial then the failure or refusal may, on the basis of such inferences, be treated as potentially corroborative of any material evidence. The idea was regarded as an extreme crime control measure. One academic condemned it, stating that:

> The most disreputable aspect of this is that it is lifted virtually holus bolus from the recommendation of the British Criminal Law Revision Committee, which in turn was rejected by the House of Lords. Not even Mrs Thatcher in the revamped Police and Criminal Evidence Bill has seen fit to revive it.
>
> (Asmal 1983:8)

In fact, the Irish provisions differed from the CLRC recommendations – significantly this meant that the original two potential provisions had now become four.

In England, the police continued to lobby for the curtailment of the right of silence as crime and industrial unrest grew throughout the 1970s. The Royal Commission on Criminal Procedure (1981) rejected the findings of the CLRC about the right of silence – largely on the grounds of protecting the innocent (see Chapter 2). It recommended that it be retained as part of a regime that balanced enhanced rights for suspects and increased powers for the police. Police and judicial criticism of the right of silence in England intensified following the passage of PACE, especially enhanced access to legal advice. The issue was revived unexpectedly by the Home Secretary and then the equally abrupt decision to introduce the Criminal Evidence (Northern Ireland) Order 1988 (see Chapter 2). The Northern Ireland Order 1988 combined adverse inferences from failure to answer police questions and to testify from the CLRC with the 'failure to account' provisions from the Irish Criminal Justice Act. It went further in allowing inferences simply from a failure to account for the object, substance, mark or location and also allowed the inferences to be viewed as corroboration. Although ostensibly introduced in response to terrorism, the Order applied to all suspects, a measure that Jackson and Daly (2016:287, 288) describe as 'the catalyst for th[e] fragmentation' of the two-tiered system between 'emergency' and 'ordinary' crime, leading to 'a normalisation and convergence of treatment'. Kevin McNamara, the Shadow Secretary of State for Northern Ireland, accused the government of using Northern Ireland as a laboratory for repressive experiments that subsequently would be transferred to the mainland (Carvel and Hearst 1988). The Royal Commission on Criminal Justice (1993) was asked to consider the right of silence and recommended no change. The government rejected its recommendation and the CJPOA duly followed. This broadly introduced the four inferences from Northern Ireland to England and Wales, and for all offences.

The aftershocks

The erosion of the right of silence gathered strength from the transfer of the English experience between similar jurisdictions. Elements of the CJPOA borrowed directly from legislation in Ireland, which subsequently amended its laws to follow the more expansive English model. Jackson and Daly (2016:282) argue that whilst Ireland was less swayed by the 'punitive turn' exhibited in other countries, the paramilitary activity in Northern Ireland and gangland crime led to similar 're-balancing' rhetoric. Following two high-profile murders in June 1996 (the gang-related killing of investigative journalist Veronica Guerin, and Detective Garda Jerry McCabe in the course of an IRA-related armed robbery), more inferences were allowed in relation to drug-trafficking offences (s7 of the Criminal Justice [Drug Trafficking] Act 1996). Under Part 4 of the Criminal Justice Act 2007, inferences can be drawn from silence in any proceedings relating to an arrestable offence. This essentially added s34 inferences (together with some safeguards around the right to legal advice). A court may draw adverse inferences where an accused has relied at trial upon a fact that 'clearly called for an explanation' but was not given when questioned. ('Clearly called for' is the language of the ECtHR, rather than the 'reasonable to mention' of s34 CJPOA.) Police powers of detention for questioning have increased steadily and further measures were introduced regarding failure to answer questions in relation to organised crime (Criminal Justice Act 2006 as amended by the Criminal Justice [Amendment] Act 2009).

Proposals to bring Scottish law into line with the planned changes in England and Wales were published in September 1994 and echoed the concern of English ministers that:

the right to silence has been taken advantage of by professional criminals and terrorists and that the law as it concerns accused persons who
remain silent no longer strikes the correct balance between the interests of the accused and the need to convict the guilty.

The Scottish Law Commission questioned the provenance, authority and
representativeness of such views, noting that the Scottish Office had failed
to provide statistics (Arlidge 1994). Since 1995, the judge and prosecution
can comment on a failure to give evidence, although this should be in
special circumstances only but they cannot comment on silence at the
police station (*Larkin* v *HM Advocate* 2005).

Several states in Australia considered following the English provisions
but, following careful enquiries, rejected the proposals. The Australian
Law Reform Commission (1987) returned to the issue and recommended
that judges should be allowed to comment on the failure of the accused to
give evidence – essentially an English *Bathurst* (1968) direction (noting
that the defendant has not given evidence, that the jury has not heard the
defence case tested but that they must not assume guilt from this). Further
reviews took place in Victoria (1996–99), Scrutiny of Acts and Regulations
Committee (1998), Western Australia (1999) and Queensland (2003–04),
which recommended retaining the right. The New South Wales Law
Reform Commission (2000a:2.138) examined the changes in England and
Singapore and rejected them on the basis that there was no empirical
support to show that prosecutions were being impeded and that to curtail
the right would:

> undermine fundamental principles concerning the appropriate rela-
> tionship between the powers of the State on the one hand and the
> liberty of the citizen on the other, exacerbated by its tendency to sub-
> stitute trial in the police station for trial by a court of law.

In 2002 a review concluded that, 'The position in Australia seems clear.
Subject to some minority murmurs ... the right to silence in its widest
form prevails throughout Australia in the sense accepted by the courts
over the last 200 years' (Northern Territory Law Reform Committee
2002).

The issue was not settled, however. Exceptional 'Star Chamber'
powers were given in the Australian Crime Commission Act 2002 relating
to the investigation of serious and organised crime. In these cases, wit
nesses are served with a summons which it is a contempt of court to
reveal, and are compelled to answer questions. (These powers were
extended in 2008 to the investigation of child abuse in the Northern
Territory.) The Northern Territory Law Reform Committee (2002:3)
marked a turning point. It was charged with looking at 'whether and

how far the UK legislation could or should be adopted'. It gave a one-word answer to the question ('no'), largely on the practical grounds that the State had the highest proportion of Aboriginal citizens who could be disadvantaged by such a measure and that it could ill afford the inevitable legal challenges to any such legislation. The first part of the report is supportive of the right. It noted that the prevailing climate of legal opinion was against a change and took the optimistic view that if a body of Australian citizens were asked to consider the issue, it would instinctively understand that to penalise silence 'would lead to tyranny'. Its reasoning then changed. It thought that:

> from the characteristically robust and direct viewpoint of the average Australian it would defy common sense that, if a person chooses a course of action, he should then demand that no one should question that course of action or draw inferences from it.

It observed that 'in both the UK and Singapore the changes in the legislation seem to have been seen as rational, and there appears no public outcry against them or any groundswell for repeal'. It also noted the ECtHR had not found against the provisions (Northern Territory Law Reform Committee 2002). The conclusion of this report was that: 'In an ideal world no doubt the rationale of the UK *Criminal Justice and Public Order Act* would lead inevitably to similar legislation in Australia.' It considered that 'if no injustice was seen to arise from the UK, then an Australian state might follow and ultimately the NT might do the same'. Somehow, subtly, curtailing the right of silence had shifted from erroneous to aspirational – the mark of an advanced criminal justice system – a view enhanced by the lack of objection in England and Strasbourg.

The New South Wales Law Reform Commission (2000a) concluded that legislation based on the CJPOA should not be introduced but, with leave, prosecutors should be permitted to comment upon the fact that the defendant has not given evidence. It also recommended a system of enhanced pre-trial disclosure – another English innovation. It returned to the issue in 2005–06 and concluded that, whilst the right to silence when questioned is an important rule of law principle and a fundamental human right, it may be modified or abrogated when in the public interest (paras 35–36). In 2013, the Evidence Amendment (Evidence of Silence) Act was passed, which essentially introduced the CJPOA provisions, along with another amendment requiring defence disclosure. The Attorney General dismissed the 'scaremongering' of opponents 'despite a ruling from the European Court of Human Rights, which found similar laws in the UK were consistent with the right to a fair trial' (Daly 2007).

More recently in Scotland, following the ruling in *Cadder* v *HM Advocate* (2010), the Carloway Review (2011) considered the possibility of adverse inferences to counterbalance the requirement for access to legal advice (Ferguson 2011). It concluded, however, that 'judging from the experience in England and Wales, the scheme would have to be of labyrinthine complexity' (7.5.24). It was also concerned that:

> this type of system is effectively moving part of the trial out of the court room and into the police station. Rather, as appears to be the position in some inquisitorial systems, what occurs in the police station becomes almost determinative of the case.

It also adopted a more principled-based approach, concluding that 'the introduction of adverse inference would not fit well with the presumption of innocence, the right to silence and the privilege against self-incrimination as understood and applied in Scotland'.

Whilst some countries clearly felt that the sponsorship of England, and subsequently the endorsement of the ECtHR, gave legitimacy to an idea initially seen as beyond the pale, others were disappointed at institutions that should be showing leadership. The Law Commission of India found that changes to the right of silence would be unconstitutional and concluded tartly that: 'It is indeed rather surprising that when China is introducing this principle into its laws some democracies like UK and Australia are introducing laws deviating from the old tradition as to right to silence' (2000:46).

Collateral damage to the lawyer–client relationship

> Restricting the right of silence is now said to be necessary as a refinement of the balance which PACE had swung too far in favour of the suspect. The fundamental weakness of this approach is that it conceives of criminal justice essentially as a legal rather than also as a social institution, and does so in legalistic rather than sociological terms.
>
> (Dixon 1991b:253)

Following Dixon's argument, this book examines the right of silence in the political, social as well as legal context in which the changes took place. Pronouncements made by investigatory bodies and abstract principles are important, but how and why laws are introduced, used and affect the working practices of criminal justice practitioners and the experiences of suspects is also significant.

The galvanising factor for many of those advocating the CJPOA changes was an increase in police station legal representation (even though the majority of suspects were unrepresented, most legal representatives were not especially adversarial and many were not even qualified). Complaints that the police were handicapped by PACE ignored the realities of the custodial encounter, in which the police have almost total authority. Police conduct in interviews has improved immeasurably – some have attributed this to the CJPOA reducing the need for a confession, but the trend predated it and is as likely to be due to improved training and tape recording of interviews. Tape recording of interviews and legal advice were opposed at first but officers came to realise that they are not a problem in a well-conducted interview. As Dixon (2010:432) noted, 'despite the fears of many, the sky remained in the heavens, suspects continued to confess, and police effectiveness was not reduced. On the contrary, the general response of police was retrospectively to welcome the new criminal process.'

It is curious, therefore, that these stereotypical attitudes about recalcitrant suspects, a presumption that suspects are guilty, the innocent having nothing to hide and the suspicion of legal representatives appear to have shifted from the police station to the courtroom (Quirk 2013:477). Whilst the direct effects of the Act have been limited by the relatively small numbers of suspects making no comment, the changes have an effect on the lawyer–client relationship in ways that were not envisaged when the law changed. The Court of Appeal has described the police interview and trial as a 'benign *continuum*' in which the suspect is engaged from the beginning (*Howell* 2003); a characterisation few suspects are likely to recognise and of course without the safeguards that apply at trial (Jackson 2001c:147; Leng 2001c). The protective benefit of legal advice, a fundamental requirement of a fair trial, is undermined by curtailing one of the few bargaining tools that legal representatives had. By making custodial legal advice of potential evidential significance, perhaps requiring representatives to testify at the trial of their clients, the CJPOA has compromised the lawyer–client relationship, thus further eroding the protective benefits of legal advice and tipping the balance even further against suspects. The Courts went even further in *Seaton* (2010) and allowed incursions into legal professional privilege – previously also regarded as a fundamental protection for defendants (Quirk 2013). Although the performance of para-legal staff has improved in many cases, the service provided continues to fall short of the protective function it is supposed to offer, leaving suspects further disadvantaged. Those suspects who get legal advice have been short-changed by the provisions, most are still unrepresented and the slow increase in representation seems likely to reverse given recent cuts to legal aid.[3]

---

3 In New South Wales, the silence provisions cannot be used if a lawyer is not present during police questioning. This has led to suggestions that – presumably more experienced – clients are being advised not to have representation during the interview.

In New South Wales, the Law Society has argued for the repeal of the right of silence provisions as they have not been used in three years, but experience from elsewhere suggests that it might be too early to make such a call. In every jurisdiction where the right of silence has been curtailed, an initially cautious judicial interpretation has yielded to a more expansive approach. After five years, Yeo (1983:100) considered that 'the amendments have not materially assisted the Singapore police force and prosecuting officers in their combat against crime' (see also Heong 1981:24). The provisions were upheld against constitutional challenges (*Haw Tua Tau* v *Public Prosecutor* 1982; *Jaykumal* v *Public Prosecutor* 1980–81) and the judiciary gained in confidence until '[t]he destruction of the privilege as a potential constitutional concept was complete' (Hor 2007:76) when it was declared that the privilege against self-incrimination was not part of the fundamental rules of natural justice in Singapore (*Public Prosecutor* v *Mazlan bin Maidun* 1992). After 20 years, Tan (1997:473) found that the numbers volunteering information or testifying had remained broadly similar but '[w]hat is dramatically different today, however, is the attitude of the courts in drawing adverse inferences'. He places the readiness of the courts to draw inferences from pre-trial and trial silence 'within the context of the gradual erosion in Singapore of the right to silence and the privilege against self-incrimination' (1997:476). He examines other developments in criminal law, such as the lowering of the standard to be met by the prosecution case at the close of its case to establishing a *prima facie* case which is not inherently incredible. Palakrishnan (1999:17) observed that, without safeguards, miscarriages of justice such as the Guildford Four and Birmingham Six might follow. In Northern Ireland, initial judicial interpretation was cautious and lacked coherency (Jackson 1991; Jackson *et al.* 2000) but within a few years it had reached the point where 'in some cases silence is almost taken as presumptive of guilt' (JUSTICE 1994:5).

Judicial decisions affect the prevailing climate in which suspects are investigated and tried; the appellate level 'is where the governing norms are made explicit' (Packer 1968:232). According to Packer, the crime control model tends to be driven by Parliament and due process protected by the judiciary (1968:173). In England, senior judicial figures advocated the curtailing of the right of silence (see Chapter 2) and interpreted the CJPOA in a manner that appeared to echo attitudes and behaviours that PACE had sought with much success to change. The judges appeared to have few qualms about the profound nature of the changes – unlike, for example, the 'supergrass' provisions in Northern Ireland (allowing suspects to be convicted solely on the evidence of a co-accused who turns 'Queen's Evidence') where judges were uneasy about convicting individuals without sufficiently robust evidence and were discomforted by criticism that these cases were incompatible with common law standards of fairness and due process (Greer 1995). In contrast, judges in England and Northern Ireland seemed unmoved by criticism from the United Nations Human Rights Committee (1995), which 'notes with concern' that the CJPOA provisions 'violates various provisions of Article 14 of the Covenant [fair trial], despite a range of safeguards built into the legislation and the rules enacted thereunder'. Human Rights Watch (Hall and Human Rights Watch 1997:8), JUSTICE (1994) and Amnesty International (1993) also criticised the provisions.

Following the Auld Review of the Criminal Courts, judges have been given increased responsibility for case management and the Criminal Procedure Rules have been drafted to ensure that the 'criminal justice system is accessible, fair and efficient' (s69(4)(a) of the Courts Act 2003). This is a significant change in the role of the judge. The first 'overriding objective' of the Criminal Practice Direction is set out in full as a stark indication of how the priorities of the courts, even at the rhetorical level, have changed:

> 1A.1 The presumption of innocence and an adversarial process are essential features of English and Welsh legal tradition and of the defendant's right to a fair trial. But it is no part of a fair trial that questions of guilt and innocence should be determined by procedural manoeuvres. On the contrary, fairness is best served when the issues between the parties are identified as early and as clearly as possible. As Lord Justice Auld noted, a criminal trial is not a game under which a guilty defendant should be provided with a sporting chance. It is a search for truth in accordance with the twin principles that the prosecution must prove its case and that a defendant is not obliged to inculpate himself, the object being to convict the guilty and acquit the innocent.

Participants in criminal trials, including defendants, now have a duty to ensure that the case is dealt with efficiently and expeditiously. Significant credit is given for early guilty pleas which, together with the case management procedures, have forced defences to be produced earlier. Swingeing cuts to legal aid have reduced the number of providers and have cut eligibility for legal aid. As a result, the number of unrepresented defendants at the police station and at trial seems likely to increase.[4]

Judicial interpretation of the law has developed a presumption that defendants should cooperate fully in the investigation and trial process,

---

4 Currently, defendants with a household disposable income of £22,325 or more are not eligible for state-funded legal representation at the magistrates' court and those with a disposable income of £37,500 or more are not eligible for legal aid for a Crown Court trial (Legal Aid Agency 2014).

and that those who do not have something to hide. The language used by the Court of Appeal suggests that judges 'have imported to the courtroom the traditional police suspicion of defendants and their legal representatives' (Quirk 2013:468). From the outset, the Court made it clear that it would not permit a 'coach and horses' to be driven through the provisions (*Cowan* 1995 at 380) and the decisions of the ECtHR have had a more limited influence than many expected. The 'common sense' judgments of the ECtHR in determining the fairness of proceedings fails to explore how suspects experience, and criminal justice practitioners implement, these provisions. No concession is made for a solicitor trying to advise when the police will not disclose their evidence or for suspects with learning difficulties having to testify, for example. This has made the police interview part of a continuum to trial – whether benign or not is disputed – but without the benefit of the courtroom safeguards (Jackson 2001c:147; Leng 2001c) and defendants are expected to expose themselves to cross-examination. Section 34 inferences are no longer restricted to subsequent fabrication but can be used, in evidence, for punitive as well as evidential purposes, against suspects for not fully cooperating with the police, and the threshold for excluding inferences for suspects who do not testify has been set so high as to be ineffective. The police had been criticised for fulfilling their obligations to the letter rather than the spirit of PACE (see Chapter 3). The CJPOA does the same: suspects appear to be in receipt of protections that fulfil the requirements of a fair trial, such as a high burden of proof and legal advice, but the protections are devalued by the quandary in which the lawyer is now placed and the potential evidential implications of a suspect's silence.

The right will rise again?

The notion of a golden age of criminal justice is a seductive but unrealistic notion. The last 30 years have been a turbulent period for criminal justice in England and Wales but it is important to remember that significant improvements have been made in the safeguards offered to those under investigation and on trial for criminal offences. The concept of what constitutes a fair trial has developed rapidly through statutory and common law changes – in particular, PACE 1984 – and advancements in both European and domestic human rights law. Crime became increasingly politicised, oddly enough as crime rates began to fall for the first time (since 1995, crime has fallen back to the level of the early 1980s but fear of crime remained disproportionately high). The right of silence was one of the first 'crime control' targets. Once it was curtailed, that was, of course, not enough. The subsequent pace of change has been unrelenting. 'The disclosure revolution' (Leng 1997:216) followed within a year of the right of silence provisions coming into force (1 April 1995). The Criminal

Procedure and Investigations Act 1996 (CPIA), creating the first compulsory defence disclosure scheme, was passed at a speed described as an 'ambush of Parliament' (Leng and Taylor 1996:6). It ostensibly targeted the same unquantified mischief as the CJPOA; '[t]he spectre of the ambush defence has been perhaps the single most powerful factor in the campaign to abolish the right to silence in police interrogation and to require early disclosure of the defence case' (Leng 1995:706). Concern about the CPIA and its potential for causing injustice grew rapidly amongst practitioners and academics (Leng 1995; Sprack 1997; British Academy of Forensic Sciences/Criminal Bar Association 1999; Plotnikoff and Woolfson 2001; Quirk 2006). As with the CJPOA, the disclosure regime was seen as inappropriate in an adversarial system (Redmayne 1997) and striking at the common law rules of fairness (Leng 1997). Once the CJPOA had made the initial breach into defendants' rights, opposition to other measures was easier to overcome. Opposition to the CPIA was dismissed on the basis that defence disclosure required little more from suspects than the incursions into the right of silence made by the CJPOA.

Inferences at charge is another example of how the case law has developed, reflecting a 'marked shift in emphasis towards an overtly inquisitorial procedure, as compared with the primary legislation and the 1995 edition of the [PACE] code' (Archbold 2016). At first, the Court of Appeal quashed convictions where inferences had been drawn from no comment interviews conducted after the police had sufficient evidence to charge (*Pointer* 1997; *Gayle* 1999). It then departed from its previous reasoning, (*Elliott* 2002; *Ioannou* 1999; *McGuinness* 1999; *Sed* 2004). The Codes of Practice were redrafted to allow questioning to continue beyond the point at which the police have sufficient evidence to charge (Cape 2003).

Criminal justice bills have followed the CJPOA at least annually, most echoing the rhetoric of redressing the balance of a system tipped too far in favour of the criminal. The changes to the centuries-old 'double jeopardy' provisions (allowing defendants to be prosecuted for a second time following an acquittal), limiting the right to trial by a jury and allowing jurors to know about a defendant's previous convictions demonstrate how previously untouchable principles have become targets to demonstrate the unflinching commitment of successive governments to tackling crime. Unsuccessful attempts were also made to introduce compulsory identity cards, to extend pre-charge detention to 90 days and to create the most extensive criminal justice DNA database in the world. This is in addition to the much higher levels of CCTV, speed cameras and regular police surveillance of non-violent protestors in the UK (see Tonry 2010).

The trend towards penal or populist punitiveness (Bottoms 1995) has been characterised by a move away from abstract notions to common sense ideas of what ordinary people know (in this case, that silence is inherently suspicious rather than in accordance with the presumption of innocence). As Campbell (2008:560) notes, 'crime control measures seem driven by intuition, political pragmatism and instinct rather than grounded on empirical expert research or principled debate'. The CJPOA began a trend to allowing more evidence before juries (Auld Report 2001; Phillips 2007). The regular 're-balancing' claims were flawed in both principle and practice. In an adversarial system, the disparity in power and resources between the individual and the State makes such compensatory measures necessary in order to ensure a fair contest. Tonry details 'the unhappy consequences of England's shift from substantive to expressive crime and antisocial behaviour policies'. He blames the Labour Party for its profoundly illiberal policies but, in fairness, this process began with the CJPOA. Tonry (2010) argues that these:

> policies and rhetoric have weakened support within the British public and within British culture for the rule of law and for fundamental beliefs about relations between the citizen and the State. Formerly unthinkable policies have become commonplace, and arguments against them have become less than fully credible. The associated risks to civil rights and liberties are considerable.

Since the events of 11 September 2001, the USA and UK governments have challenged fundamental principles such as *habeas corpus* and the prohibition on evidence obtained by torture. They have created previously untenable new procedures, such as 'extraordinary rendition', 'enhanced interrogation' and the military tribunals at Guantánamo Bay. Whilst governments have a duty to protect their citizens, public fear can be exploited to overcome political or principled opposition to eroding the rights of suspects. Seidman (2007) explains the prohibition against torture, a concept which was controversially re-defined by the US government, in terms of a right to silence, as 'essential in preserving the distinction between mind and body on which human freedom depends'. Then Prime Minister Tony Blair argued that: 'The whole of our system starts from the proposition that its duty is to protect the innocent from being wrongly convicted.... But surely our primary duty should be to allow law-abiding people to live in safety' (quoted in BBC News 2005:110–111). Some of these changes may have occurred anyway (and the US has gone further than the UK in such measures) so the CJPOA cannot be causative of all the changes. They are, however, an important reminder of the first principles that should be considered in criminal justice, and the presumption of innocence – in part due to the CJPOA – has fallen down that list. By undermining fundamental safeguards such as the right of silence, the CJPOA made it easier in the future to challenge other fundamental safeguards?

Conclusion

'Issues of evidence in particular are not confined to the technical nuts and bolts of making a system run more smoothly, but go to the heart of the rights of individuals' (Jackson and Summers 2012:5). The right of silence is seen as more than an ordinary evidential rule. It is often described as speaking to something in the national character. Lord Salman (*HL Debs*, Col 1604, 14–15 February 1973) thought the CLRC proposals were an attack on 'the very roots of British justice'. The Northern Territory Law Reform Committee (2002) considered the views of the 'average Australian' on the subject. The changes in Singapore were regarded as an expression of 'Asian Values' and a post-colonial freedom to create a 'Singapore model of Criminal' (Hor 1997). The former Prime Minister, Lee Kuan Yew, said when opening the Singapore Academy of Law:

> In English doctrine, the rights of the individual must be the paramount consideration. We shook ourselves free from the confines of English norms which did not accord with the customs and values of Singapore society. In criminal law legislation, our priority is the security and well-being of law-abiding citizens rather than the rights of the criminal to be protected from incriminating evidence.
>
> (31 August 1990, cited in Hor 1997:66)

Leng (2001c:132) argues that the CJPOA 'represents a re-negotiation of the relationship between citizen and state' but it was not a one-off deal. The arguments of principle that were made against the provisions, set out in Chapter 1, of themselves, proved insufficient to resist the changes. It is still, however, instructive to consider the effects of the CJPOA against these claims. The right of silence was not solely a protective measure. It was also a practical expression of the principle that it is for the prosecution to discharge the burden of proof, without assistance from the accused. The CJPOA provisions sit uneasily with the presumption of innocence, in some cases making it easier for the Crown to discharge the burden of proof. Ashworth (2006:243) explains that the presumption of innocence operates at the criminal trial (where the prosecution bears the burden of proving guilt beyond reasonable doubt) but European human rights law also supports a 'wider, sense of the presumption of innocence: that pre-trial procedures should be conducted, so far as possible, as if the defendant were innocent'. It is this latter part that has changed under the CJPOA. The formal doctrine that the legal burden of proof rests throughout on the prosecution remains unchanged (Redmayne 1997:85; Jackson 2001a:145). This burden is eased, however, by the 'normative expectation' (Leng 2001a:246) created by these provisions, that the accused will cooperate with the investigation and trial process. This hinders the adversarial preparation of the defence and is part of the armoury of increasingly inquisitorial powers given to the police, evidence from which may then be deployed in an adversarial context (Cape 2003:369). It is argued the CJPOA goes beyond mere procedural change and distorts the adversarial system under which individuals are investigated and tried. Suspects' rights to a fair trial, now guaranteed formally under Article 6 of the ECHR, appear stronger than ever. In reality, however, the working practices of, and relationships between, suspects, the police and legal representatives have been distorted by this legislation, which has made it easier for the prosecution to discharge the burden of proof. In effect, for the first time, suspects are expected to cooperate actively with the investigation and trial process, an assumption of 'coerced participation' which runs contrary to the principle that it is for the prosecution to prove its case (Leng 2001c:128).

Distinctions based on the guilty and innocent imply that there is no value in protecting the guilty from self-incrimination (Redmayne 2007:221). Whilst Redmayne examines the harm done to personal integrity, this book develops this argument to look at the harm done to the integrity of the criminal justice system. There is a danger of 'mission creep' in these crime control policies whereby 'policies that were initially widely seen as radical intrusions into individual liberty and as profoundly illiberal became accepted in time as normal and then led to adoption of broader policies that at the outset would have been unimaginable' (Tonry 2010). The arguments against the introduction of section 34, however weighty, cannot without more be relied on to justify its repeal (Birch 1999:770). Practitioners qualifying since 1994 are likely to accept inferences as the norm and, until recently, there had been few academic articles on the subject. Clause 11 of the Liberal Democrats' draft Freedom Bill 2009 proposed the 'repeal of provisions which restrict the right to silence' but attracted little attention and the document was soon removed from the Liberal Democrats' website. The coalition government decided not to include it in the Protection of Freedoms Bill 2010–11 because the current arrangements 'strike the right balance' (email correspondence between the author and the Ministry of Justice, dated 1 August 2011).

There are possible signs of change. The police were formidable opponents of the right of silence, regarding it as a challenge to their authority and as an obstacle to solving crime. That influence appears to have declined, however, and a divide appears to have opened between the police, who have faced enormous cuts in their budgets, and the government. The 2015 general election was the first for over 30 years in which crime was not one of the main issues. The European Union has adopted a series of directives requiring that suspects be given information in a written 'Letter of Rights' of a number of procedural rights, including the right to remain silent.[5] The United Nations General Assembly passed a resolution[6] drawn from 'international standards and recognized good practices' (at para 6). Under Guideline 3, states are called upon to introduce measures to 'promptly inform every person detained, arrested, suspected or accused of, or charged with a criminal offence of his or her right to remain silent' (at para 43(a)). The person should be advised of his or her 'rights and the implications of waiving them in a clear and plain manner' (para 43(i)).

England led the world in establishing the right of silence as part of a fair trial – it then became a leader in its retrenchment. Moisidis (2008) argues that 'criminal discovery has gone from inquisitorial English origins, in which the accused was compelled to speak and bear witness against himself, to the accused being silenced by defence counsel as the prosecution was put to proof'. He argues that recent changes have moved back towards an 'accused speaks' model (Moisidis 2008:3). The CJPOA introduced the worrying innovation of the notion of a fulcrum in developing criminal justice systems, at which point rights should be ceded. This also has had a damaging effect on countries with less well developed suspects' rights. The re-balancing notion was clearly flawed but it suggests that new regimes would be better off setting out rights as fully as possible from the outset, as augmenting them later may give a sense that rights can be traded. One of the areas of concern is that the curtailment of the right of silence is seen as something that only a fully functioning justice system can undertake, rather than being a retrograde step. As a Malaysian scholar explained:

> In this modern era, the police no longer can afford to resort to harsh methods of interrogation to extract confessions. Advancement in the society calls for changes in the methods of police investigation. Curtailment of the right to silence of sophisticated criminals is certainly a move in the right direction.

To celebrate the improvements in the treatment of suspects should not mean having to concede the protections that helped shape that progression. Such an argument sets a dangerous precedent – it might equally be argued that the burden of proof could be shifted or reduced because it was laid on the prosecution to be discharged beyond reasonable doubt at a time when defendants were much less protected. However limited in

---

5 Directive 2012/13/EU of the European Parliament and of the Council of 22 May 2012 on the Right to Information in Criminal Proceedings, OJ L 142/1 (1 June 2012).

6 *United Nations Principles and Guidelines on Access to Legal Aid in Criminal Justice Systems.* A/Res/67/187. www.unodc.org/documents/justice-and-prison-reform/UN_principles_and_guidlines_on_access_to_legal_aid.pdf.

scope the CJPOA might appear, this encroachment did not just change a rule of evidence; it altered the very nature of the system. The right of silence had a distinguished history 'as a "bench mark" of British justice' (Jackson 1991); its curtailment became a benchmark for crime control measures across the globe.

Legislation: Criminal Justice and Public Order Act 1994 (as enacted)

Inferences from accused's silence

34 Effect of accused's failure to mention facts when questioned or charged

(1) Where, in any proceedings against a person for an offence, evidence is given that the accused—

    (a) at any time before he was charged with the offence, on being questioned under caution by a constable trying to discover whether or by whom the offence had been committed, failed to mention any fact relied on in his defence in those proceedings; or

    (b) on being charged with the offence or officially informed that he might be prosecuted for it, failed to mention any such fact,

being a fact which in the circumstances existing at the time the accused could reasonably have been expected to mention when so questioned, charged or informed, as the case may be, subsection (2) below applies.

(2) Where this subsection applies—

    (a) a magistrates' court, in deciding whether to grant an application for dismissal made by the accused under section 6 of the [1980 c. 43.] Magistrates' Courts Act 1980 (application for dismissal of charge in course of proceedings with a view to transfer for trial);

    (b) a judge, in deciding whether to grant an application made by the accused under—

        (i) section 6 of the [1987 c. 38.] Criminal Justice Act 1987 (application for dismissal of charge of serious fraud in respect of which notice of transfer has been given under section 4 of that Act); or

        (ii) paragraph 5 of Schedule 6 to the [1991 c. 53.] Criminal Justice Act 1991 (application for dismissal of charge of violent or sexual offence involving child in respect of which notice of transfer has been given under section 53 of that Act);

(c) the court, in determining whether there is a case to answer; and

(d) the court or jury, in determining whether the accused is guilty of the offence charged,

may draw such inferences from the failure as appear proper.

(3) Subject to any directions by the court, evidence tending to establish the failure may be given before or after evidence tending to establish the fact which the accused is alleged to have failed to mention.

(4) This section applies in relation to questioning by persons (other than constables) charged with the duty of investigating offences or charging offenders as it applies in relation to questioning by constables; and in subsection (1) above 'officially informed' means informed by a constable or any such person.

(5) This section does not—

(a) prejudice the admissibility in evidence of the silence or other reaction of the accused in the face of anything said in his presence relating to the conduct in respect of which he is charged, in so far as evidence thereof would be admissible apart from this section; or

(b) preclude the drawing of any inference from any such silence or other reaction of the accused which could properly be drawn apart from this section.

(6) This section does not apply in relation to a failure to mention a fact if the failure occurred before the commencement of this section.

(7) In relation to any time before the commencement of section 44 of this Act, this section shall have effect as if the reference in subsection (2) (a) to the grant of an application for dismissal was a reference to the committal of the accused for trial.

35 Effect of accused's silence at trial

(1) At the trial of any person who has attained the age of fourteen years for an offence, subsections (2) and (3) below apply unless—

(a) the accused's guilt is not in issue; or

(b) it appears to the court that the physical or mental condition of the accused makes it undesirable for him to give evidence;

but subsection (2) below does not apply if, at the conclusion of the evidence for the prosecution, his legal representative informs the court that the accused will give evidence or, where he is unrepresented, the court ascertains from him that he will give evidence.

(2) Where this subsection applies, the court shall, at the conclusion of the evidence for the prosecution, satisfy itself (in the case of proceedings on indictment, in the presence of the jury) that the accused is aware that the stage has been reached at which evidence can be given for the defence and that he can, if he wishes, give evidence and that, if he chooses not to give evidence, or having been sworn, without good cause refuses to answer any question, it will be permissible for the court or jury to draw such inferences as appear proper from his failure to give evidence or his refusal, without good cause, to answer any question.

(3) Where this subsection applies, the court or jury, in determining whether the accused is guilty of the offence charged, may draw such inferences as appear proper from the failure of the accused to give evidence or his refusal, without good cause, to answer any question.

(4) This section does not render the accused compellable to give evidence on his own behalf, and he shall accordingly not be guilty of contempt of court by reason of a failure to do so.

(5) For the purposes of this section a person who, having been sworn, refuses to answer any question shall be taken to do so without good cause unless—

(a) he is entitled to refuse to answer the question by virtue of any enactment, whenever passed or made, or on the ground of privilege; or
(b) the court in the exercise of its general discretion excuses him from answering it.

(6) Where the age of any person is material for the purposes of subsection (1) above, his age shall for those purposes be taken to be that which appears to the court to be his age.

(7) This section applies—

(a) in relation to proceedings on indictment for an offence, only if the person charged with the offence is arraigned on or after the commencement of this section;
(b) in relation to proceedings in a magistrates' court, only if the time when the court begins to receive evidence in the proceedings falls after the commencement of this section.

36 Effect of accused's failure or refusal to account for objects, substances or marks

(1) Where—

    (a) a person is arrested by a constable, and there is—

        (i) on his person; or

        (ii) in or on his clothing or footwear; or

        (iii) otherwise in his possession; or

        (iv) in any place in which he is at the time of his arrest, any object, substance or mark, or there is any mark on any such object; and

    (b) that or another constable investigating the case reasonably believes that the presence of the object, substance or mark may be attributable to the participation of the person arrested in the commission of an offence specified by the constable; and

    (c) the constable informs the person arrested that he so believes, and requests him to account for the presence of the object, substance or mark; and

    (d) the person fails or refuses to do so,

then if, in any proceedings against the person for the offence so specified, evidence of those matters is given, subsection (2) below applies.

(2) Where this subsection applies—

    (a) a magistrates' court, in deciding whether to grant an application for dismissal made by the accused under section 6 of the [1980 c. 43.] Magistrates' Courts Act 1980 (application for dismissal of charge in course of proceedings with a view to transfer for trial);

    (b) a judge, in deciding whether to grant an application made by the accused under—

        (i) section 6 of the [1987 c. 38.] Criminal Justice Act 1987 (application for dismissal of charge of serious fraud in respect of which notice of transfer has been given under section 4 of that Act); or

        (ii) paragraph 5 of Schedule 6 to the [1991 c. 53.] Criminal Justice Act 1991 (application for dismissal of charge of violent or sexual offence involving child in respect of which notice of transfer has been given under section 53 of that Act);

    (c) the court, in determining whether there is a case to answer; and

    (d) the court or jury, in determining whether the accused is guilty of the offence charged,

may draw such inferences from the failure or refusal as appear proper.

(3) Subsections (1) and (2) above apply to the condition of clothing or footwear as they apply to a substance or mark thereon.

(4) Subsections (1) and (2) above do not apply unless the accused was told in ordinary language by the constable when making the request mentioned in subsection (1)(c) above what the effect of this section would be if he failed or refused to comply with the request.

(5) This section applies in relation to officers of customs and excise as it applies in relation to constables.

(6) This section does not preclude the drawing of any inference from a failure or refusal of the accused to account for the presence of an object, substance or mark or from the condition of clothing or footwear which could properly be drawn apart from this section.

(7) This section does not apply in relation to a failure or refusal which occurred before the commencement of this section.

(8) In relation to any time before the commencement of section 44 of this Act, this section shall have effect as if the reference in subsection (2) (a) to the grant of an application for dismissal was a reference to the committal of the accused for trial.

37 Effect of accused's failure or refusal to account for presence at a particular place

(1) Where—

   (a) a person arrested by a constable was found by him at a place at or about the time the offence for which he was arrested is alleged to have been committed; and
   (b) that or another constable investigating the offence reasonably believes that the presence of the person at that place and at that time may be attributable to his participation in the commission of the offence; and
   (c) the constable informs the person that he so believes, and requests him to account for that presence; and
   (d) the person fails or refuses to do so,

   then if, in any proceedings against the person for the offence, evidence of those matters is given, subsection (2) below applies.

(2) Where this subsection applies—

   (a) a magistrates' court, in deciding whether to grant an application for dismissal made by the accused under section 6 of the [1980 c. 43.] Magistrates' Courts Act 1980 (application for dismissal of charge in course of proceedings with a view to transfer for trial);

(b) a judge, in deciding whether to grant an application made by the accused under—

    (i) section 6 of the [1987 c. 38.] Criminal Justice Act 1987 (application for dismissal of charge of serious fraud in respect of which notice of transfer has been given under section 4 of that Act); or

    (ii) paragraph 5 of Schedule 6 to the [1991 c. 53.] Criminal Justice Act 1991 (application for dismissal of charge of violent or sexual offence involving child in respect of which notice of transfer has been given under section 53 of that Act);

(c) the court, in determining whether there is a case to answer; and

(d) the court or jury, in determining whether the accused is guilty of the offence charged,

may draw such inferences from the failure or refusal as appear proper.

(3) Subsections (1) and (2) do not apply unless the accused was told in ordinary language by the constable when making the request mentioned in subsection (1)(c) above what the effect of this section would be if he failed or refused to comply with the request.

(4) This section applies in relation to officers of customs and excise as it applies in relation to constables.

(5) This section does not preclude the drawing of any inference from a failure or refusal of the accused to account for his presence at a place which could properly be drawn apart from this section.

(6) This section does not apply in relation to a failure or refusal which occurred before the commencement of this section.

(7) In relation to any time before the commencement of section 44 of this Act, this section shall have effect as if the reference in subsection (2) (a) to the grant of an application for dismissal was a reference to the committal of the accused for trial.

38 Interpretation and savings for sections 34, 35, 36 and 37

(1) In sections 34, 35, 36 and 37 of this Act—

(a) 'legal representative' means an authorised advocate or authorised litigator, as defined by section 119(1) of the [1990 c. 41.] Courts and Legal Services Act 1990; and

(b) 'place' includes any building or part of a building, any vehicle, vessel, aircraft or hovercraft and any other place whatsoever.

(2) In sections 34(2), 35(3), 36(2) and 37(2), references to an offence charged include references to any other offence of which the accused could lawfully be convicted on that charge.

(3) A person shall not have the proceedings against him transferred to the Crown Court for trial, have a case to answer or be convicted of an offence solely on an inference drawn from such a failure or refusal as is mentioned in section 34(2), 35(3), 36(2) or 37(2).

(4) A judge shall not refuse to grant such an application as is mentioned in section 34(2)(b), 36(2)(b) and 37(2)(b) solely on an inference drawn from such a failure as is mentioned in section 34(2), 36(2) or 37(2).

(5) Nothing in sections 34, 35, 36 or 37 prejudices the operation of a provision of any enactment which provides (in whatever words) that any answer or evidence given by a person in specified circumstances shall not be admissible in evidence against him or some other person in any proceedings or class of proceedings (however described, and whether civil or criminal).

   In this subsection, the reference to giving evidence is a reference to giving evidence in any manner, whether by furnishing information, making discovery, producing documents or otherwise.

(6) Nothing in sections 34, 35, 36 or 37 prejudices any power of a court, in any proceedings, to exclude evidence (whether by preventing questions being put or otherwise) at its discretion.

Methods

Region X is a large, predominantly urban, multi-racial area, outside London. The police requested that it was not identified. Locations within the region are described by the police as Operational Command Units (OCU). The region is divided into nine areas (shown by a letter), each containing two or three OCUs (distinguished by a number). Most interviews took place in A (a large town with a second tier Crown Court), B (the major city in the region with a first tier Crown Court) and C (a smaller city with a third tier Crown Court). I conducted 100 semi-structured interviews in total all but one between April and June 1999: 26 legal representatives, 26 prosecutors, 17 police officers, 16 barristers, 6 clerks to the justices, 5 lay magistrates, 2 stipendiary magistrates (now called District Judges (Magistrates' Court)) and 2 judges. Three hundred questionnaires were distributed by the police and 100 were completed. Each interviewee was allocated an identifying code. The first part of each code denotes the interviewee's job: a (P) indicates that the legal executive is a former police officer. Police officers are labelled according to rank, Detective Constable, Police Sergeant etc., as are Executive Officers (non-legally qualified CPS caseworkers), Principal, Branch or Senior Crown Prosecutors. The other titles are self-explanatory (Justice of the Peace/magistrate (JP), clerk (the legal adviser to lay magistrates), judge, stipe.). The second part of the label shows which operational command unit (the police divisions for the region) the person worked in (A–J). The number distinguishes the respondents. For legal representatives, it shows the firm that they work for and the final Roman numeral differentiates between respondents from the same firm. Thus Sol A/2/ii is the second solicitor interviewed from firm 2 in Town A. The questionnaire responses are prefixed with Questionnaire followed by the officer's rank, if known, and an identifying number (1–100). Despite repeated efforts, it was not possible to get permission from the police or CPS to conduct a follow-up study.

Solicitors and barristers were mostly approached by letter. I contacted most of the firms and chambers that did criminal work in Town A and a range from City B. Interviews were conducted at 6 of the 10 magistrates' courts. Most interviews were recorded and transcribed in full (officers at one police station did not want to be recorded, so handwritten notes were taken).

One of the police officers I interviewed offered to collate some statistics relating to the incidence of 'no comment' interviews. Recordings of police interviews with suspects are transcribed, often in précis, by civilian staff. The interviewing officer completes an accompanying form, highlighting the salient points in the interview that must be transcribed verbatim. One of the categories on this cover sheet is whether a 'no comment' answer has been given to a significant question. Over a two-month period, this officer arranged for the typists in his station to record the total number of interviews they transcribed and those in which the officers had indicated that there had been a significant refusal to answer questions. I requested that this be repeated at an area-wide level. This was done for a six-week period (between 14 June and 25 July 1999).

Bibliography

Agnew, S. E., Powell, M. B. and Snow, P. C. (2006), 'An examination of the questioning styles of police officers and caregivers when interviewing children with intellectual disabilities'. *Legal and Criminological Psychology* 11/1: 35.

Ainsworth, J. (2012), 'Why do innocent people confess to crimes they did not commit? A consideration of the linguistic and psychological characteristics of false confessions and forensic linguistic suggestions for reforms to prevent conviction of the innocent'. *International Conference on Law, Language and Discourse: Multiculturalism, Multimodality, and Multidimensionality*, plenary address, Hangzhou, China, April.

Ainsworth, P. (2002), *Psychology and Policing*. Cullompton: Willan.

Allen, M. J. and Cooper, S. (1995), 'Howard's way – a farewell to freedom'. *The Modern Law Review* 58/3: 25.

Allen, R. J. (1996), 'The Simpson Affair, reform of the criminal justice process, and Magic Bullets'. *Colorado Law Review* 67: 989.

Allen, R. J. and Mace, M. K. (2003), 'The self-incrimination clause explained and its future predicted'. *The Journal of Criminal Law and Criminology* 94/2: 50.

Alschuler, A. W. (1996), 'A peculiar privilege in historical perspective: The right to remain silent'. *Michigan Law Review* 94/8: 2625.

Amann, D. M. (1998), 'A whipsaw cuts both ways: The privilege against self-incrimination in an international context'. *UCLA Law Review* 45/5: 1201.

Amnesty International. (1993), *United Kingdom: Northern Ireland: The Right of Silence.* 1 February 1993, Index number: EUR 45/001/1993.

Amnesty International. (1995), *United Kingdom: Summary of Human Rights Concerns (August 1995)*. Amnesty International report: EUR 45/006/1994. London: Amnesty International.

Anon. (1990), 'Detectives taught to read suspect's body language'. *Guardian*, 19 June, p. 4.

Anon. (2008), 'Case comment. Right to silence; confessions – Canada'. *Criminal Law Review* 3: 248.

Anscombe, G. E. M. and Feldman, J. (1972), 'On the nature of justice in a trial'. *Analysis* 33/2: 33.

Archbold. (2016), *Archbold Magistrates' Courts Criminal Practice 2016*. London: Sweet & Maxwell.

Arlidge, J. (1994), 'Scottish review backs suspect's right to silence'. *The Independent*, 28 October.

Ashworth, A. (1988), 'Criminal justice and the criminal process'. *British Journal of Criminology* 28/2: 12.

Ashworth, A. (1989), 'Curtailing the right of silence'. *Criminal Law Review* October: 677.

Ashworth, A. (1998), *The Criminal Process: An Evaluative Study.* Oxford: Clarendon Press.

Ashworth, A. (2006), 'Four threats to the presumption of innocence'. *International Journal of Evidence & Proof* 10: 37.

Asmal, K. (1983), 'Dublin letter: A squalid extension of southern police powers'. *Fortnight* December: 7.

Association of Chief Police Officers. (1993), *Right to Silence Briefing Paper.* London: ACPO.

Auburn, T., Drake, S. and Willig, C. (1995), ' "You punched him, didn't you?": Versions of violence in accusatory interviews'. *Discourse & Society* 6/3: 353.

Auld, The Right Honourable Lord Justice. (2001), *Review of the Criminal Courts of England and Wales Report.* London: The Stationery Office.

Australian Law Reform Commission. (1975), *Criminal Investigation: An Interim Report.* Canberra: Australian Government Publishing Service.

Australian Law Reform Commission. (1987), *Evidence, Draft Evidence Bill.* Canberra: Australian Law Reform Commission.

Baksi C. (2014), 'Criminal lawyers warn of "advice deserts" as they stage walk-out'. *The Law Society Gazette,* 7 March.

Baldwin, J. (1990), 'Police interviews on tape'. *New Law Journal* 140: 2.

Baldwin, J. (1991), 'Summarising tape recordings of police interviews'. *Criminal Law Review.* 671.

Baldwin, J. (1992a), 'Legal advice in the police station'. *New Law Journal* 142: 1762.

Baldwin, J. (1992b), 'Preparing the record of taped interview', *Royal Commission on Criminal Justice Research Study No. 2.* London: HMSO.

Baldwin, J. (1992c), 'Video taping police interviews with suspects: A national evaluation'. *Police Research Series Paper No. 1.* London: Home Office Police Department.

Baldwin, J. (1993), 'The role of legal representatives at the police station', *Royal Commission on Criminal Justice Research Study.* London: HMSO.

Baldwin, J. and Maloney, T. (1993), *Supervision of Police Investigation in Serious Criminal Cases.* Royal Commission on Criminal Justice, Research Study No. 4. London: HMSO.

Baldwin, J. and McConville, M. (1979), *Jury Trials.* Oxford: Clarendon Press.

Bandalli, S. (1998), 'Abolition of the presumption of doli incapax and the criminalisation of children'. *Howard Journal of Criminal Justice* 37/2: 114.

Bassiouni, M. C. (1992–93), 'Human rights in the context of criminal justice: Identifying international procedural protections in national constitutions'. *Duke Journal of Comparative and International Law* 3/2: 235.

Baum, L. M. (2001), 'Pursuing justice in a climate of moral outrage: An evaluation of the rights of the accused in the Rome Statute of the International Criminal Court'. *Wisconsin International Law Journal* 19/2: 33.

BBC News. (2005), 'Prime Minister Tony Blair's keynote speech to the Labour Party's 2005 conference in Brighton'. *BBC News,* 27 September. http://news.bbc.co.uk/1/hi/uk_politics/4287370.stm.

BBC Radio 4. (2014), 'From Inside: The Guildford Four'. *Archive on 4,* BBC Radio 4 broadcast, 4 October.

Bedward, J. and Baldwin, J. (1991), 'Summarising tape recordings of police interviews'. *Criminal Law Review* September: 671.

Behrens, J. L. (2009), 'When law fails: Making sense of miscarriages of justice'. *Law Library Journal* 101/3: 391.

Belloni, F. and Hodgson, J. (2000), *Criminal Injustice: An Evaluation of the Criminal Justice Process in Britain*. Basingstoke: Macmillan.

Bennett, His Honour Judge HG, QC, Chairman. (1978–79), *Report of the Committee of Inquiry into Police Interrogation Procedures in Northern Ireland*. London: HMSO.

Bennett, T. (2000), *Drug Use Among Arrestees*. Home Office Research, Development and Statistics Directorate Research Findings No. 70. London: Home Office.

Bennun, M. E. (1973), 'Defendants who fail to give evidence'. *The Modern Law Review* 36/5: 554.

Benson, D. and Jordan, A. (2011), 'What have we learned from policy transfer research? Dolowitz and Marsh revisited'. *Political Studies Review* 9/3: 13.

Bentham, J. (1825), *A Treaty on Judicial Evidence*, ed. E. Dumont. London: Baldwin, Craddock and Joy.

Bentley, E. and US Congress, House Committee on Un-American Activities. (1971), *Thirty Years of Treason: Excerpts from Hearings Before the House Committee on Un-American Activities, 1938–1968*. New York: Viking Press.

Berg, C. (2013), 'Anything you don't say may be used against you'. *ABC Opinion*, 26 March.

Berger, M. (1994), 'Of policy, politics, and Parliament: The legislative rewriting of the British right to silence'. *American Journal of Criminal Law* 22: 391.

Berger, M. (1999), 'Reforming confession law British style: A decade of experience with adverse inferences from silence'. *Columbia Human Rights Law Review* 31: 243.

Berger, M. (2006), 'Europeanizing self-incrimination: The right to remain silent in the European Court of Human Rights'. *Columbia Journal of European Law* 12: 340.

Berger, M. (2012), 'The right to silence in the Hague International Criminal Courts'. *University of San Francisco Law Review* 47/1: 54.

Beune, K., Giebels, E. and Sanders, K. (2009), 'Are you talking to me? Influencing behaviour and culture in police interviews'. *Psychology Crime & Law* 15/7: 597.

Bevins, A. (1993), 'Crime rate shows tenfold increase in past 40 years'. *The Independent*, 11 February.

Bingham, A., Cochran, J. K., Boots, D. P. and Heide, K. M. (2013), 'Public support for preventive/corrective remedies against miscarriages of justice in capital cases'. *Justice Quarterly* 30/4: 594.

Birch, D. (1997), 'Case comment. Appellant advised by solicitor not to comment in interview – no evidence before jury as to reasons for solicitor's advice'. *Criminal Law Review* June: 449.

Birch, D. (1999), 'Suffering in silence: A cost-benefit analysis of section 34 of the Criminal Justice and Public Order Act 1994'. *Criminal Law Review* October: 769.

Birch, D. (2003), Case comment. Evidence: Criminal Justice and Public Order Act 1994 s.34 – silence of defendant at interview. *Criminal Law Review* June: 405.

Björk, M. (2008), 'Fighting cynicism: Some reflections on self-motivation in police work'. *Police Quarterly* 11/1: 88.

Blair, C. (2003), 'Miranda and the right to silence in England'. *Tulsa Journal of Comparative & International Law* 11/1: 1.

Blake, M. and Ashworth, A. (1996), 'The presumption of innocence in English criminal law'. *Criminal Law Review* May: 306.

Blake, M. and Ashworth, A. (2004), 'Ethics and the criminal defence lawyer'. *Legal Ethics* 7/2: 23.

Blake, N. (1990), 'The case for retention', in S. Greer and R. Morgan, eds, *The Right to Silence Debate*. Bristol: Bristol and Bath Centre for Criminal Justice.

Blumenson, E. (2006), 'The challenge of a global standard of justice: Peace, pluralism, and punishment at the International Criminal Court'. *Columbia Journal of Transnational Law* 44/3: 801.

Bottomley, A. K., Coleman, C., Dixon, D., Gill, M. and Wall, D. (1991), *The Impact of PACE: Policing in a Northern Force*. Hull: Centre for Criminology and Criminal Justice.

Bottoms, A. E. (1995), 'Philosophy and politics of punishment and sentencing', in C. Clarkson and R. Morgan, eds, *The Politics of Sentencing Reform*. Oxford: Oxford University Press.

Box, S. (1987), *Recession, Crime and Unemployment*. London: Macmillan.

Boyle, J. (1993), 'Crime does not pay'. *Solicitors Journal* 137/48: 1279.

Bridges, L. (2007), *Evaluation of the Public Defender Service in England and Wales/by Lee Bridges [et al.]; with the Assistance of Alan Paterson [et al.]*. London: The Stationery Office.

Bridges, L. (2010), 'Toward a culture of complacency – criminal justice under New Labour'. *Criminal Justice Matters* 79/1: 22.

Bridges, L. and Bunyan, T. (1983), 'Britain's new urban policing strategy: The police and criminal evidence bill in context'. *Journal of Law and Society* 10/1: 85.

Bridges, L. and Cape, E. (2008), *CDS Direct: Flying in the Face of Evidence*. London: Centre for Crime and Justice Studies.

Bridges, L. and Choongh, S. (1998), *Improving Police Station Legal Advice*. London: Law Society and Legal Aid Board, Research Study No. 31.

Bridges, L. and McConville, M. (1994), 'Keeping faith with their own convictions: The Royal Commission on Criminal Justice'. *The Modern Law Review* 57/1: 75.

Bridges, L., Cape, E., Fenn, P., Mitchell, A., Moorhead R. and Sherr, A. (2007), *Evaluation of the Public Defender Service in England and Wales*. London: Legal Services Commission.

Bridges, L., Suffrin, B., Whetton, J. and White, R. (1975), *Legal Services in Birmingham*. Birmingham: University of Birmingham, Institute of Judicial Administration.

British Academy of Forensic Sciences/Criminal Bar Association. (1999), *Survey of the Practising Independent Bar into the Operation in Practice of the Criminal Procedure and Investigations Act 1996 Disclosure Provisions*. London: BAFS.

Brooks, N. (1978), 'The Law Reform Commission of Canada's Evidence Code'. *Osgoode Hall Law Journal* 16/2: 80.

Brown, D. (1989), *Detention at the Police Station under the Police and Criminal Evidence Act 1984*. Research study. London: Home Office.

Brown, D. (1991), *Investigating Burglary: The Effects of PACE*. Home Office Research Study No. 123. London: HMSO.

Brown, D. (1994), 'The incidence of right of silence in police interviews: The research evidence reviewed'. *Research Bulletin* 35: 57. London: Home Office Research and Statistics Department.

Brown, D. (1997), *PACE Ten Years On: A Review of the Research.* Home Office Research Study No. 155. London: HMSO.

Brown, D., Ellis, T. and Larcombe, K. (1992), *Changing the Code: Police Detention under the Revised PACE Codes of Practice.* Home Office Research Study No. 129. London: Home Office.

Brown-Blake, C. and Chambers, P. (2007), 'The Jamaican Creole speaker in the UK criminal justice system'. *International Journal of Speech Language and the Law* 14/2: 269.

Bruce, D., Savage, K. and De Waal, J. (2000), 'A duty to answer questions: The police, the Independent Complaints Directorate and the right to remain silent'. *South African Journal on Human Rights* 16: 71.

Bruinooge, J. P. (1974), 'The impact of divergent evidentiary standards on the exercise of foreign criminal jurisdiction in the United Kingdom'. *The Air Force Law Review* 16: 32.

Bryan, I. (1997), 'Shifting images: Police–suspect encounters during custodial interrogations'. *Legal Studies* 17/2: 215.

Bucke, T. and Brown, D. (1997), *In Police Custody: Police Powers and Suspects' Rights under the Revised PACE Codes of Practice.* Home Office Research Study No. 174. London: Home Office.

Bucke, T., Street, R. and Brown, D. (2000), *Right of Silence: The Impact of the Criminal Justice and Public Order Act 1994.* Home Office Research Study 199. London: Home Office.

Bush, K. (2008), 'When law fails: Making sense of miscarriages of justice'. *Library Journal* 133/20: 143.

Börk, M. (2008), 'Fighting cynicism: Some reflections on self-motivation in police work'. *Police Quarterly* 11/1: 88.

Callen, C. R., Doran, S. and Jackson, J. D. (2009), 'Evidence during the ten years of ICE'. *International Commentary on Evidence* 6/2: 1.

Campbell, L. (2008), 'Criminal justice and penal populism in Ireland'. *Legal Studies* 28/4: 559.

Campbell, L. (2010), 'Responding to gun crime in Ireland'. *British Journal of Criminology* 50/3: 414.

Campeau, H. (2015), ' "Police culture" at work: Making sense of police oversight'. *British Journal of Criminology* 55/4: 669.

Cape, E. (1997), 'Sidelining defence lawyers: Police station advice after Condron'. *The International Journal of Evidence and Proof* 1: 386.

Cape, E. (1999), 'Detention without charge: What does "sufficient evidence to charge" mean?' *Criminal Law Review* November: 874.

Cape, E. (2003), 'The revised PACE Codes of Practice'. *Criminal Law Review* June: 355.

Cape, E. (2006), 'Rebalancing the criminal justice process: Ethical challenges for criminal defence lawyers'. *Legal Ethics* 9/1: 24.

Cape, E. and Ardill, N. (2004), 'A rebalancing act?'. *Criminal Justice Matters* 57/1: 16.

Cape, E. and Luqmani, J. (1995), *Defending Suspects at Police Stations: The Practitioner's Guide to Advice and Representation.* London: Legal Action Group.

Cape, E. and Maastrichts Europees Instituut Voor Transnationaal Rechtswetenschappelijk, O. (2010), *Effective Criminal Defence in Europe: Executive Summary and Recommendations.* Antwerp, Oxford, Portland: Intersentia.

Cape, E. and Webb, J. (2006), 'The ethics of criminal justice professionals in an era of change'. *Legal Ethics* 9/1: 5.

Cape, E. and Young, R. (2008), *Regulating Policing: The Police and Criminal Evidence Act 1984 Past, Present and Future.* London: Bloomsbury.

Carlisle, M. (1972), 'The Criminal Law Revision Committee's report on evidence'. *Journal of the Society of Public Teachers of Law* 12: 224.

Carloway, Lord. (2011), *The Carloway Review: Report and Recommendations.* Edinburgh: The Scottish Government.

Carter, E. (2011), *Analysing Police Interviews: Laughter, Confessions and the Tape.* London: Bloomsbury.

Caruso, D. (2012), 'Return of the wrongly convicted: The test for post-conviction executive references in Australia', in A. Sarat, ed., *Studies in Law, Politics, and Society, Vol. 57.* Bingley: Emerald Insight.

Carvel, J. and Hearst, D. (1988), 'King ends the right to silence', *Guardian*, 21 October, p. 1.

Cassell, P. G. (1995), 'All benefits, no costs: The grand illusion of Miranda's defenders'. *Northwestern University Law Review* 90: 1084.

Cassell, P. G. (1999–2000), 'The statute that time forgot: 18 U.S.C. 3501 and the overhauling of Miranda'. *Iowa Law Review* 85/1: 175.

Cassell, P. G. and Fowles, R. (1997), 'Handcuffing the cops: A thirty-year perspective on Miranda's harmful effects on law'. *Stanford Law Review* 50: 1055.

Castles, A. C. (1977), 'Letter from Australia'. *Hong Kong Law Journal* 7: 100.

Cavanaugh, K. A. (2002), 'Emergency rule, normalcy exception: The erosion of the right to silence in the United Kingdom'. *Cornell International Law Journal* 35/3: 491.

Chakrabarti, S. (2008), 'A thinning blue line? Police independence and the rule of law'. *Policing* 2/3: 367.

Chan, J. (2008), 'Police culture: A brief history of a concept'. in T. Anthony and C. Cunneen, eds, *The Critical Criminology Companion.* Sydney: Hawkins Press.

Charman, S. and Savage, S. P. (2009), 'Mothers for justice? Gender and campaigns against miscarriages of justice'. *British Journal of Criminology* 49/6: 900.

Chartres, J. (1975), 'Six Birmingham Bomb Murderers Get Life Sentences'. *The Times*, 16 August.

Chase, C. A. (1995), 'Hearing the sounds of silence in criminal trials: A look at recent British law reforms with an eye toward reforming the American criminal justice system'. *University of Kansas Law Review* 44: 929.

Chaulk, S. J., Eastwood, J. and Snook, B. (2014), 'Measuring and predicting police caution comprehension in adult offenders'. *Canadian Journal of Criminology and Criminal Justice* 56/3: 323.

Chiu, J. W. K. (2009), 'Criminal interrogation and the right to remain silent: A study of the Hong Kong customs service'. *International Journal of Police Science & Management* 11/2: 217.

Choo, A. L. T. (2005), *Evidence.* New York: Oxford University Press.

Choo, A. L. T. (2013), *The Privilege Against Self-Incrimination and Criminal Justice.* London: Bloomsbury.

Choo, A. L. T. (2015), *Evidence*, 4th ed. New York: Oxford University Press.

Choo, A. L. T. and Jennings A. F. (2003), 'Silence on legal advice revisited: *R v Howell*'. *The International Journal of Evidence and Proof* 7: 185.

Choo, A. L. T. and Mellors, M. (1995), 'Undercover police operations and what the suspect said (or didn't say)', in M. Allen, ed., *Web Journal of Current Legal Issues*. London: Blackstone.

Choongh, S. (1997), *Policing as Social Discipline*. Oxford: Clarendon Press.

Choongh, S. (1998), 'Policing the dross: A social disciplinary model of policing'. *British Journal of Criminology* 38/4: 623.

Christian, L. (1983), *Policing by Coercion*. London: GLC Police Committee Support Unit.

Christie, N. (2000), *Crime Control as Industry*, 3rd ed. London: Routledge.

Clare, I. C. H. and Gudjonsson, G. H. (1995), 'The vulnerability of suspects with intellectual disabilities during police interviews: A review and experimental study of decision-making'. *Mental Handicap Research* 8: 110.

Clare, I. C. H., Gudjonsson, G. H. and Harari, P. M. (1998), 'Understanding of the current police caution (England and Wales)'. *Journal of Community & Applied Social Psychology* 8/5: 323.

Clarke, D. and Milne, R. (2001), *National Evaluation of the PEACE Investigative Interviewing Scheme*. Police Research Award Scheme Report. London: Home Office.

Cleary, H. M. D. (2014), 'Police interviewing and interrogation of juvenile suspects: A descriptive examination of actual cases'. *Law and Human Behavior* 38/3: 271.

Coldrey, J. (1991), 'The right to silence: Should it be curtailed or abolished?'. *Common Law World Review* 20: 51.

Cole, S. A. (2009), 'Cultural consequences of miscarriages of justice'. *Behavioral Sciences & the Law* 27/3: 431.

Coles, J. (1990a), 'Court frees Winchester Three: King statement prejudiced trial judge rules'. *Guardian*, 28 April, p. 1.

Coles, J. (1990b), 'Media coverage shown in court'. *Guardian*, 28 April, p. 4.

Colville Report. (1990), *Review of the Northern Ireland (Emergency Provisions) Acts 1978 and 1987*. Cm 1115. London: HMSO.

Committee for the Prevention of Torture or Degrading Treatment or Punishment. (1994), *Report to the Government of the United Kingdom on the Visit to Northern Ireland Carried Out by the European Committee for the Prevention of Torture or Degrading Treatment or Punishment on its Visit to Northern Ireland from 20–29 July, 1993*. London: Committee for the Prevention of Torture (CPT).

Cooke, M. (1995), 'Understood by all concerned? Anglo/Aboriginal legal translation'. *Translation and the Law, Amsterdam/Philadelphia: John Benjamins* 37: 66.

Cordner, S. (2012), 'Forensic pathology and miscarriages of justice'. *Forensic Science Medicine and Pathology* 8/3: 316.

Cotterill, J. (2005), '"You do not have the right to say anything": Instructing the jury on the defendant's right to silence in the English justice system'. *Multilingua – Journal of Cross-Cultural and Interlanguage Communication*, 24: 7.

Council of Europe, Convention on Human Rights. (1970), *Report of the Committee of Experts on Human Rights to the Committee of Ministers on the Problems Arising from the Co-existence of the UN Covenants on Human Rights and the European Convention on Human Rights*. Strasbourg: Council of Europe.

Coyle, I. R. (2011), 'The cogency of risk assessments'. *Psychiatry Psychology and Law* 18/2: 270.

Crank, J. P. (1998), *Understanding Police Culture*. Cincinnati: Anderson Publishing.

Creta, V. M. (1997–98), 'The search for justice in the former Yugoslavia and beyond: Analyzing the rights of the accused under the statute and the rules of procedure and evidence of the International Criminal Tribunal for the Former Yugoslavia'. *Houston Journal of International Law* 20/2: 38.

Criminal Law and Penal Methods Reform Committee of South Australia. (1974), *Second Report: Criminal Investigations*, Chairman: Dame R. Mitchell. Adelaide: Government Printer.

Criminal Law Revision Committee. (1972), *Eleventh Report: Evidence (General)* (Cmnd. 4991). London: HMSO.

Croquet, N. A. J. (2011), 'The International Criminal Court and the treatment of defence rights: A mirror of the European Court of Human Rights jurisprudence?'. *Human Rights Law Review* 11: 91.

Cross, R. (1974), 'An attempt to update the law of evidence: The 11th report of the English Criminal Law Revision Committee'. *Israel Law Review* 9: 1.

Crowder, P. and Lawrence, I. (1972), *The Conviction of the Guilty*. London: Conservative Political Centre.

Cummins, I. (2011), ' "The other side of silence": The role of the appropriate adult post-Bradley'. *Ethics and Social Welfare* 5/3: 7.

Daly, Y. (2007), 'Silence and solicitors: Lessons learned from England and Wales'. *Irish Criminal Law Journal* 17/2: 2.

Daly, Y. M. (2014), 'The right to silence: Inferences and interference'. *Australian and New Zealand Journal of Criminology* 47/1: 59.

Damaška, M. R. (1973), 'Evidentiary barriers to conviction and two models of criminal procedure: A comparative study'. *Faculty Scholarship Series*. Paper 1591. http://digitalcommons.law.yale.edu/fss_papers/1591.

Davies, G. and Griffiths, L. (2008), 'Eyewitness identification and the English courts: A century of trial and error'. *Psychiatry, Psychology and Law* 15/3: 435.

DeFrancia, C. (2001), 'Due process in international criminal courts: Why procedure matters'. *Virginia Law Review* 87/7: 1381.

Denning, L. (1987), 'Free justice from silence'. *The Sunday Times*, 20 September, p. 31.

Dennis, I. (1993), 'Miscarriages of justice and the law of confessions: Evidentiary issues and solutions'. *Public Law* Summer: 291.

Dennis, I. (1995), 'The Criminal Justice and Public Order Act 1994: The evidence provisions'. *Criminal Law Review* January: 4.

Dennis, I. (1997), 'Rectitude rights and legitimacy: Reassessing and reforming the privilege against self-incrimination in English law'. *Israel Law Review* 31: 24.

Dennis, I. (2002), 'Silence in the police station: The marginalisation of section 34'. *Criminal Law Review* January: 25.

Dennis, I. (2009), 'Instrumental protection, human right or functional necessity? Reassessing the privilege against self-incrimination'. *The Cambridge Law Journal* 54/2: 342.

Dennis, I. (2013), *The Law of Evidence*, 5th ed. London: Thomson Sweet & Maxwell).

Denyer, R. L. (2010), 'The changing role of the judge in the criminal process'. *International Journal of Evidence and Proof* 14/2: 96.

Devlin, P. (1986), *Easing the Passing: The Trial of Doctor John Bodkin Adams*. London: Faber.

Dick, P. (2006), 'The psychological contract and the transition from full to part-time police work'. *Journal of Organizational Behavior* 27/1: 37.

Dick, P. and Hyde, R. (2006), 'Line manager involvement in work-life balance and career development: Can't manage, won't manage?'. *British Journal of Guidance & Counselling* 34/3: 345.

Dickson, B. (1984), *The Legal System of Northern Ireland*. Belfast: SLS Legal.

Dillon, M. (1990), *The Dirty War*. London: Hutchinson.

Dixon, D. (1991a), 'Politics, research and symbolism in criminal justice: The right to silence and the Police and Criminal Evidence Act 1984'. *Anglo-American Law Review* 20/1: 23.

Dixon, D. (1991b), 'Common sense, legal advice and the right to silence'. *Public Law* 2: 22.

Dixon, D. (1992), 'Legal regulation and policing practice'. *Social and Legal Studies* 1/4: 27.

Dixon, D. (1997), *Law in Policing*. Oxford: Clarendon Press.

Dixon, D. (1999), 'Police investigative procedures: Changing legal and political contexts of policing practices', in C. Walker and K. Starmer, eds, *Miscarriages of Justice: A Review of Justice in Error*. London: Blackstone.

Dixon, D. (2010), 'Questioning suspects: A comparative perspective'. *Journal of Contemporary Criminal Justice* 26/4: 426.

Dixon, D., Bottomley, A. K., Coleman, C., Gill, M. and Wall, D. (1989), 'Reality and rules in the construction and regulation of police suspicion'. *International Journal of the Sociology of Law* 17/2: 21.

Dixon, D., Bottomley, K., Coleman, C., Gill, M. and Wall, D. (1990), 'Safeguarding the rights of suspects in police custody'. *Policing and Society* 1/2: 115.

Dobinson, I. (1997), 'What impact has the return to Chinese sovereignty had on Hong Kong's criminal justice system'. *Current Issues in Criminal Justice* 9: 180.

Dolowitz, D. P. (2000), *Policy Transfer and British Social Policy: Learning from the USA?* Maidenhead: Open University Press.

Dolowitz, D. P. (2003), 'A policy-maker's guide to policy transfer'. *The Political Quarterly* 74/1: 10.

Doran, S., Jackson, J. D. and Seigel, M. L. (1995), 'Rethinking adversariness on nonjury criminal trials'. *American Journal of Criminal Law* 23: 1.

Dressler, J. (2000), 'Some brief thoughts (mostly negative) about "Bad Samaritan" laws'. *Santa Clara Law Review* 40/4: 18.

Drew, K. J. (1989), 'Criminal investigation – the police perspective'. *Current Issues in Criminal Justice* 1: 46.

Du Plessis, J. R. (1988), 'An inquisitorial system in practice – visits to German criminal courts'. *South African Law Journal* 105: 305.

Duff, P. (2009), 'Straddling two worlds: Reflections of a retired criminal cases review commissioner'. *Modern Law Review* 72/5: 693.

Dyer, C. (1990a), 'Lane "ruled himself out of appeal"'. *Guardian*, 28 April, p. 4.

Dyer, C. (1990b), 'Police forced to question their interviewing tactics'. *Guardian*, 19 June, p. 4.

Dyer, C. (2008), 'Southall's secret case files show no reason to suspect miscarriages of justice'. *BMJ (Clinical Research ed.)* 337: a987.

Eady, D. (2008), 'Re-thinking miscarriages of justice: Beyond the tip of the iceberg'. *Criminology & Criminal Justice* 8/2: 227.

Easton, S. (1998a), 'Legal advice, common sense and the right to silence'. *International Journal of Evidence & Proof* 2: 109.

Easton, S. (1998b), *The Case for the Right to Silence*. Farnham: Ashgate.

Easton, S. (1991), *The Right to Silence*. Aldershot: Avebury.

Easton, S. (2014), *Silence and Confessions : The Suspect as the Source of Evidence*. Basingstoke: Palgrave MacMillan.

Eastwood, J. and Snook, B. (2010), 'Comprehending Canadian police cautions: Are the rights to silence and legal counsel understandable?'. *Behavioral Sciences & the Law* 28/3: 366.

Eastwood, J. and Snook, B. (2012), 'The effect of listenability factors on the comprehension of police cautions'. *Law and Human Behavior* 36/3: 177.

Eastwood, J., Snook, B. and Chaulk, S. J. (2010), 'Measuring reading complexity and listening comprehension of Canadian police cautions'. *Criminal Justice and Behavior* 37/4: 453.

Ede, R. and Shepherd, E. (1997), *Active Defence: A Solicitor's Guide to Police and Defence Investigation and Prosecution and Defence Disclosure in Criminal Cases*. London: Law Society.

Edgerton, G. (1996), 'Quelling the "oxygen of publicity": British broadcasting and "the troubles" during the Thatcher years'. *Journal of Popular Culture* 30/1: 115.

Edwards, A. (1995), 'Inferences from silence: More trouble than they're worth'. *Archbold News* 5: 6.

Edwards, D. (2008), 'Intentionality and mens rea in police interrogations: The production of actions as crimes'. *Intercultural Pragmatics*. 5/2: 177.

Edwards, D. and Stokoe, E. (2011), '"You don't have to answer": Lawyers' contributions in police interrogations of suspects'. *Research on Language & Social Interaction* 44/1: 21.

Egharevba, S. (2006), 'African immigrants' perception of police in Finland: Is it based on the discourse of race or culture?'. *International Journal of the Sociology of Law* 34/1: 42.

Eisenhardt, K. M. and Graebner, M. E. (2007), 'Theory building from cases: Opportunities and challenges'. *Academy of Management Journal* 50/1: 25.

Elks, L. (2008), *Righting Miscarriages of Justice?: Ten Years of the Criminal Cases Review Commission*. London: JUSTICE.

Ericson, R. V. (2007), 'Rules in policing – five perspectives'. *Theoretical Criminology* 11/3: 367.

Etter, B. (2013), 'The contribution of forensic science to miscarriage of justice cases'. *Australian Journal of Forensic Sciences* 45/4: 368.

Evans, P. (1972), 'Criminal law revision proposals received with heavy criticism'. *The Times*, 28 June, p. 1.

Evans, R. (1993), *The Conduct of Police Interviews with Juveniles*. Royal Commission on Criminal Justice Research Study No. 8. London: HMSO.

Ewing, K. (2010), *Bonfire of the Liberties: New Labour, Human Rights, and the Rule of Law*. Oxford: Oxford University Press.

Falvey, J. L. J. (1995–96), 'United Nations justice or military justice: Which is the oxymoron? An analysis of the rules of procedure and evidence of the International Tribunal for the Former Yugoslavia'. *Fordham International Law Journal* 19: 54.

Fennell, P. W. H. (1994), 'Mentally disordered suspects in the criminal justice system'. *Journal of Law and Society* 21/1: 57.

Fenner, S., Gudjonsson, G. H. and Clare, I. C. H. (2002), 'Understanding of the current police caution (England and Wales) among suspects in police detention'. *Journal of Community & Applied Social Psychology* 12/2: 83.

Fenwick, H. (1995a), 'Curtailing the right to silence: Access to legal advice and section 78'. *Criminal Law Review* February: 132.

Fenwick, H. (1995b), 'Evading access to legal advice'. *Journal of Criminal Law* 59: 198.

Ferguson, P. R. (2011), 'Repercussions of the Cadder case: The ECHR's fair trial provisions and Scottish criminal procedure'. *Criminal Law Review* October: 743.

Field, S. and Thomas, P. A. (1994), 'Introduction: Justice and efficiency? The Royal Commission on Criminal Justice'. *Journal of Law and Society* 21/1: 1.

Findlay, M. (1995), 'International rights and Australian adaptations: Recent developments in criminal investigation'. *Sydney Law Review* 17: 278.

Findlay, M. (2001), 'Juror comprehension and complexity'. *British Journal of Criminology* 41/1: 21.

Fisher, H. (1977), *Fisher Report*. London: The Stationery Office.

Fitzpatrick, B. and Taylor, N. (2001), 'Human rights and the discretionary exclusion of evidence'. *Journal of Criminal Law* 65: 349.

Foote, D. H. (1986), 'Prosecutorial discretion in Japan: A response'. *UCLA Pacific Basin Law Journal* 5: 96.

Foote, D. H. (1991), 'Confessions and the right to silence in Japan'. *Georgia Journal of International and Comparative Law* 21: 415.

Forrester, M. and Ramsden, C. H. (2000), 'Discursive ethnomethodology: Analysing power and resistance in talk'. *Psychology, Crime & Law* 6/4: 281.

Fox, D. (2009), 'The right to silence as protecting mental control'. *Akron Law Review* 42: 763.

Fox, D. (2011), 'The right to silence protects mental control'. in M. Freeman, ed., *Law and Neuroscience: Current Legal Issues*. Oxford: Oxford University Press.

Friend, A. and Metcalf, A. (1981), *Slump City: The Politics of Mass Unemployment*. London: Pluto Press.

Fulton, K. (2006), *Unsung Hero: How I Saved Dozens of Lives as a Secret Agent Inside the IRA*. London: John Blake Publishing Ltd.

Garland, D. (2001), *The Culture of Control: Crime and Social Order in Contemporary Society*. Oxford: Oxford University Press.

Garrett, B. L. (2010), 'The substance of false confessions'. *Stanford Law Review* 62/4: 1051.

George, B. J. (1968), 'Right of Silence in Japanese Law'. *Washington Law Review* 43/5: 1147.

Gerstein, R. S. (1979), 'The self-incrimination debate in Great Britain'. *The American Journal of Comparative Law* 27/1: 81.

Gibb, F. (1987), 'New DPP faces uphill fight'. *The Times*, 2 October, p. 5.

Gibbons, T. (1985), 'The conditions of detention and questioning by the police'. *Criminal Law Review* September: 558.

Glasbeek, H. J. and Prentice, D. D. (1968), 'Criminal suspects illusory right of silence in British Commonwealth'. *Cornell Law Review* 53/3: 473.

Glover, R. (2015), *Murphy on Evidence*, 14th ed. Oxford: Oxford University Press.

Godsey, M. A. (2002), 'Miranda's final frontier – the international arena: A critical analysis of United States v. Bin Laden, and a proposal for a new Miranda exception abroad'. *Duke Law Journal* 51/6: 1703.

Goethals, K., Gunn, J. and Calcedo-Barba, A. (2012), 'Selling forensic psychiatry: Recruiting for the future, establishing services'. *Criminal Behaviour and Mental Health* 22/4: 261.

Gooderson, R. (1968), 'Previous consistent statements'. *Cambridge Law Journal* 26/1: 64.

Gray, D. and Griffin, C. (2014), 'A journey to citizenship: Constructions of citizenship and identity in the British Citizenship Test'. *British Journal of Social Psychology* 53/2: 16.

Gray, N. S., O'Connor, C., Williams, T., Short, J. and MacCulloch, M. (2001), 'Fitness to plead: Implications from case-law arising from the Criminal Justice and Public Order Act 1994'. *Journal of Forensic Psychiatry & Psychology* 12/1: 52.

Great Britain. Northern Ireland Office. (1994), *Criminal Appeals and Arrangements for Dealing with Alleged Miscarriages of Justice in Northern Ireland.* Belfast: Northern Ireland Office.

Great Britain, Scientific Committee and West, T. S. (1992), *The Guildford and Woolwich Inquiry. An Examination of Some Scientific Issues in the Case of the Maguire Seven.* London: Home Office.

Green, M. S. (1999), 'The privilege's last sound: The privilege against self-incrimination and the right to rebel against the State'. *Brooklyn Law Review* 65: 627.

Greenawalt, K. (1981), 'Silence as a moral and constitutional right'. *William and Mary Law Review* 23/1: 15.

Greenwood, H. (2012), *The Narrative Construction of Miscarriages of Justice: The Influence of Adversarial and Inquisitorial Investigative Models of Truth-findings.* Cardiff: Cardiff University.

Greer, C. and McLaughlin, E. (2012), ' "This is not justice". Ian Tomlinson, institutional failure and the press politics of outrage'. *British Journal of Criminology* 52/2: 274.

Greer, D. S. (1980), 'The admissibility of confessions under the Northern Ireland (Emergency Provisions) Act'. *Northern Ireland Law Quarterly* 31: 205.

Greer, S. (1990), 'The right to silence: A review of the current debate'. *Modern Law Review* 53/6: 22.

Greer, S. (1994a), 'Miscarriages of criminal justice reconsidered'. *Modern Law Review* 57: 58.

Greer, S. (1994b), 'The right to silence, defence disclosure and confession evidence'. *Journal of Law and Society* 21: 17.

Greer, S. (1995), *Supergrasses: A Study in Anti-Terrorist Law Enforcement in Northern Ireland.* Oxford: Clarendon Press.

Greer, S. and Morgan, R. (1990), *The Right to Silence Debate.* Bristol: Centre for Criminal Justice, University of Bristol.

Gregory, W. O. (1994), 'Reilly, England limits the right to silence and moves towards an inquisitorial system of justice'. *The Journal of Criminal Law and Criminology* 84/2: 411.

Griew, E. (1971), 'Proposed reforms of the law of evidence in criminal cases in England and Wales'. *University of Wales Australia Law Review* 10: 243.

Griffiths, A. and Milne, B. (2006), 'Will it end in tiers? Police interviews with suspects in Britain', in T. Williamson, ed., *Investigative Interviewing: Rights, Research and Regulation.* Cullompton: Willan.

Grisso, T., Steinberg, L., Woolard, J., Cauffman, E., Scott, E., Graham, S., Lexcen, F., Dickon Reppucci, N. and Schwartz, R. (2003), 'Juveniles' competence to stand trial: A comparison of adolescents' and adults' capacities as trial defendants'. *Law and Human Behavior* 27/4: 30.

Griswold, E. N. (1955), *The 5th Amendment Today*. Cambridge MA: Harvard University Press.

Griswold, E. N. (1960), 'Right to be let alone'. *Northwestern University Law Review* 55: 216.

Gross, O. and Ní Aoláin, F. (2006), *Law in Times of Crisis: Emergency Powers in Theory and Practice*. Cambridge: Cambridge University Press.

Grubin, D. (1996), 'Silence in court: Psychiatry and the Criminal Justice and Public Order Act 1994'. *Journal of Forensic Psychiatry & Psychology* 7/3: 647.

Gudjonsson, G. (1992), *The Psychology of Interrogations, Confessions and Testimony*. Chichester: John Wiley and Sons.

Gudjonsson, G., Clare, I. and Rutter, S. (1994), 'Psychological characteristics of suspects interviewed at police stations: A factor-analytic study'. *Journal of Forensic Psychiatry & Psychology* 5/3: 517.

Gudjonsson, G. H. (1994), *Suspicion and Silence: The Right to Silence in Criminal Investigations*. London: Blackstone Press.

Gudjonsson, G. H. (2002), 'Unreliable confessions and miscarriages of justice in Britain'. *International Journal of Police Science & Management* 4/4: 332.

Gudjonsson, G. H. (2006), 'Sex offenders and confessions: How to overcome their resistance during questioning'. *Journal of Clinical Forensic Medicine* 13/4: 203.

Gudjonsson, G. H. (2010), 'Psychological vulnerabilities during police interviews. Why are they important?'. *Legal and Criminological Psychology* 15/2: 161.

Gudjonsson, G. H., Clare, I., Rutter, S. and Pearse, J. (1993), *Persons at Risk During Interviews in Police Custody: The Identification of Vulnerabilities*. RCCJ Research Study. London: HMSO.

Gudjonsson, G. H., Hayes, G. D. and Rowlands, P. (2000), 'Fitness to be interviewed and psychological vulnerability: The views of doctors, lawyers and police officers'. *The Journal of Forensic Psychiatry* 11/1: 74.

Guttel, E. and Teichman, D. (2012), 'Criminal sanctions in the defense of the innocent'. *Michigan Law Review* 110/4: 597.

Hall, A. (2010), 'Where do the advocates stand when the goal posts are moved?'. *International Journal of Evidence and Proof* 14/2: 107.

Hall, J. and Human Rights Watch. (1997), *To Serve Without Favor: Policing, Human Rights, and Accountability in Northern Ireland*. Helsinki: Human Rights Watch.

Halliburton, R. (1999), 'When the law attacks the lawyers'. *New Statesman*, 23 August: 13.

Hallsworth, S. and Young, T. (2008), 'Death and life are in the power of the tongue' (Proverbs 18:21)'. *Theoretical Criminology* 12: 21.

Harkin, G. and Ingram, M. (2004), *Stakeknife: Britain's Secret Agents in Ireland*. Dublin: The O'Brien Press.

Harlow, B. (1993), 'Speaking from the dock'. *Callaloo* 16/4: 874.

Harvey, J. C. O. E. C. C. (1967), *The Interrogation of Suspects*. London: Justice.

Hawkins, K. (2003), 'Order, rationality and silence: Some reflections on criminal justice decision-making', in L. Gelsthorpe and N. Padfield, eds, *Exercising Discretion: Decision-making in the Criminal Justice System and Beyond*. Cullompton: Willan.

Haworth, K. (2006), 'The dynamics of power and resistance in police interview discourse'. *Discourse & Society* 17/6: 739.

Haworth, K. (2010), 'Police interviews in the judicial process: Police interviews as evidence', in M. Coulthard and A. Johnson, eds, *The Routledge Handbook of Forensic Linguistics*. Abingdon: Routledge.

Haworth, K. (2013), 'Audience design in the police interview: The interactional and judicial consequences of audience orientation'. *Language in Society* 42/1: 45.

Helmholz, R. H., Gray, C. M. and Alschuler, A. W., eds (1997), *The Privilege Against Self-Incrimination: Its Origins and Development*. Chicago: University of Chicago Press.

Henham, R. (1995), 'Criminal justice and the trial and sentencing of white collar offenders'. *Journal of Criminal Law* 59: 83.

Heong, S. Y. M. (1981), 'My Lord, the defendant chooses to remain silent'. *Malaya Law Review* 23: 10.

Herrmann, F. R. and Speer, B. M. (2007), 'Standing mute at arrest as evidence of guilt: The right to silence under attack'. *American Journal of Criminal Law* 35: 1.

Heydon, G. (2011), 'Silence: Civil right or social privilege? A discourse analytic response to a legal problem'. *Journal of Pragmatics* 43/9: 2308.

Heydon, G. (2012), 'Helping the police with their enquiries: Enhancing the investigative interview with linguistic research'. *The Police Journal: Theory, Practice and Principles* 85/2: 101.

Heydon, J. D. (1973), 'Confessions and silence'. *Sydney Law Review* 7: 375.

Heydon, J. D. (1977), 'Current trends in the law of evidence'. *Sydney Law Review* 8: 305.

Ho, H. L. (2013), 'The privilege against self-incrimination and right of access to a lawyer: A comparative assessment'. *Singapore Academy of Law Journal* 25: 826.

Hobbs, D. (1989), *Doing the Business: Entrepreneurship, the Working Class and Detectives in the East End of London*. Oxford: Oxford University Press.

Hodgson, J. (1992), 'Tipping the scales of justice: The suspect's right to legal advice'. *Criminal Law Review.* 854.

Hodgson, J. (1994), 'Adding injury to injustice: The suspect at the police station'. *Journal of Law and Society* 21: 85.

Hodgson, J. (1997), 'Vulnerable suspects and the appropriate adult'. *Criminal Law Review* November: 785.

Hodgson, J. (2002), 'Constructing the pre-trial role of the defence in French criminal procedure: An adversarial outsider in an inquisitorial process'. *International Journal of Evidence & Proof* 6: 1.

Hodgson, J. (2010), 'The future of adversarial criminal justice in twenty-first century Britain'. *North Carolina Journal of International Law and Commercial Regulation* 35: 320.

Holdaway, S. (1980), 'The police station'. *Urban Life and Culture* 1: 22.

Holdaway, S. (1983), *Inside the British Police: A Force at Work*. Oxford: Blackwell Publishing Ltd.

Holtz, L. E. (1987), 'Miranda in a juvenile setting: A child's right to silence'. *Journal of Criminal Law and Criminology* 78: 534.

Home Office. (1989), *Report of the Working Group on the Right to Silence*. London: HMSO.

Hope, J. (1996), 'A constitutional right to a fair trial: Implications for the reform of the Australian criminal justice system'. *Federal Law Review* 24: 173.

Hor, M. (1993), 'The privilege against self-incrimination and fairness to the accused'. *Singapore Journal of Legal Studies* 1993: 35

Hor, M. (2007), 'Criminal due process in Hong Kong and Singapore: A mutual challenge'. *Hong Kong Law Journal* 37/1: 16.

House of Commons. (1977), *Report of an Inquiry by the Hon. Sir Henry Fisher into the Circumstances Leading to the Trial of Three Persons Arising out of the Death of Maxwell Confait and the Fire at 27 Doggett Road, London SE6* (Fisher Report). London: HMSO.

House of Lords. (2009), *Surveillance: Citizens and the State, Volume I: Report.* London: HMSO.

Howard, M. (1995), 'Crime and punishment: Restoring the balance'. Frank Newsam Memorial Lecture, Bramshill College, 19 April.

Hoyle, C. (1998), *Negotiating Domestic Violence: Police, Criminal Justice and Victims.* Oxford: Oxford University Press.

Human Rights Committee. (1995), *19th Annual Report* (A/50/40). New York, 3 October.

Hunt, A. and Young, R. (1995), 'Criminal justice and academics: Publish and be ignored'. *Holdsworth Law Review* 17: 193.

Hurd, D. (1987), Lecture (untitled) to the Police Foundation. London: Police Foundation.

Ingraham, B. L. (1995), 'The right of silence, the presumption of innocence, the burden of proof, and a modest proposal: A reply to O'Reilly'. *Journal of Criminal Law and Criminology* 86: 559.

Innes, M. (2003), *Investigating Murder: Detective Work and the Police Response to Criminal Homicide.* Oxford: Oxford University Press.

Innes, M. (2014), *Signal Crimes: Social Reactions to Crime, Disorder, and Control.* Oxford: Oxford University Press.

Ipp, D. A. (1998), 'Lawyers' duties to the court'. *Law Quarterly Review* 114/Jan: 45.

Irving, B. L. and Hilgendorf, E. L. (1980), *Police Interrogation: The Psychological Approach: A Case Study of Current Practice.* London: HMSO.

Irving, B. and McKenzie, I. (1989), *Police Interrogation.* London: Police Foundation.

Jackson, J. (1989), 'Recent developments in criminal evidence'. *Northern Ireland Legal Quarterly* 40: 26.

Jackson, J. (1991), 'Curtailing the right of silence: Lessons from Northern Ireland'. *Criminal Law Review* 1991: 404.

Jackson, J. (1993), 'Inferences from silence: From common law to common sense'. *Northern Ireland Legal Quarterly* 44: 103.

Jackson, J. (1994), 'The right of silence: Judicial responses to Parliamentary encroachment'. *Modern Law Review* 57: 270.

Jackson, J. (1996), 'Analysing the new evidence scholarship: Towards a new conception of the law of evidence'. *Oxford Journal of Legal Studies* 16/2: 20.

Jackson, J. (1997), 'Truth and compromise in criminal justice: A critique of trial practice and lawyers' ethics'. *Northern Ireland Legal Quarterly* 48: 321.

Jackson, J. (1998), 'Hearsay: The sacred cow that won't be slaughtered'. *International Journal of Evidence & Proof* 2: 166.

Jackson, J. (2001a), 'Silence legislation in Northern Ireland: The impact after ten years'. *Journal of Civil Liberties* 6/2: 134.

Jackson, J. (2001b), 'Understanding miscarriages of justice'. *Journal of Law and Society* 28/2: 4.

Jackson, J. (2001c), 'Silence and proof: Extending the boundaries of criminal proceedings in the United Kingdom'. *International Journal of Evidence & Proof* 5: 145.

Jackson, J. (2003), 'Justice for all: Putting victims at the heart of criminal justice?'. *Journal of Law and Society* 30/2: 309.

Jackson, J. (2005), 'The effect of human rights on criminal evidentiary processes: Towards convergence, divergence or realignment?'. *Modern Law Review* 68/5: 737.

Jackson, J. (2009), 'Re-conceptualizing the right of silence as an effective fair trial standard'. *International and Comparative Law Quarterly* 58/4: 835.

Jackson, J. and Daly, Y. (2016), 'The criminal justice process: From questioning to trial', in D. Healy, C. Hamilton, Y. Daly and M. Butler, eds, *The Routledge Handbook of Irish Criminology.* London: Routledge.

Jackson, J. and Doran, S. (1993), 'Conventional trials in unconventional times: The Diplock court experience'. *Criminal Law Forum* 4/3: 503.

Jackson, J. and Doran, S. (1995), *Judge Without Jury: Diplock Trials in the Adversary System.* Oxford: Oxford University Press.

Jackson, J. and Doran, S. (1997), 'Addressing the adversarial deficit in non-jury criminal trials'. *Israel Law Review* 31: 645.

Jackson, J. and Summers, S. J. (2012), *The Internationalisation of Criminal Evidence: Beyond the Common Law and Civil Law Traditions.* Cambridge: Cambridge University Press.

Jackson, J., Wolfe, M. and Quinn, K. (2000), *Legislating Against Silence: The Northern Ireland Experience.* Belfast: Northern Ireland Statistics & Research Agency.

Jaworski, A. (2005), 'Introduction: Silence in institutional and intercultural contexts'. *Multilingua: Journal of Cross-Cultural and Interlanguage Communication* 24/1–2: 1.

Jenkins, S. (2013a), 'Methodological challenges of conducting "insider" reflexive research with the miscarriages of justice community'. *International Journal of Social Research Methodology* 16/5: 373.

Jenkins, S. (2013b), 'Miscarriages of justice and the discourse of innocence: Perspectives from appellants, campaigners, journalists, and legal practitioners'. *Journal of Law and Society* 40/3: 329.

Jenkins, S. (2013c), 'Secondary victims and the trauma of wrongful conviction: Families and children's perspectives on imprisonment, release and adjustment'. *Australian and New Zealand Journal of Criminology* 46/1: 119.

Jennings, A. (2001), 'Self-incrimination and the right to silence', in K. Starmer, M. Strange and Q. Whitaker, eds, *Criminal Justice and Police Powers.* Oxford: Oxford University Press.

Jennings, A. and Emanuel, D. (2001), 'Adverse inferences from silence – an update'. *Archbold News* 9, 30 November.

Jennings, A., Ashworth, A. and Emerson, B. (2000), 'Silence and safety: The impact of human rights law'. *Criminal Law Review* November: 879.

Jiang, N. (2013), 'The presumption of innocence and illegally obtained evidence: Lessons from wrongful convictions in China?'. *Hong Kong Law Journal* 43: 745.

Johnson, A. (2002), 'So...?: Pragmatic implications of so-prefaced questions in formal police interviews', in J. Cotterill, ed., *Language in the Legal Process.* Basingstoke: Palgrave Macmillan.

Johnson, A. (2008), ' "From where we're sat...": Negotiating narrative transformation through interaction in police interviews with suspects'. *Text & Talk* 28/3: 327.

Jones, C. E. (2010), 'A reason to doubt: The suppression of evidence and the inference of innocence'. *Journal of Criminal Law & Criminology* 100/2: 415.

Jones, D. (2011), 'Miscarriages of justice: The role of homicide review'. *Medicine Science and the Law* 51/2: 63.

Jones, T. and Newburn, T. (2002), 'Policy convergence and crime control in the USA and the UK: Streams of influence and levels of impact'. *Criminology and Criminal Justice* 2: 31.

Jörg, N., Field, S. and Brants, C. (1995), 'Are inquisitorial and adversarial systems converging?', in P. Fennell, C. Harding, N. Jörg and B. Swart, eds, *Criminal Justice in Europe: A Comparative Study*. Oxford: Clarendon Press.

Judge, Lord of Draycote. (2008), *The Criminal Justice System in England and Wales: Time for Change?* Speech to the University of Hertfordshire, 4 November.

Judges, D. P. and Cribari, S. J. (2009), 'Response article. Speaking of silence: A reply to making defendants speak'. *Minnesota Law Review* 94: 800.

Judicial Studies Board. (2010), *Crown Court Bench Book: Directing the Jury*. March. London: Judicial Studies Board.

JUSTICE. (1967), *The Interrogation of Suspects*. Report of the Justice Committee on Evidence. London: JUSTICE.

JUSTICE. (1994), *Right of Silence Debate: The Northern Ireland Experience*. London: JUSTICE.

JUSTICE and Committee on the Administration of Justice. (1994), *Right of Silence Debate: The Northern Ireland Experience*. London: JUSTICE. West Yorkshire Police. (1989), *West Yorkshire Police Study for the Home Office Working Group*. Unpublished.

Karstedt, S. (2002), 'Durkheim, Tarde and beyond: The global travel of crime policies'. *Criminal Justice* 2/2: 111.

Kassin, S. M. (2008), 'The psychology of confessions'. *Annual Review of Law and Social Science* 4/1: 193.

Kassin, S. M., Appleby, S. C. and Perillo, J. T. (2010), 'Interviewing suspects: Practice, science, and future directions'. *Legal and Criminological Psychology* 15/1: 39.

Kaye, T. (1991), *Unsafe and Unsatisfactory? Report of the Independent Inquiry into the Working Practices of the West Midlands Police Serious Crime Squad*. London: Civil Liberties Trust.

Keel, P. (1987), 'Senior police to call for end to right of silence'. *Guardian*, 22 September, p. 2.

Kemp, V. (2010), *Transforming Legal Aid: Access To Criminal Defence Services*. London: Legal Services Commission.

Kemp, V. (2012), *Bridewell Legal Advice Study – BLAST: An Innovation in Police Station Legal Advice*. London: Legal Services Research Centre.

Kemp, V. (2013), 'No time for a solicitor: Implications for delays on the take-up of legal advice'. *Criminal Law Review* 2013: 19.

Kemp, V. (2014), 'PACE, performance targets and legal protections'. *Criminal Law Review* 2014/1: 278.

Kemp, V. and Balmer, N. (2008), *Criminal Defence Services: Users' Perspectives. An Interim Report*. Legal Services Research Centre, Research Paper No. 21. http://lsrc.org.uk/publications.

Kemp, V., Pleasence, P. and Balmer, N. (2011), 'Children, young people and requests for police station legal advice: 25 years on from PACE'. *Youth Justice* 11/1: 28.

Kemp, V., Pleasence, P. and Balmer, N. J. (2012), 'Whose time is it anyway? Factors associated with duration in police custody'. *Criminal Law Review* 735.

Keong, C. S. (1996), 'The criminal process – the Singapore model'. *Singapore Law Review* 17: 433.

Killian, J. H., Costello, G. A. and Thomas, K. R., eds (2004), *The Constitution of the United States of America: Analysis and Interpretation: Analysis of Cases Decided by the Supreme Court of the United States to June 28, 2002.* Congressional Research Service, Library of Congress, Washington: USGPO.

Kirby, T. (1994), 'Plans to abolish right to silence criticised by police'. *The Independent*, 2 February.

Kleining, J. (1996), *The Ethics of Policing.* Cullompton: Willan.

Klockars, C. (1980), 'The Dirty Harry problem'. *The Annals* 452 (November): 33.

Klug, F., Starmer, K. and Weir, S. (1996), 'Civil liberties and the Parliamentary watchdog: The passage of the Criminal Justice and Public Order Act 1994'. *Parliamentary Affairs* 49/4: 536.

Knepper, W. (2012), 'In/justice and necro-natality in Edwidge Danticat's Brother, I'm Dying'. *Journal of Commonwealth Literature* 47/2: 191.

Kurzon, D. (1995), 'Right of silence: A model of interpretation'. *Journal of Pragmatics* 23/1: 15.

Kurzon, D. (2007), 'Towards a typology of silence'. *Journal of Pragmatics* 39/10: 1673.

Kyle, D. (2004), 'Correcting miscarriages of justice: The role of the Criminal Cases Review Commission'. *Drake Law Review* 52: 657.

Lamble, S. (2013), 'The quiet dangers of civilized rage: Surveying the punitive aftermath of England's 2011 riots'. *South Atlantic Quarterly* 112/3: 577.

Landau, J. (2007), 'The right against self-incrimination and the right to silence under Article 6'. *Judicial Review* 12/4: 261.

Langbein, J. H. (1994), 'The historical origins of the privilege against self-incrimination at common law'. *Michigan Law Review* 92/5: 1047.

Langbein, J. H. (1997), 'The privilege and common law criminal procedure: The sixteenth to the eighteenth centuries', in R. H. Helmholz, C. M. Gray and A. W. Alschuler, eds, *The Privilege Against Self-Incrimination: Its Origins and Development.* Chicago: University of Chicago Press.

Langer, M. (2004), 'From legal transplants to legal translations: The globalization of plea bargaining and the Americanization thesis in criminal procedure'. *Harvard International Law Journal* 45/1.

Larsen, N. (1995), 'Silence may be guilt'. *Juta's Business Law* 3/4: 183.

Lassiter, G. D. (2010), 'Psychological science and sound public policy: Video recording of custodial interrogations'. *American Psychologist* 65/8: 768.

Law Commission of India. (2000), *Report on Article 20(3) of the Constitution of India and the Right to Silence,* Law Comm No 180, May 2000, No:6(3) (76) /2002 –LC (LS).

Law Reform Commission of Western Australia. (1999), *Review of the Civil and Criminal Justice System.* Final Report. Recommendation 251.

Law Society. (1994), 'Advice to practitioners from the Criminal Law Committee of the Law Society'. *Criminal Practitioners Newsletter*, October.

Law Society. (1997), 'Law Society advice to practitioners', *Criminal Practitioners Newsletter*, July.

Law Society. (2006), 'Changes in the law relating to silence', *Criminal Practitioners Newsletter*, January.

Legal Aid Agency. (2014), *Criminal Legal Aid: Means Testing*, available at www.gov.uk/guidance/criminal-legal-aid-means-testing.

Leigh, L. H. (1997), 'The right to a fair trial and the European Convention on Human Rights', in D. Weissbrodt and R. Wolfrum, eds, *The Right to a Fair Trial*. Berlin: Springer-Verlag.

Leng, R. (1993), 'The right to silence in police interrogation: A study of some of the issues underlying the debate', *Royal Commission on Criminal Justice Research Study*. London: HMSO.

Leng, R. (1994), 'The right-to-silence debate', in D. Morgan and G. Stephenson, eds, *Suspicion and Silence: The Right to Silence in Criminal Investigations*. London: Blackstone.

Leng, R. (1995), 'Losing sight of the defendant: The government's proposals on pre-trial disclosure'. *Criminal Law Review* September: 704.

Leng, R. (1997), 'Defence strategies for information deficit: Negotiating the CPIA'. *International Journal of Evidence & Proof* 1/4: 215.

Leng, R. (2001a), 'Silence in court: From common sense to common law'. *International Journal of Evidence & Proof* 6: 7.

Leng, R. (2001b), 'Silence pre-trial, reasonable expectations and the normative distortion of fact-finding'. *International Journal of Evidence & Proof* 5: 240.

Leng, R. (2001c), 'The right to silence reformed: A re-appraisal of the Royal Commission's influence'. *Journal of Civil Liberties* 6/2: 28.

Leng, R. and Taylor, R. (1996), *Blackstone's Guide to the Criminal Procedure and Investigations Act 1996*. London: Blackstone Press Ltd.

Leo, R. A. (2000), 'Questioning the relevance of Miranda in the twenty-first century'. *Michigan Law Review* 99: 1000.

Leo, R. A. (2005), 'Rethinking the study of miscarriages of justice: Developing a criminology of wrongful conviction'. *Journal of Contemporary Criminal Justice* 21/3: 201.

Leo, R. A. (2008), *Police Interrogation and American Justice*. Cambridge, MA: Harvard University Press.

Leshem, S. (2010), 'The benefits of a right to silence for the innocent'. *Rand Journal of Economics* 41/2: 398.

Levy, L. W. (1968), *Origins of the Fifth Amendment: The Right Against Self-incrimination*. Oxford: Oxford University Press.

Lidstone, K. W. and Early, T. L. (2008), 'Questioning freedom: Detention for questioning in France, Scotland and England'. *International and Comparative Law Quarterly* 31/03: 488.

Liebman, J. S., Blackburn, S., Mattern, D. and Waisnor, J. (2013), 'The evidence of things not seen: Non-matches as evidence of innocence'. *Iowa Law Review* 98/2: 577.

Linneberg, A. (2009), 'Law, simulation, and society from Ibsen to Treholt'. *Law & Literature* 21/1: 24.

Littlechild, B. (1995), 'Reassessing the role of the appropriate adult'. *Criminal Law Review* July: 540.

Livingstone, S. (1994), 'The House of Lords and the Northern Ireland conflict'. *Modern Law Review* 57: 333.

Lloyd-Bostock, S. (2000), 'The effects on juries of hearing about the defendant's previous criminal record: A simulation study'. *Criminal Law Review* September: 734.

Lloyd-Bostock, S. (2006), 'The effects on lay magistrates of hearing that the defendant is of "good character", being left to speculate, or hearing that he has a previous conviction'. *Criminal Law Review* March: 189.

Loader, I. and Mulcahy, A. (2001), 'The power of legitimate naming. Part I: Chief constables as social commentators in post-war England'. *British Journal of Criminology* 41/1: 41.

Loftus, B. (2009), *Police Culture in a Changing World*. Oxford: Oxford University Press.

Lords, H. O. (2009), *Surveillance: Citizens and the State, Volume I: Report*. London: The Stationery Office.

Lustig, R. (1981), 'Commission feared police would reject tape recording plan', *Observer*, 11 January.

Luzzati, S. (2010), 'On the admissibility of statements made by the defendant prior to trial: Remarks on the ICTY Appeals Chamber's decisions in Halilovic and Prlic et al.'. *Journal of International Criminal Justice* 8/1: 221.

MacKenzie, J. (1990), 'Silence in Hampshire'. *New Law Journal* 18 May.

MacNair, M. R. (1990), 'The early development of the privilege against self-incrimination'. *Oxford Journal of Legal Studies* 10/1: 66.

Maguire, M. (1988), 'Effects of the "PACE" provisions on detention and questioning', *British Journal of Criminology* 28/1: 19.

Maguire, M. and Norris, C. (1992), *The Conduct and Supervision of Criminal Investigations*. Royal Commission on Criminal Justice Research Study No. 5. London: HMSO.

Maguire, M. and Norris, C. (1994), 'Police investigations: Practice and malpractice'. *Journal of Law and Society* 21: 72.

Maidment, M. (2013), 'When law fails: Making sense of miscarriages of justice'. *Punishment & Society-International Journal of Penology* 15/3: 332.

Mansfield, M. (1995), *Counsel*, January–February 1995, p. 30.

Mark, R. (1966), 'A matter of conviction'. *Criminal Law Review* 311.

Mark, R. (1973), 'Minority Verdict', The 1973 Dimbleby Lecture, London: BBC.

Markesinis, B. S. (1994), *The Gradual Convergence*. Oxford: Clarendon Press.

Marks, A. (2013), 'Expert evidence of drug traces: Relevance, reliability and the right to silence'. *Criminal Law Review* 10: 16.

Martinsen, R. (1974), 'What works? Questions and answers about prison reform'. *The Public Interest* 35: 43.

Matia Portilla, F. J. (2012), 'Is there a fundamental right to silence? On the limits of article 10.2 EC'. *Revista Espanola De Derecho Constitucional* 32/94: 355.

Mayers, L. (1959), *Shall We Amend the Fifth Amendment?* London: Harper.

McBarnet, D. (1978), 'The Fisher Report on the Confait case: Four issues'. *The Modern Law Review* 41/4: 455.

McCartney, C. (2013), *Forensic Identification and Criminal Justice*. London: Routledge.

McConville, M. (1992), 'Videotaping interrogations: Police behaviour on and off camera'. *Criminal Law Review* August: 532.

McConville, M. and Baldwin, J. (1982), 'The role of interrogation in crime discovery and conviction'. *The British Journal of Criminology* 22/2: 165.

McConville, M. and Bridges, L. (1994), *Criminal Justice in Crisis*. Aldershot: Edward Elgar.

McConville, M. and Hodgson, J. (1993), *Custodial Legal Advice and the Right to Silence*. London: HMSO.

McConville, M. and Marsh, L. (2015), 'Adversarialism goes West: Case management in criminal courts'. *International Journal of Evidence & Proof* 19/3: 18.

McConville, M., Hodgson, J., Bridges, L. and Pavlovic, A. (1994), *Standing Accused: The Organisation and Practices of Criminal Defence Lawyers in Britain*. Oxford: Oxford University Press.

McConville, M., Sanders, A. and Leng, R. (1991), *The Case for the Prosecution: Police Suspects and the Construction of Criminality*. London: Routledge.

McElree, F. and Starmer, K. (1993), 'The right to silence', in C. Walker and K. Starmer, eds, *Justice in Error*, London: Blackstone Press.

McEvoy, K. (2000), 'Law, struggle and political transformation in Northern Ireland'. *Journal of Law and Society* 27/4: 542.

McEvoy, K. (2001), *Paramilitary Imprisonment in Northern Ireland: Resistance, Management and Release*. Oxford: Oxford University Press.

McEwan, J. (1998), *Evidence and the Adversarial Process – The Modern Law*, 2nd ed. Oxford: Hart Publishing.

McEwan, J. (2007), 'Striking a balance in unlawfully obtained confession cases: United Kingdom pragmatism against principle'. *San Diego Law Review* 44: 597.

McInerney, P. (2014), 'The privilege against self-incrimination from early origins to Judges' Rules: Challenging the "Orthodox view"'. *The International Journal of Evidence & Proof* 18/2: 38.

McKenzie, I. K. and Irving, B. (1987), 'Police interrogation – the effects of PACE (Police and Criminal Evidence Act 1984)'. *Policing* 3/1: 4.

McKenzie, I. and Irving, B. (1988), 'The right to silence'. *Policing* 4: 88.

McKinnon, I. and Grubin, D. (2010), 'Health screening in police custody'. *Journal of Forensic and Legal Medicine* 17/4: 209.

McKittrick, D. (1988), 'Judges tackled King over right to silence'. *The Independent*, 29 December, p. 1.

McLaughlin, E., Muncie, J. and Hughes, G. (2001), 'The permanent revolution: New Labour, new public management and the modernization of criminal justice'. *Criminology and Criminal Justice* 1/3: 301.

McNee, D. S. (1983), *McNee's Law/Sir David McNee*. London: Collins.

McNicol, S. B. (1984), 'Strategies for reform of the law relating to police interrogations'. *The International and Comparative Law Quarterly* 33/2: 265.

Medford, S., Gudjonsson, G. H. and Pearse, J. (2003), 'The efficacy of the appropriate adult safeguard during police interviewing'. *Legal and Criminological Psychology* 8/2: 14.

Metropolitan Police. (1989), *Metropolitan Police Study for the Home Office Working Group*. Unpublished.

Miller, C. J. (1973), 'Silence and confessions: What are they worth?'. *Criminal Law Review* 343.

Milne, B. and Powell, M. (2010), 'Investigative interviewing', in J. M. Brown and E. A. Campbell, eds, *The Cambridge Handbook of Forensic Psychology*. Cambridge: Cambridge University Press.

Ministry of Justice and Gove, Rt Hon M. (2016), Written statement to Parliament:

'Changes to criminal legal aid contracting', delivered on 28 January. London: Ministry of Justice.

Mirfield, P. (1995), 'Two side effects of section 34 to section 37 of the Criminal Justice and Public Order Act 1994'. *Criminal Law Review* August: 612.

Mirfield, P. (1997), *Silence, Confessions and Improperly Obtained Evidence.* Oxford: Oxford University Press.

Mitchell, B. (1983), 'Confession and police interrogation of suspects'. *Criminal Law Review* 596.

Moglen, E. (1994), 'Taking the 5th: Reconsidering the origins of the constitutional privilege against self-incrimination'. *Michigan Law Review* 92/5: 1086.

Moisidis, C. (2008), *Criminal Discovery. From Truth to Proof and Back Again.* Sydney: Institute of Criminology Press.

Moore, L. (2009), 'Rethinking miscarriages of justice: Beyond the tip of the iceberg'. *Critical Social Policy* 29/2: 296.

Morgan, D. and Stephenson, G. M. (1995), *Suspicion and Silence: The Right to Silence in Criminal Investigations.* London: Blackstone Press.

Morgan, G., Dagistanli, S. and Martin, G. (2010), 'Global fears, local anxiety policing, counterterrorism and moral panic over "Bikie gang wars" in New South Wales'. *Australian and New Zealand Journal of Criminology* 43/3: 580.

Morgan, R. (1996), 'The process is the rule and punishment is the process'. *Modern Law Review* 59: 306.

Morgan, R., Reiner, R. and McKenzie, I. K. (1991), *Police Powers and Police: A Study of the Work of Custody Officers.* Full final report to the ESRC. Unpublished.

Morris, P. (1980), 'Police interrogation review of the literature', *Royal Commission Research Study.* London: HMSO.

Mortimer A. (1994), 'Asking the right questions'. *Policing* 10: 111.

Moston, S. (1990), 'The ever-so gentle art of police interrogation', paper presented at British Psychological Society Annual Conference, University College, Swansea, 5 April.

Moston, S. (2009), 'Investigative interviewing of suspects in Australia', in T. Williamson, B. Milne and S. P. Savage, eds, *International Developments in Investigative Interviewing.* Cullompton: Willan.

Moston, S. and Engelberg, T. (1993), 'Police questioning techniques in tape recorded interviews with criminal suspects'. *Policing and Society* 3/3: 15.

Moston, S., Stephenson, G. M. and Williamson, T. M. (1992), 'The effects of case characteristics on suspect behaviour during police questioning'. *British Journal of Criminology* 32/1: 23.

Moston, S., Stephenson, G. M. and Williamson, T. M. (1993), 'The incidence, antecedents and consequences of the use of the right to silence during police questioning'. *Criminal Behavior and Mental Health* 3/1: 18.

Moston, S. J. and Stephenson, G. M. (1994), 'Helping the police with their enquiries outside the police station', in D. Morgan and G. Stephenson, eds, *Suspicion and Silence: The Right to Silence in Criminal Investigations.* London: Blackstone.

Mulcahy, L. (2013), 'Putting the defendant in their place: Why do we still use the dock in criminal proceedings?'. *British Journal of Criminology* 53/6: 1139.

Mullin, J. (1994), 'Several arrests after protesters try to pierce riot police cordons placed around Parliament'. *Guardian,* 20 October, p. 6.

Muncie, J. (2005), 'The globalization of crime control – the case of youth and juvenile justice: Neo-liberalism, policy convergence and international conventions'. *Theoretical Criminology* 9/1: 35.

Munday, R. (1996), 'Inferences from silence and European human rights law'. *Criminal Law Review* June: 370.

Murray, J. (2010), 'Assessing allegations: Judicial evaluation of testimonial evidence in international tribunals'. *Chicago Journal of International Law* 10: 769.

Nakane, I. (2007), 'Problems in communicating the suspect's rights in interpreted police interviews'. *Applied Linguistics* 28/1: 87.

Nakane, I. (2011), 'The role of silence in interpreted police interviews'. *Journal of Pragmatics* 43/9: 2317.

National Appropriate Adult Network. (2011), *Guide for Appropriate Adults*. National Appropriate Adult Network. London: Home Office.

National Council for Civil Liberties. (1972), *Civil Liberties and the Judges' Rules*. London: NCCL.

Naughton, M. (2012), *Rethinking Miscarriages of Justice: Beyond the Tip of the Iceberg*. Basingstoke: Palgrave Macmillan.

Needham, K. (2015), 'Abolishing right to silence proved unworkable, says NSW Labor', *The Sydney Morning Herald*, 7 June.

Nellis, M. (2000), 'Law and order: The electronic monitoring of offenders', in D. Dolowitz, ed., *Policy Transfer and British Social Policy*. Buckingham: Open University Press.

Newman, D. (2013), *Legal Aid Lawyers and the Quest for Justice*. Oxford: Hart Publishing.

Newburn, T. (1995), *Crime and Criminal Justice Policy*. London: Longman.

Newburn, T. (2002), 'Atlantic crossings: "Policy transfer" and crime control in the USA and Britain'. *Punishment and Society* 4/2: 165.

Newburn, T. (2003), *Crime and Criminal Justice Policy*. London: Pearson Education.

Newburn, T. and Jones, T. (2004), 'The convergence of US and UK crime control policy: Exploring substance and process', in R. Sparks, ed., *Criminal Justice and Political Cultures*. Cullompton: Willan.

Newburn, T. and Jones, T. (2005), 'Symbolic politics and penal populism: The long shadow of Willie Horton'. *Crime Media Culture* 1/1: 72.

Newburn, T. and Jones, T. (2007), *Policy Transfer and Criminal Justice: Exploring US Influence over British Crime Control Policy*. Maidenhead: Open University Press.

Newbury, P. and Johnson, A. (2006), 'Suspects' resistance to constraining and coercive questioning strategies in the police interview'. *The International Journal of Speech, Language and the Law* 13/2: 27.

New South Wales Law Reform Commission. (1998), *The Right to Silence*. Sydney: New South Wales Law Reform Commission.

New South Wales Law Reform Commission. (2000a), *The Right to Silence*. Sydney: New South Wales Law Reform Commission.

New South Wales Law Reform Commission. (2000b), *The Right to Silence and Pretrial Disclosure in NSW*. Research report/New South Wales Law Reform Commission 10. Sydney: New South Wales Law Reform Commission.

Ní Aoláin, F. (1995–96), 'The fortification of an emergency regime'. *Albany Law Review* 59/4: 1353.

Nobles, R. and Schiff, D. (2002), *Understanding Miscarriages of Justice: Law, the Media and the Inevitability of a Crisis*. New York: Oxford University Press.

Nobles, R. and Schiff, D. (2008), 'Absurd asymmetry – a comment on *R* v *Cottrell and Fletcher and BM, KK and DP (Petitioners)* v *Scottish Criminal Cases Review Commission'. Modern Law Review* 71/3: 464.

Norris, C. (1989), 'Avoiding trouble: The police officer's perception of encounters with the public', in M. Weatheritt, ed., *Police Research: Some Future Prospects.* Aldershot: Avebury.

Northern Territory Law Reform Committee. (2002), *Report on the Right to Silence.* Darwin: Northern Territory Law Reform Committee.

Office for National Statistics. (2010), *ONS Survey of Psychiatric Morbidity among Prisoners in England and Wales, 1997.* UK Data Archive. London: ONS.

Ogletree, C. J. (1986), 'Are confessions really good for the soul?: A proposal to Mirandize Miranda'. *Harvard Law Review* 100: 1826.

Open Society Justice Initiative. (2013), *Globalizing Torture: CIA Secret Detention and Extraordinary Rendition.* New York: Open Society Justice Initiative.

O'Reilly, G. W. (1994), 'England limits the right to silence and moves towards an inquisitorial system of justice'. *Journal of Criminal Law and Criminology* 85: 402.

O'Reilly, G. W. (1997), 'Comment on Ingraham's "moral duty" to talk and the right to silence'. *Journal of Criminal Law & Criminology* 87/2: 521.

Ormerod, D. and Birch, D. (2004), 'The evolution of the discretionary exclusion of evidence'. *Criminal Law Review* October: 767.

Ostermann, A. C. (2007), 'Georgina Heydon, The language of police interviewing: A critical analysis'. *Language in Society* 36/3: 462.

Owusu-Bempah, A. (2011), 'Judging the desirability of a defendant's evidence: An unfortunate approach to s.35(1)(b) of the Criminal Justice and Public Order Act 1994'. *Criminal Law Review* September: 690.

Owusu-Bempah, A. (2014), 'Silence in suspicious circumstances'. *Criminal Law Review* 2: 10.

Packer, H. (1968), *The Limits of the Criminal Sanction.* Stanford, CA: Stanford University Press.

Page, M., Taylor, J. and Blenkin, M. (2012), 'Reality bites: A ten-year retrospective analysis of bitemark casework in Australia'. *Forensic Science International* 216/1–3: 82.

Palakrishnan (1999), 'The right to silence'. *The Singapore Law Gazette.*

Paoli, L. (2003), *Mafia Brotherhoods: Organized Crime, Italian Style.* Oxford: Oxford University Press.

Paoline, E. A. (2003), 'Taking stock: Toward a richer understanding of police culture'. *Journal of Criminal Justice* 31/3: 199.

Paoline III, E. A. (2004), 'Shedding light on police culture: An examination of officers' occupational attitudes'. *Police Quarterly* 7/2: 205.

Parker, G. (1974), 'National Law Reform Commission'. *Criminal Law Quarterly* 17: 31.

Pattenden, R. (1991), 'Should confessions be corroborated?'. *Law Quarterly Review* 107: 317.

Pattenden, R. (1995), 'Inferences from silence'. *Criminal Law Review* August: 602.

Pattenden, R. (1998), 'Silence: Lord Taylor's legacy'. *Evidence and Proof,* 2: 141.

Pattenden, R. and Skinns, L. (2010), 'Choice, privacy and publicly funded legal advice at police stations'. *Modern Law Review* 73/3: 349.

Payne-James, J. J., Green, P. G., Green, N., McLachlan, G. M. C., Munro, M. H. W. M. and Moore, T. C. B. (2010), 'Healthcare issues of detainees in police custody in London, UK'. *Journal of Forensic and Legal Medicine* 17/1: 7.

Pearce, J., Gudjonsson, G., Clare, I. C. H. and Rutter, S. (1998), 'Police interviewing and psychological vulnerabilities: Predicting the likelihood of a confession'. *Journal of Community and Applied Social Psychology* 8: 1.

Pearse, J. and Gudjonsson, G. (1996a), 'How appropriate are appropriate adults?'. *Journal of Forensic Psychiatry & Psychology* 7/3: 570.

Pearse, J. and Gudjonsson, G. (1996b), 'A review of the role of the legal adviser in police stations'. *Criminal Behaviour and Mental Health* 6/3: 231.

Pearse, J. and Gudjonsson, G. (1997a), 'Police interviewing and legal representation: A field study'. *Journal of Forensic Psychiatry & Psychology* 8/1: 200.

Pearse, J. and Gudjonsson, G. (1997b), 'Police interviewing techniques at two south London police stations'. *Psychology, Crime and Law* 3/1: 63.

Peerenboom, R. (2004), *Asian Discourses of Rule of Law*. London: RoutledgeCurzon.

Pejic, J. and Lesnie, V. (2000), *What Is a Fair Trial? A Basic Guide to Legal Standards and Practice*. New York: Lawyers Committee for Human Rights.

Phillips, C. and Brown, D. (1998), *Entry into the Criminal Justice System: A Survey of Police Arrests and their Outcomes*. Home Office Research Study. London: Home Office.

Phillips, E. (2011), 'Miscarriages of justice and the forensic expert: The impact of the law commission's reforms'. *The Medico-Legal Journal* 79/Pt 3: 94.

Phillips, L. O. W. M. (2007), 'Trusting the jury'. *Criminal Bar Association Kalisher Lecture*, 23 October.

Pierpoint, H. (2000), 'How appropriate are volunteers as "appropriate adults" for young suspects? The "appropriate adult" system and human rights'. *Journal of Social Welfare and Family Law* 22/4: 18.

Pierpoint, H. (2006), 'Reconstructing the role of the appropriate adult in England and Wales'. *Criminology and Criminal Justice* 6/2: 219.

Pierpoint, H. (2008), 'Quickening the PACE: The use of volunteers as appropriate adults'. *Policing and Society: an International Journal* 18/4: 14.

Pityana, N. B. (2004), 'Liberation, civil rights and democracy: Perspectives on a decade of democracy'. *Ten Years of Democracy in Southern Africa: Historical Achievement, Present State, Future Prospects*, University of South Africa, Pretoria, 23–25 August.

Pleasence, P. and Quirk, H. (2002), *Criminal Case Profiling Study: Final Report*. LSRC Research Paper (Criminal) No. 1, available at http://webarchive.nationalarchives.gov.uk/20100210214359/http:/www.lsrc.org.uk/publicationslist.html.

Pleasence, P., Kemp, V. and Balmer, N. J. (2011), 'The justice lottery? Police station advice 25 years on from PACE'. *Criminal Law Review* 2011: 3.

Plimmer, J. (1997), 'Confession rate'. *Police Review* February: 3.

Plotnikoff, J. and Woolfson, R. (2001), *'A Fair Balance'? Evaluation of the Operation of Disclosure Law*. RDS Occasional Paper No. 76. London: Home Office.

Policy Studies Institute. (1983), *Police and People in London;* i, D. J. Smith, *A Survey of Londoners*; ii, S. Small, *A Group of Young Black People*; iii, D. J. Smith, *A Survey of Police Officers*; iv, D. J. Smith and J. Gray, *The Police in Action*. London: Policy Studies Institute.

Powell, M. B. (2000), 'PRIDE: The essential elements of a forensic interview with an Aboriginal person'. *Australian Psychologist* 35/3: 186.

Powell, M. B. (2002), 'Specialist training in investigative and evidential interviewing: Is it having any effect on the behaviour of professionals in the field?'. *Psychiatry, Psychology and Law* 9/1: 11.

Quinn Jr, T. P. (1994), 'Judicial interpretation of silence: The Criminal Evidence Order of 1988'. *Case Western Reserve Journal of International Law* 26: 365.

Quinn, K. and Jackson, J. (2003), 'The detention and questioning of young persons by the police in Northern Ireland'. *Northern Ireland Office Research and Statistical Series: Report No 9.* Belfast: Northern Ireland Office.

Quinn, K. and Jackson, J. (2007), 'Of rights and roles: Police interviews with young suspects in Northern Ireland'. *British Journal of Criminology* 47/2: 234.

Quirk, H. (2006), 'The significance of culture in criminal procedure reform: Why the revised disclosure scheme cannot work'. *International Journal of Evidence & Proof* 10/1: 42.

Quirk, H. (2007), 'Identifying miscarriages of justice: Why innocence in the UK is not the answer'. *Modern Law Review* 70/5: 759.

Quirk, H. (2013), 'Twenty years on: The right of silence and legal advice: The spiralling costs of an unfair exchange'. *Northern Ireland Legal Quarterly* 64/4: 465.

Radelet, M. L. (2009), 'When law fails: Making sense of miscarriages of justice'. *Judicature* 93/2: 77.

Ranson, D. (2009), 'Forensic experts and miscarriages of justice: The inquiry into pediatric forensic pathology in Ontario'. *Journal of Law and Medicine* 17/1: 22.

Rassin, E. (2010), 'Blindness to alternative scenarios in evidence evaluation'. *Journal of Investigative Psychology and Offender Profiling* 7/2: 153.

RCPPP (1929), *Report of the Royal Commission on Police Powers and Procedure.* London: HM Stationery Office.

Redmayne, M. (1997), 'Process gains and process values: The Criminal Procedure and Investigations Act 1996'. *The Modern Law Review* 60/January: 79.

Redmayne, M. (2007), 'Rethinking the privilege against self-incrimination'. *Oxford Journal of Legal Studies* 27/2: 209.

Redmayne, M. (2008), 'English Warnings'. *Cardozo Law Review* 30: 1047.

Reiner, R. (1985), *The Politics of the Police,* 1st ed. Brighton: Wheatsheaf Books.

Reiner, R. (1992), 'Police research in the United Kingdom: A critical review'. *Crime and Justice* 15: 435.

Reiner, R. (2000), *The Politics of the Police,* 3rd ed. Oxford: Oxford University Press.

Reiner, R. (2010), *The Politics of the Police,* 4th ed. Oxford: Oxford University Press.

Reprieve. (2015), 'Government concedes policies on lawyer-client snooping were unlawful', *Reprieve,* 18 February, www.reprieve.org.uk/press/government-concedes-polices-on-lawyer-client-snooping-were-unlawful/.

Ricciardelli, R., Bell, J. G. and Clow, K. A. (2009), 'Student attitudes toward wrongful conviction'. *Canadian Journal of Criminology and Criminal Justice* 51/3: 411.

Robert, R. (2000), *The Politics of the Police.* Oxford: Oxford Press.

Roberts, D. (1995), 'Legal advice, the unrepresented suspect and the courts: Inferences from silence under the Criminal Justice and Public Order Act 1994'. *Criminal Law Review* June: 483.

Roberts, J. V. and Hough, M. (2013), 'Sentencing riot-related offending: Where do the public stand?'. *British Journal of Criminology* 53/2: 234.

Roberts, P. and Zuckerman, A. (2010), *Criminal Evidence.* Oxford: Oxford University Press.

Roberts, S. (2009), 'Re-thinking miscarriages of justice: Beyond the tip of the iceberg'. *Theoretical Criminology* 13/2: 274.

Roberts, S. (2010), 'Wrongful convictions: International perspectives on miscarriages of justice'. *International Sociology* 25/2: 253.

Robertson, J. (2013), 'Understanding how forensic science may contribute to miscarriages of justice'. *Australian Journal of Forensic Sciences* 45/2: 109.

Robertson, R. (2006), 'The increasing monopolization of identity by the State: The case of the UK and the US'. *Nationalism and Ethnic Politics* 12/3: 373.

Robinson, C. D. (1968), 'Police and prosecutor practices and attitudes relating to interrogation as revealed by pre-and post-Miranda questionnaires: A construct of police capacity to comply'. *Duke Law Journal* 3: 425.

Rock, F. (2010), 'Witnesses and suspects in interviews: Collecting oral evidence: The police, the public and the written word', in M. Coulthard and A. Johnson, eds, *The Routledge Handbook of Forensic Linguistics, Routledge Handbooks in Applied Linguistics*. London: Routledge.

Rogers, R., Harrison, K. S., Shuman, D. W., Sewell, K. W. and Hazelwood, L. L. (2007), 'An analysis of Miranda warnings and waivers: Comprehension and coverage'. *Law and Human Behavior* 31/2: 177.

Rogers, R., Hazelwood, L. L., Sewell, K. W., Harrison, K. S. and Shuman, D. W. (2008), 'The language of Miranda warnings in American jurisdictions: A replication and vocabulary analysis'. *Law and Human Behavior* 32/2: 124.

Royal Commission on Criminal Justice (Chair: Viscount Runciman of Doxford). (1993), *Report*, Cm 2263. London: HMSO.

Royal Commission on Criminal Procedure (Chair: Sir Cyril Phillips) (1981), *Report*, Cmnd 8092. London: HMSO.

Ruddock, P. (2004), 'Australia's legislative response to the ongoing threat of terrorism'. *University of New South Wales Law Journal* 27: 254.

Rushin, S. (2011), 'Rethinking Miranda: The post-arrest right to silence'. *California Law Review* 99/1: 151.

Ryan, M. (2003), *Penal Policy and Political Culture in England and Wales*. Winchester: Waterside.

Samuels, A. (1972), 'Interrogation of the suspect'. *Northern Ireland Legal Quarterly* 23: 512.

Samuels, A. and Barrister, J. P. (1992), 'The right of silence'. *Medicine, Science, and the Law* 32/2: 95.

Sanders, A. (2008), 'Can coercive powers be effectively controlled or regulated? The case for anchored pluralism', in E. Cape and R. Young, eds, *Regulating Policing: The Police and Criminal Evidence Act 1984 Past, Present and Future*. Oxford: Hart.

Sanders, A. and Bridges, L. (1990), 'Access to legal advice and police malpractice'. *Criminal Law Review.* 494.

Sanders, A. and Young, R. (1994), *Criminal Justice*. London: Butterworths.

Sanders, A. and Young, R. (2008), 'Police powers', in T. Newburn, ed., *Handbook of Policing*. Cullompton: Willan.

Sanders, A., Bridges, L., Mulvaney, A. and Crozier, G. (1989), *Advice and Assistance at Police Stations under the 24-hour Duty Solicitor Scheme*. London: Lord Chancellors Department.

Sanders, A., Young, R. and Burton, M. (2010), *Criminal Justice*, 4th ed. Oxford: Oxford University Press.

Sarat, A. (2008), 'Memorializing miscarriages of justice: Clemency petitions in the killing state'. *Law & Society Review* 42/1: 183.

Schabas, W. (2010), *The International Criminal Court: A Commentary on the Rome Statute*. Oxford: Oxford University Press.

Schabas, W. A. (2015), *The European Convention on Human Rights: A Commentary*. Oxford: Oxford University Press.

Schwikkard, P. J. (1998), 'The presumption of innocence: What is it?'. *South African Journal of Criminal Justice* 11: 396.

Schwikkard, P. J. (2001), 'Is it constitutionally permissible to infringe the right to remain silent'. *International Journal of Evidence & Proof* 5: 32.

Schwikkard, P. J. (2003), 'Silence and common sense'. *Acta Juridica* 2003: 92.

Schwikkard, P. J. (2009), 'The muddle of silence'. *International Commentary on Evidence* 6/2: 4.

Scope. (2014), *Current Attitudes Towards Disabled People*. Milton Keynes: Scope.

Scott, I. R. (1974), 'Accused's evidence as corroboration'. *The Modern Law Review* 37/2: 205.

Seet, M. (2015), 'Case comment: Suspected terrorists and the privilege against self-incrimination'. *Cambridge Law Journal* 74/2: 4.

Seidman, L. M. (2007), *Silence and Freedom*. Stanford: Stanford University Press.

Seidmann, D. J. (2008), 'The effects of a right to silence', in H. M. Mialon and P. H. Rubin, eds, *Economics, Law and Individual Rights*. London: Routledge.

Seidmann, D. J. and Stein, A. (2000), 'The right to silence helps the innocent: A game-theoretic analysis of the Fifth Amendment privilege'. *Harvard Law Review* 114/2: 431.

Selby, H. (1995), *Tomorrow's Law*. Leichhardt, NSW: Federation Press.

Sharpe, S. (1997), 'Judicial discretion and investigative impropriety'. *The International Journal of Evidence and Proof* 1: 149.

Sharpe, S. (1998a), 'Inferences from silence revisited'. *Justice of the Peace* 162: 563.

Sharpe, S. (1998b), *Judicial Discretion and Criminal Investigation*. London: Sweet and Maxwell.

Shepherd, E. (1990), *Investigative Interviewing: A Trainer's Workbook*. London: Investigative Science Associates.

Shepherd, E., Ede, R. and Hickman, J. (2007), *Active Defence*. London: Law Society.

Shepherd, E., Mortimer, A. and Mobasheri, R. (1995), 'The police caution: Comprehension and perception in the general population'. *Expert Evidence* 4: 60.

Sim, J. (1982), 'Scarman: The police counter-attack', *The Socialist Register*, London: The Merlin Press, 57.

Singh, H. (1974), 'Conflicting interests: A need to revise values'. *Malaya Law Review* 16: 218.

Singh, H. (1975), 'Reforms in the law of evidence: Some observations'. *Malaya Law Review* 17: 160.

Singh, S. (1994), 'Understanding the long-term relationship between police and policed', in M. McConville and L. Bridges, eds, *Criminal Justice in Crisis*. Aldershot: Edward Elgar.

Skeen, A. (1993), 'A bill of rights and the presumption of innocence'. *South African Journal on Human Rights* 9: 525.

Skinns, L. (2009a), ' "I'm a detainee; Get me out of here": Predictors of access to custodial legal advice in public and privatized police custody areas in England and Wales'. *British Journal of Criminology* 49/3: 19.

Skinns, L. (2009b), ' "Let's get it over with": Early findings on the factors affecting detainees' access to custodial legal advice'. *Policing and Society* 19/1: 21.

Skinns, L. (2010), 'Stop the clock? Predictors of detention without charge in police custody areas'. *Criminology and Criminal Justice* 10/3: 18.

Skinns, L. (2011), *Police Custody: Governance, Legitimacy and Reform in the Criminal Justice Process*. Cullompton: Willan.

Skolnick, J. (1966), *Justice Without Trial*. New York: Wiley.

Skolnick, J. (2008), 'Enduring issues of police culture and demographics'. *Policing and Society* 18/1: 35.

Smith, T. (2012), 'Zealous advocates: The historical foundations of the adversarial criminal defence lawyer'. *Law, Crime & History* 2/1: 1.

Smith, T. H. (1981), *Approach to Criminal Evidence Law Reform (from Criminal Evidence Law Reform – Proceedings, P 39–53, 1981 – See NCJ-84738)*. Sydney: Australia Law Reform Commission.

Smyth, M. B. (2007), 'A critical research agenda for the study of political terror'. *European Political Science* 6/3: 260.

Snook, B., Eastwood, J. and MacDonald, S. (2010), 'A descriptive analysis of how Canadian police officers administer the right-to-silence and right-to-legal-counsel cautions'. *Canadian Journal of Criminology and Criminal Justice* 52/5: 545.

Social and Community Planning Research. (1996), *British Social Attitudes Survey, 1994* [data collection]. Colchester, Essex: UK Data Service. SN: 3572.

Softley, P. (1980), *Police Interrogation: An Observational Study in Four Police Stations*. London: HMSO.

Sonnemans, J. and Van Dijk, F. (2012), 'Errors in judicial decisions: Experimental results'. *Journal of Law Economics & Organization* 28/4: 687.

Sparks, R. and Newburn, T. (2002), 'Introduction: How does crime policy travel?'. *Criminology and Criminal Justice* 2: 3.

Sprack, J. (1997), 'The Criminal Procedure and Investigations Act 1996: The duty of disclosure'. *Criminal Law Review.* 308.

Spurlock, P. (1950), 'The Yokohama War Crimes Trials: The truth about a misunderstood subject'. *American Bar Association Journal* 36/5: 387.

Standing Advisory Commission on Human Rights. (1989), *Fourteenth Report for the Period 1 November 1987–31 March 1989*. London: HMSO.

Stannard, J. E. (2000), 'A presumption and four burdens'. *Northern Ireland Legal Quarterly* 51: 560.

Stein, A. (2008), 'The right to silence helps the innocent: A response to critics'. *Cardozo Law Review* 30/3: 1115.

Steinberg, L., Graham, S., O'Brien, L., Woolard, J., Cauffman, E. and Banich, M. (2009), 'Age differences in future orientation and delay discounting'. *Child Development* 80/1: 28.

Stephenson, G. M. and Moston, S. J. (1994), 'Police interrogation'. *Psychology, Crime & Law* 1: 151.

Stevens, J. (2003), *Stevens Inquiry: Overview and Recommendations*, 17 April. London: HM Government.

Stockdale, J. (1993), *Management and Supervision of Police Interviews*. PRG Paper 5, London: Home Office.

Stone, D. (2004), 'Transfer agents and global networks in the "transnationalization" of policy'. *Journal of European Public Policy* 11/3: 22.

Stone, E. (1998), 'Calling a spade a spade: The embarrassing truth about the right to silence'. *Criminal Law Journal* 22/Feb: 29.

Summers, S. J. (2007), *Fair Trials: The European Criminal Procedural Tradition and the European Court of Human Rights.* Oxford; Portland: Hart

Surtees, J. (2000), *The Strange Case of Dr. Bodkin Adams: The Life and Murder Trial of Eastbourne's Infamous Doctor and the Views of Those Who Knew Him.* Seaford: SB Publishers.

Tan, A. K.-J. (1997), 'Adverse inferences and the right to silence: Re-examining the Singapore experience'. *Criminal Law Review* July: 471.

Tapper, C. (1972), 'Evidence (general). Eleventh Report of the Criminal Law Revision Committee'. *The Modern Law Review* 35/6: 4.

Taylor, Lord. (1994), 'The Tom Sergant Memorial Lecture'. *New Law Journal* 141.

Taylor, P. (1987), *Stalker: The Search for the Truth.* London: Faber and Faber.

Thomas, C. (1980), 'Suspected terrorists' right of silence angers Army in Ulster'. *The Times*, 12 February, p. 3.

Thomas, C. (2010), 'Are juries fair?'. *Ministry of Justice Research Series 1/10.* London: Ministry of Justice.

Thoresby, R. (1973), 'Is due process fleeing its English home?'. *ABAJ* 59: 1046.

Thwaites, R. (1993), 'Interviews on trial'. *Solicitors' Journal* 17 December: 1278.

Tierney, K. (1968), 'Transatlantic attitudes toward self-incrimination'. *American Criminal Law Quarterly* 6: 26.

Tonry, M. (2010), 'The costly consequences of populist posturing: ASBOs, victims, "rebalancing" and diminution in support for civil liberties'. *Punishment & Society* 12/4: 387.

Travis, A. (1993), 'Right to silence abolished in crackdown on crime'. *Guardian*, 7 October.

Tregilgas-Davey, M. I. (1997), 'Adverse inferences and the "no comment" interview'. *Solicitors Journal* 141: 500.

Twining, W. (2009), *General Jurisprudence: Understanding Law from a Global Perspective.* Cambridge; Cambridge University Press.

UN. (1993), *Report of the Secretary-General Pursuant to Paragraph 2 of Security Council Resolution UN SCOR, 48th Sess.,* UN Doc. S/25704.

UN. (1994), *Human Rights Committee, General Comment 13, Article 14 (21st session, 1984) Compilation of General Comments and General Recommendations Adopted by Human Rights Treaty Bodies,* UN Doc. HRI\GEN\1\Rev.1.

University of Sydney. (1973), 'Right of silence: Seminar (Sydney, 1972): Proceedings', *Proceedings of The Institute of Criminology,* 161. Sydney: University of Sydney, Institute of Criminology.

Van Kessel, G. (1998), 'European perspectives on the accused as a source of testimonial evidence'. *West Virginia Law Review* 100: 799.

Victoria. (1999), *Inquiry into the Right to Silence – Final Report.* Victoria: Scrutiny of Acts and Regulations Committee.

Waddington, P. A. J. (1999), 'Police (canteen) sub-culture. An appreciation'. *British Journal of Criminology* 39/2: 287.

Walker, C. (1992), *The Prevention of Terrorism in British Law,* 2nd ed. Manchester: Manchester University Press.

Walker, C. (2008), 'Post-charge questioning of suspects'. *Criminal Law Review* 7: 509.

Walker, C. (2014), *Blackstone's Guide to the Anti-Terrorism Legislation*, 3rd ed. Oxford: Oxford University Press.

Walker, C. and Starmer, K. (1999), *Miscarriages of Justice: A Review of Justice in Error*. Oxford: Oxford University Press.

Walsh, D. W. and Milne, R. (2008), 'Keeping the PEACE? A study of investigative interviewing practices in the public sector'. *Legal and Criminological Psychology* 13: 39.

Wasik, M. (1996), 'Magistrates: Knowledge of previous convictions'. *Criminal Law Review* December: 12.

Wasik, M. and Taylor, R. (1995), *Blackstones Guide to the Criminal Justice and Public Order Act 1994*. London: Blackstones.

White, R. (1975), 'The distasteful character of litigation for poor persons'. *Juridical Review* 20: 233.

Wigmore, J. (1906), *Treatise on Evidence*. Boston: Little, Brown and Company.

Wigmore, J. H. (1961), *Evidence in Trials at Common Law*. Boston: Little, Brown and Company.

Williams, C. R. (1994), 'Silence in Australia: Probative force and rights in the law of evidence'. *Law Quarterly Review* 110/Oct: 25.

Williams, G. (1960), 'Questioning by the police: Some practical considerations'. *Criminal Law Review* May: 325.

Williams, G. (1987), 'The tactic of silence', *New Law Journal* 137/6333: 1107.

Williams, G. L. (1955), *The Proof of Guilt: A Study of the English Criminal Trial*. Hamlyn Lectures, Seventh Series. London: Stevens & Sons.

Williamson, T. and Moston, S. (1990), 'The extent of silence in police interviews', in S. Greer and R. Morgan, eds, *The Right to Silence Debate*, Bristol: Bristol University Centre for Criminal Justice.

Willis, C., McLeod, J. and Naish, P. (1988), *The Tape-Recording of Interviews with Suspects: A Second Interim Report*. Home Office Research Study No. 97. London: HMSO.

Willis, C. F. (1984), *The Tape-recording of Police Interviews with Suspects: An Interim Report*. Home Office Research Study No. 82. London: HMSO.

Wilson, J. Q. (1968), *Varieties of Police Behavior*. Cambridge, MA: Harvard University Press.

Windlesham, L. (1993), *Responses To Crime*. Oxford: Oxford University Press.

Wolchover, D. (2001), *Silence and Guilt: An Assessment of Case Law on the Criminal Justice and Public Order Act 1994*. UK: Lion Court Lawyers.

Wolchover, D. (2002), 'An obituary for inferences on police station silence'. *Archbold News* 6: 3.

Wolchover, D. (2005), 'Silent triumph of the coach and horses'. *Archbold News* 9: 5.

Wolchover, D. and Heaton-Armstrong, A. (1995), 'Questioning and identification changes under PACE'. *Criminal Law Review*. 356.

Woodcock, J. (1992), *Specialist Crime and Investigating Squads, and Detection Policies Report*. Her Majesty's Inspector of Constabulary, London: Home Office.

Wright, A. M. and Alison, L. (2004), 'Questioning sequences in Canadian police interviews: Constructing and confirming the course of events'. *Psychology, Crime, and Law* 10: 137.

Wright, D. (1998), 'The solicitor in the witness box'. *Criminal Law Review*. 44.

Yeo, M. H. (1983), 'Diminishing the right to silence: The Singapore experience'. *Criminal Law Review* 1983: 89–101.

Young, R. and Sanders, A. (1994), 'The Royal Commission on Criminal Justice: A confidence trick?'. *Oxford Journal of Legal Studies* 14/3: 435.

Young, S., Goodwin, E. J., Sedgwick, O. and Gudjonsson, G. H. (2013), 'The effectiveness of police custody assessments in identifying suspects with intellectual disabilities and attention deficit hyperactivity disorder'. *BMC Medicine* 11: 248.

Zander, M. (1974), 'The Criminal Law Revision Committee Report: A survey of reactions'. *Law Society's Gazette* 2 October: 953.

Zander, M. (1979), 'The investigation of crime: A study of contested cases at the Old Bailey'. *Criminal Law Review* 203.

Zander, M. (1985), *The Police and Criminal Evidence Act 1984*. London: Sweet and Maxwell.

Zander, M. (1996), 'You have no right to remain silent: Abolition of the privilege against self-incrimination in England'. *St Louis Law Journal* 40: 18.

Zander, M. and Henderson, P. (1993), 'Crown Court study', *Royal Commission on Criminal Justice Research Study 19*. London: HMSO.

Zuckerman, A. A. S. (1973), 'Criminal Law Revision Committee 11th Report, Right of Silence'. *The Modern Law Review* 36/5: 509.

Zuckerman, A. A. S. (1989a), *The Principles of Criminal Evidence*, Oxford: Clarendon.

Zuckerman, A. A. S. (1989b), 'Trial by unfair means – the report of the Working Group on the Right of Silence'. *Criminal Law Review* December: 855.

Zuckerman, A. A. S. (1994), 'Bias and suggestibility: Is there an alternative to the right to silence?', in D. Morgan and G. Stephenson, eds, *Suspicion and Silence: The Right to Silence in Criminal Investigations*. London: Blackstone.

Index

Page numbers in *italics* denote tables.